W9-CGL-830

Resolving Traumatic Memories

Metaphors and Symbols in Psychotherapy

Resolving Traumatic Memories

Metaphors and Symbols in Psychotherapy

David J. Grove
B.I. Panzer

Irvington Publishers, Inc.
New York

For information write to: Irvington Publishers, Inc.,
Executive offices: 522 E. 82nd Street, Suite 1, New York, NY 10028
Customer service and warehouse:
195 McGregor St, Manchester, NH 03102

Library of Congress Cataloging-in-Publication Data

Grove, David J.
    Resolving traumatic memories.

    Bibliography: p.
    Includes index.
    1. Metaphor—Therapeutic use. 2. Symbolism (Psychology) 3. Post-traumatic stress disorder—Treatment. 4. Psychotherapy. I. Panzer, B. I. II. Title. [DNLM: 1. Memory. 2. Psychotherapy—methods. 3. Semantics. 4. Symbolism (Psychology)
WM 420 G883]
RC489.M47G76   1989   616.89'14   89-2060
ISBN 0-8290-2407-7
ISBN 0-8290-2417-4 (Includes two audio cassettes)

                    10 9 8 7 6 5 4 3 2

Production and design

The
BRAMBLE
COMPANY

Falls Village, Connecticut

Printed in the United States of America

Contents

Preface

Is there a therapist who has not experienced the client who fails to progress? How often are clients referred who, despite much therapeutic work, have experienced little progress with their unwanted thoughts, feelings, moods or behaviors? How many clients are resistant to traditional and Ericksonian inductions? What is the most humane, yet brief and effective, intervention when we must help the client with a recent catastrophe such as rape, mugging, robbery, burglary, automobile accident or the loss of love or a loved one? Can there be an economical treatment of the abuse and incest survivor?

What is to be done if the client's past of abuse or molestation, sin of omission or commission reaches into the present, and the future, and affectively resonates, interfering with the present process? How can the therapist most effectively deal with the client who blames past events for present difficulties? M.H. Erickson, Paul Watzlawick, and others have pointed to the need for bypassing or breaking up familiar patterns in the client's life and therapy.

David Grove's therapy is a new departure for the client and his therapeutic situation. In furthering his process, curling himself into his own story by going inside his own 'symptom', the client achieves a state of focused self-absorption. He involves himself ever deeper in his own narrative. The therapist does not intrude or induct. Most often there is no resistance. The client does what he needs to do, goes or not where he needs to go. The client does not go to a beach or forest, or cave, but into the infrastructure of his own experience, at a time and place of special interest; a time and place that holds special fascination for him, a time and place that may be but a moment in time between a particular stimulus and response.

The client's narrative contains clues to the infrastructure of his experience. These clues permit the therapist to smoothly and unintrusively enter the client's underlying non-conscious world. In formatting the client's memories, external metaphors, internal physiological symbols or semantic constructs, the client experiences— often for the first time— how it is that he makes his world, what he wants, how he knows he knows, and what beliefs and myths underlie his mind set. The client begins to experience his infrastructure and how it got that way.

This infrastructure, which exists just below the level of everyday awareness, is a strange and foreign land filled with hitherto 'unknown' elements of memories, metaphors, symbols, and semantic constructs. It is a world of knots, frogs, spiked balls, fists, and walls; a world in which mermaids and other strange denizens splash around inside our hearts, and green jelly is found inside our knees.

In order to smoothly enter this matrix of experience, this infrastructure of experience, the therapist speaks clean language. The verbal form and syntax of the therapist's clean questions are chosen according to which of the four languages of experience predominate in the client's constructs. Which sensory channels does the client favor? Where is the greatest density of the pathology located? Where does the client locate his concerns in time and space? Matching the client's practices, procedures, and constructs, the therapist's clean language facilitates a state of purposeful, focused, uncontaminated self-absorption. Having constellated the client's want, the therapist is in a position to generate permissive, brief, respectful, consensual, uninvasive, elegant, and powerful operations. By operating directly and selectively on the memories, metaphors, symbols or semantic constructs that underlie the client's complaint, the infrastructure of pathology is incisively and enduringly altered. This restructuring of underlying constructs impacts powerfully on cognition, feeling, mood, and behavior.

This precise, focused therapy is particularly applicable to clients who are troubled by memories of traumatic experiences, phobias, obsessions, and compulsions. It is the therapy to be chosen in many cases of rape, incest, and child abuse.

This book constitutes a complete description of a new approach to producing breakthrough sessions with PTSD clients. Special emphasis is on rape, incest, and child abuse. New discoveries relating to the four different ways that clients formulate their complaints are discussed. On the basis of these discoveries, a new therapeutic language, *clean language*, is formulated for the therapist's clinical use. The use of clean language can elicit trance without induction, enable the client to discover the infrastructure of his complaint, permit the therapist to communicate with the client's non-conscious functions. A healing evolution of the memories, metaphors, symbols, and semantic constructs underlying the client's disturbance is facilitated. Breakthrough sessions are frequently obtained. The structure of the client's complaint contains the seed of the healing. In many cases the client provides all the ingredients, knowledge, and energy for his own healing. The therapist merely evolves the client's own process: this is therapy on the snowball or log-jam model.

Most therapies are laborious and slow. Breakthrough sessions tend to be infrequent. Many therapists operate on a Sisyphus model of therapy. *Clean therapy* is free of the therapist's idiosyncratic language, attributions, metaphors, characterizations or therapeutic hypotheses. *Clean language* and *clean therapy* can be incorporated into many facets of most therapeutic modalities.

During the past six years, I have spent many hundreds of hours, on both sides of the Atlantic, at workshops, seminars, and presentations of many of the pre-eminent therapists and theoreticians of our day.

I first participated in a David Grove workshop during the International Symposium on Stress and Anxiety Disorders at Imperial College, London in August 1985. After the first few hours I knew that there was something innovative, unusually powerful, and effective going on. In October 1986 I persuaded David Grove to devote ten whole days to record on tape the bulk of his teachings. The content of those tapes constitutes the substance of this book. The chapters on Matrix and Want Frame have been thoroughly rewritten and revised together with David Grove. The other chapters are more representative of David Grove's flow of focused consciousness and have been produced by a process of selection, correction, and editing. For turning thirty hours of tapes into over six hundred pages of manuscript and producing three rewrites, I thank Sarah Stacey and Jacquetta Pease. I am grateful to Felix Patrikeeff, Sue Johnson, and Dale Miller for their devoted work of copy-editing and proofreading. I gladly acknowledge J.B. Forget's talent and his generosity in donating the use of his very personal composition for the jacket of this book. I also thank my publisher for his support, encouragement, and suggestions.

Most of the case material and all of the original thought is David Grove's. When I first witnessed David Grove's work with clients I was determined to learn to do what he does. My commitment is stronger than ever....

B.I. Panzer, Ph.D.
London

Clean Language

Precis

The therapist's use of clean language facilitates the client's process, ensuring that the client's meaning and resonance remain wholly intact, uncontaminated by the therapist's words. It opens the door to change. States of self-absorption and naturalistic trance are induced. The non-conscious process is constellated. Resistance is not evoked. The client's words are followed to the origins of experience. Clean language implies a participatory experience; the client feels understood. The therapist's language evokes an animated experience within the client, preserving the client's information in pristine form. The client's way of processing and storing information is revealed.

Historical Metaphor

On 20th March 1847, Ignaz Philipp Semmelweis, M.D. started his full assistantship on the medical ward of the first maternity clinic of the Vienna General Hospital. The mortality rate of women who gave birth in the medical wing operated by medical obstetricians and their students was devastating. Puerperal fever was decimating the unhappy mothers who had the ill fortune of being admitted to the medical maternity ward.

In the adjacent midwives' ward of the same first maternity clinic, abutting the medical maternity ward in the same building, happy healthy mothers were giving birth to healthy infants.

This scandal was no secret to the general public. Women in labor were dragged screaming off the streets to the medical ward of the maternity clinic on alternate days. The women of Vienna's poor would rather give birth on the street than be admitted to the medical obstetrics service.

These were the conditions confronting Semmelweis from 27th February 1846 to the end of May 1847. During this period Semmelweis studied and observed methods, practices, and procedures in both maternity services. He performed hundreds of autopsies. After a great deal of thought, and by the process of elimination, Semmelweis came to the conclusion that the essential difference between the two services was the presence of the medical practitioners on the medical ward and the absence of the medical practitioners on the midwifery ward. Could it be that the physicians were carrying the cause of puerperal fever to the unfortunate women? Semmelweis could propose no other logical hypothesis.

By 7th June 1847 Semmelweis had set up portable wash basins and ordered the attending physicians and students to thoroughly scrub their hands with liquid chloride solution on entering the ward. He set up further portable wash basins ordering the physicians to scrub their hands between each obstetrical examination. Semmelweis personally supervised the scrubbing. The physicians were outraged. Within thirty days the death rate plummeted from 18% to 2.45%. Semmelweis was hounded out of his hospital in October 1850 by his incensed medical colleagues. He returned to Hungary and, although honored by various academic and professional appointments, it is said that his battles in Vienna were the cause of repeated mental breakdown.

During the second week of December 1985, a physician, who can fairly be described as America's most famous psychiatrist, asked a question of his patient. This famous physician is fully trained in medical psychiatry and psychoanalysis, the author of many excellent books on his speciality, the originator of a valuable and innovative approach to one of the most difficult and prevalent of psychiatric illnesses, the holder of prestigious professorial appointments and many awards, and a kind and competent clinician. In front of a vast audience of clinicians, he asked his demonstration patient: 'WHAT HAVE YOU GOT GOING THROUGH YOUR MIND THAT'S CON-CRETE?'

Client's language. Therapists have always used clients' language and clients' behavior as their prime material. To some therapists, the clients' language is a clue to the underlying process. Dr. Aaron Beck, to his great credit, gives full credit and recognition to what the client says. He asks him to examine his experience more carefully and then gives complete credit to what the client says about his experience. In our attention to clients' language, we examine not only the auditory, visual, and kinesthetic channels that the client uses, but we also pay serious attention to *how the client uses language* to describe experiences and inner realities. Clients have a number of ways of doing this.

The therapist's use of clean language allows the client to tell his story in one of the four language forms. These forms are ways in which clients can make sense of their world. They are modes of describing their own internal experience. These languages of experience differ from how we normally talk about external reality. These are the languages that are found inside a *matrix* (see p. 26 et seq.) and they are vital constituents of the internal reality. These languages can act like a lens through which we can magnify and freeze time, extend the significance into the matrix and make manifest a *there* that is there in the client's own unique way of expressing his internal reality.

The four languages in which cognitions and experiences are expressed are memories, metaphors, symbols, and semantics. A client may express his internal reality in one or more of these four languages. In these languages we seek to discover the medium through which a particular message of the client's immediate experiential reality is delivered. We want to discover which of these appears to be the predominant language. That is, the *one* most favored language in which the client is delivering this information and in which his experience of any particular event is characterized. The density is a measure of how much time a client devotes to, or what proportion of his reality is delivered in, each of these four languages.

Memories. The first of these languages is memories. A memory is the recall of any event in the past. The client relates particular events that have occurred. There may also be anticipatory memories about the future or expectation of things that might happen. Memories are the recall of events real or imagined. As the therapist listens to the information, he hears the narrative of a recall of the events and a description of what happened. The client usually delivers his version of what is wrong in terms of memory and relates it to the past: when a husband is talking about his relationship with his wife and he focuses on: "If only I had not hit her then, we would not be having this difficulty now," the husband is identifying this past event as the main cause that is affecting him now.

Symbols. The next language is internal symbols. These are derived symbols. They are different from Jungian symbols in that they are idiosyncratic rather than universal. Each client's symbol is an internal experience: a physiological or psychological feeling that is located within the boundary of his body. It has an anatomy. It is located within the body.

A husband who faces a problem with his wife, instead of talking about memories, could talk very much about his physiology: "I'm so *upset* with the fact that I hit my wife and in our relationship now, it is so *tensed* it is like every time we meet and talk I have got this *knot in my stomach* that gets me all *tensed* and we just do not have a relationship any more." He speaks in terms of his physiology and internal symbols, which are his predominant language.

Metaphors. Another language is that of metaphors. These metaphors do not have universal application. They are derived from the client's own experience and are external to the body: "I have a *cloud hanging over me*, life is a *bowl of cherries*, every *cloud has a silver lining."* A husband presenting in the language of metaphors might say: "Ever since it happened we have no communication. It is like there is *a wall between us.* Every time I try to talk to my wife it is like trying to *talk through a brick wall."* The *wall* is the metaphor. The density of his language is in metaphors. The issue is not the feeling, or that he has memories, or what he did. He is concerned by the *wall* that is between them now.

Semantics. The fourth language is semantics. What is important in this language is the *private* definition of the words. In a language these words have a meaning, from which is derived the experience of the client talking in his particular language. A husband might say: "Well, she really deserved what I did to her, she is so immature. If she was more mature then we would not have a problem. The problem is really in the communication. It does not really have anything to do with what I did, but we are not communicating now and I just think it is her immaturity that does it. Things are not right between us and if only she would change and grow up, then we would not have a problem. And the family unit is not what it ought to be." Here the client is presenting his wife's immaturity. Semantics is a bit tricky. The other languages are delivered *with* words. In semantics it is the words and not the meanings that have the most important effect. When the client speaks in terms of metaphor and he is talking about a brick wall, the words do not really mean that much. It is the *idea* of the brick wall and what is *visualized* that is important.

When the client is talking in terms of symbols— about the knot in his stomach, for example— it is what the client feels that is important. The words that he uses are not important. It is the symbol, the *knot* in his stomach, that is at issue.

When we talk about the language of memories, the words simply give information. It is the *memory* itself which is most significant rather than the words used.

These are some of the distinctions between the four different languages and how they make sense. One presenting problem can be presented in four different ways. Our first goal is to discover which of these four languages the client uses primarily.

As we develop a matrix we want to identify the reality of the client's language and develop his experience wholly within his language. For instance, normally we would not ask questions such as: 'How do you feel?' or questions having to do with behavior, or having to do with cognitions about why the client did something. We want to find how the client expresses his experience and in what language. Then we can use his language to make the intervention. At the external— video tape— level the husbands beating their wives could behaviorally be exactly the same. In terms of four different husbands, the experience, and the way that it is structured internally within the client's matrix of experience, is quite different. The objective for the therapist is to talk and work entirely in the client's language. The therapist delivers his clinical intervention within the client's frame of reference.

The therapist adopts the client's use of language in order to elicit information from the client and deliver information to the client. The therapist does not invite the client to learn the therapist's language. It is important to use the language of the client because the mixing of metaphors does not make for effective therapy.

Discovering the client's chosen language assists us in designing an intervention that will fit the client's experience. A woman has been raped. She talks about this trauma. We might normally assume that we have to deal with the event of the rape, the sorts of abuse that occurred, and work with her on this issue. As we listen for the language in which she expresses her experience we might make an entirely different intervention. If she is presenting the density of her communications in terms of the memory of the rape, she might say: "I saw him coming down the street and that look in his eyes; and then I knew and I keep seeing this when I wake up at night. I can feel his hands on me. I can feel the roughness and the smell and I keep reliving it over and over again." Here the client is in a language of memories, and to work with the actual event of the trauma could make for a good outcome.

The client may, in fact, present in a different way. Although the rape happened, what she is talking about is the feeling of anger that she now feels for the perpetrator. This anger is like a *hot flash* that *burns in her chest* and *flashes up to her face* like *fire*. The basis of presenting now is symbolic. There is this *burning sensation* of wanting to get even and kill the perpetrator; whereas in the memory of the actual event her physiology at that time was when *she was frozen* and she *felt like concrete* unable to do anything. Here we have two different physiological sets: the frozen concrete feeling that actually occurs at the point of the rape, and then a couple of days later she gets this physiological set of the fire burning in her chest. When she gets angry— and this is a different moment— she now has a different language. It is no longer the language of memories: it is more the language of this physiology, the symbolic physiology, the fire in her body.

Another client presents in a language that is more metaphorical. After the rape she feels degraded and worthless. She was going to be a nun, but now in the sight of God she is no longer worthy. She is *like a disused blob of mud* and completely unworthy. The *blob of mud* that she feels she has been thrown into is her metaphor. Her density is not about the rape, it is not about the feelings immediately after, or those she is having or about the perpetrator. Rather, it is about her metaphor and of feeling degraded in the eyes of God. It will not help her very much if we deal with her memory of the rape, or if we agree with her anger because her density and her language are in terms of the oriented metaphor. It is *future-oriented* and now she says she cannot achieve what she saw as her purpose in life.

A client who presents more semantically may present evenly with all of these language forms. She may be equally valenced in terms of the memory. She will talk it over and over and over again: the idea of being raped; all men are like that, and she will never associate with them again. They are brutes. She is using words to describe her whole experience, and the experience is contained in these words. The semantic form of it is what is important. There is a different intervention required here because the density occurs at a different point in time and in a different language as well.

Therapist's language. Different psychotherapies have paid different degrees of attention to the words that therapists use in talking to their clients. The two schools that readily come to mind as having paid considerable attention to the exact way in which therapists express themselves are the NLP and Ericksonian therapists. Both talk about matching and pacing in their striving to speak in the same language as the client. NLP therapists emphasize submodalities and whether the client's greatest density is in visual, auditory or kinesthetic terms. We believe that our emphasis on clean language— which allows the client to remain in the alpha state, to remain on the level of matrix, and in the mental set in which he finds himself— goes beyond the efforts of these schools.

Clean language is a prerequisite in developing the client's matrix of experience and in discerning the particular language that the client uses to refer to his reality. The shape and the structure of questions will limit the ways in which the client can respond and can leave a form of tunnel vision which will restrict his response pattern. Were we to ask: 'And how do you feel about that?' this would tend to limit the client's response. It would presuppose that the most valued way which he can answer pertains to a feeling. In fact, what the client may have wanted to answer could have been in terms of a cognitive construct. By asking about feelings, we would tend to limit the spectrum of response. We would not get the client to express his experience in his own language. We have to be careful about the shape of the question and the category of language that we use because we do not want to restrict the ways in which the client responds.

The first objective is for the therapist to keep the language clean and allow the client's language to manifest itself. The second objective is that the clean language used by the therapist be a facilitatory language; in the sense that it will ease entry into the matrix of experience, and into that altered state that may be helpful for the client to internally access his experience.

When a client is in a matrix, he is also in an altered state. When he is out of the matrix he tends to be out of the alpha state. At the first level of the matrix, the client will be in an alpha state, internally oriented and paying attention to the internal rather than the external environment. By using clean language to ask clean questions, we uncover the infrastructure of the client's reality.

Trance. Clean language facilitates whatever *experience* the client needs. We do not maintain that clients need to go into trance. This is perhaps another distinction embodied in the structure of using clean language. It may be very conducive to a trance. We do not resort to artifice, techniques, injunctions or direct instructions to encourage the client's trance.

In traditional hypnosis, a trance is facilitated through the language, rhythm, and the injunctions the therapist uses. As distinct from this traditional approach, clean language can produce an alpha state simply because the language is not valenced. It is not loaded in any particular direction to distract the client from entering an appropriate state in the most natural way. There is no artificial support for the alpha state and the altered state is facilitated because it is directed toward a goal. The client, in approaching a particular goal in himself, creates an environment in which the alpha state is induced. The structure of the questions induces the altered state, as contrasted with direct instructions or injunctions given to the client about going into a trance. In order to discover answers to the clean questions, the client goes naturally into an alpha state. This is different from trying to induce a trance in order to do something. The alpha state is a by-product of the direction that our questions orient.

In addressing himself to a matrix that is in either past, present or future, the therapist maintains congruency with that time. The therapist would bring a client out of the alpha state if he were to mismatch the verb tenses or talk about one thing in a different time frame. To maintain clean language there needs to be congruency in the structure of the therapist's language with the client's orientation in time.

The structure of the therapist's question induces the alpha state indirectly, without mentioning anything about the trance. The trance is often a prerequisite in finding the answer. Clients alter their state in going somewhere to get that answer. That somewhere is where we want to leave them, and that happens to be where they may develop in the trance.

With clean language we can perform complete interventions by asking questions. We may never need to make a statement of fact or give a direction. By asking clean questions we shape the location and the direction of the client's search for the answer. In asking a question we do not impose upon the client any value, construct or presupposition about what he should answer. We are only asking a question. Perhaps the client will discover an answer and perhaps not. That is a different perspective to giving a direct injunction.

The client is free to find an answer and may keep the answer to himself. It may not be necessary for the client to share his memories, thoughts or feelings, or express them to the therapist. In many therapies the object of asking questions is to gather information from the client. Using our approach, however, we may not need the information. The questions are not asked to gather information or to understand the client's perspectives. We ask our questions so that the client can understand his perspective internally, in his own matrix.

If we were to ask for information, the client might come out of the matrix or out of the alpha state and tell us this and that. This would be a very slow way of conducting therapy. Our clean questions tend to shape the client's internal reality. We want to leave our questions embedded in the client's experience. If the client were to come out of matrix to explain matters, a different environment would be created.

Our questions will have given a form, made manifest some particular aspect of the client's internal experience in a way that he has not experienced before. The experience is alive and real; not just contained in words or dissipated in answers. We structure an environment internally: the client is going to *experience* rather than *describe* what the experience is like. We give less value to the client giving us information or describing the internal experience. Our real object in getting the client to search for this kind of answer is that it helps to structure, manifest, and evoke the client's internal experience.

Our common use of trance is as a focused state. We normally do not want the client to be in a deep trance in our intervention. We prefer our client in a state of conversational trance. Each question can put the client into a trance state. In order to get an answer based on memories, the client may have to go into a trance state to get his information. Every time the client goes inside, as in a daydream, he is going into a trance. It can be very effective in therapy to use these facilitatory states in producing neurological changes.

We work with the client inside his experience because the ideas, and questions, go straight down. We want some feedback with the use of trance as well. There must be a degree of precision about our work and we need the work to be participatory. We want the client to communicate to us when he has done his task. Our questions are shaped in discreet units so that when we ask for information we do so in such a way that the client has to go inside to get it.

'So when you were there at that time, how long did that take? And as you find out that information, you might like to see if there were any other times and just tell me the number of other times that that happened.' That questioning puts the client inside. He has to sort out other experiences within that time. These words also convey to him that we do not want him to tell us about what happened: all we want him to tell us is how many times it has happened. He only has to come out with a number and that helps keep him inside his internal experience. Should a therapist say: 'Now, tell me what happened,' the client is unlikely to be in trance because he is going to be out conversing and narrating.

'So think of all the things that happened then, and take your time now, and stay inside, and when you have thought of all those things, just let me know when you have done that.' That statement allows the client to go inside and to know he does not have to tell us what happened. All he has to do is let us know that he has finished thinking of those things. This helps shape the client's experience and puts him into trance. It is his own natural trance; he goes in, he does his work, and comes out to tell us it is done. We do not want to interrupt him while he is doing that.

All we need to know are simple bits of symbolic information. How many times did it happen? Were there any particular colors? We want the client in *subjective* reality because that is where the change is going to occur. With our words, our injunctions, and our questions, we want the client to go inside, where change will occur, right then and there, in front of us. This is the same phenomenon as when a client goes away and says a week later: "Well, I thought about what you said last time and it really made a difference."

Why did he have to wait until that thought made a difference? We want to provide an environment in which our words hit home right now, in front of us, so that we can influence the quality of the experience. Usually, clients go where they are not distracted by the presence of the therapist to think about words, and only then do those words go down and effect a change. We want that alteration to happen right here in front of us and that is why we are *not present in clean language.*

A client who is very verbal may need to say the words. There may then have to be some question/answer exchange. For a client who is very physiologically oriented, talking about it makes it difficult to access that particular physiology. The therapist surrounds the physiological factor with his words instead and may not need answers to his questions. As the client goes to find the answers, the experience is created inside him.

The purpose of questions formulated in clean language is to develop the client's internal process: the process needed to generate the desired internal experience. The internal experience need not necessarily be shared with the therapist.

The more the client has to share with the therapist, the more cumbersome and more inefficient the process becomes.

This is because the client has to translate out of the matrix into external reality and qualify what his experience is. Generally it is difficult to put experience into words. Thus we leave the experience in the client's own language of experience, and clean language helps to facilitate this. The object of the operation is to give form to the client's experience. It is most important, wherever possible, to give it a form other than the form of words. If we ask questions and expect answers, we evoke the form of words. If we ask questions that do not require verbal answers, we give the matrix experiential form inside the client's experience. That form is much closer to the client's internal reality than is the form of words. We give a lower value to words and descriptions, and a higher value to the experience being there, constellated inside the client. The client can say that he knows that the experience is now there, and he *knows* the experience.

Clean language encourages and defines the client's internal process. It is couched in the client's sensory channel and terms, allowing the client to explore further and know about his own experience. Questions couched in 'normal' language ask the client to *comment* on his experience. Every time he does that he comes out of a state of self-absorption to perform an intellectual task which interrupts the process we are working to encourage and to facilitate.

The first question. In initially asking clean questions, the therapist wants to be undefined about what it is he wants. He is waiting for something to distill out of the client's experience and that he can then extend down into the matrix. The therapist is not sure where the client is going to be focused in time and to what level of experience the client is going to relate. The therapist defines his information from the client in terms of: 'What is it that you want?' This allows the client to respond in some abstraction about the future that is totally undefined. The client may need to know that that is his reality. This orients the client in a particular reference and the therapist keeps him there. In starting off with clean questions the therapist needs

TABLE 1

Some Aspects of Clean Language

Questions	Clean Questions
What can I do for you?	What do you need to have happen?
How can I help?	What would be helpful?
What seems to be the matter?	What do you want?
What is your problem?	What would you like?
What brings you here (today)?	What would you want (to happen here today)?
How do you feel?	Are you experiencing anything now?
What is going through your mind?	Is there anything (you are thinking)?
What is on your mind?	Is there something you are thinking?
I am listening.	Is there something you want to say?
What are you thinking?	Are you thinking anything?
How do you feel about that?	And when that happened, how did you feel?
What does it remind you of?	And when that happened, how does that affect you?
Tell me what happened.	And when that happened …?
What do you think/feel?	Is there anything happening?
Can you get in touch with that feeling?	And when you have that feeling, what does that feel like? And where do you feel it?
How does that make you feel?	And when that happened did you have any feeling?
Are you angry/do you feel angry?	What is that feeling like?
You must have a lot of anger.	Did you feel anything when that happened?
I want you to …	And what can you suggest you could do …?

Words	Clean Words
addiction, habit, compulsion	What is it that you don't want to do?
depression, anxiety, phobia, obsession, pathology	What is it that you don't want to think/feel?

to slide in gently; to be unsure and undefined in what it is that he actually requires from the client.

There are several ways in which the therapist might ask the first question: 'What would you like?' 'What is it that you want?' 'Is there something you would like?' 'What is it that you would like to have happen here?' The last is quite clean but does restrict the client. We may obtain more important information if we ask: 'What is it that you want?' This allows the client to respond in some abstraction about the future that is totally undefined. The client may need to know that that is his reality. This can be much more useful than getting the client to answer a more pragmatic question.

'What brings your here?' This has a good degree of cleanliness, but it is about bringing here. 'What brought you here?' implies that it was a problem that forced the client to come here and is therefore limiting. 'What is it that you want?' is going to get a very different answer. 'What brings you here?' will focus the client in terms of defining a problem which impels him here. 'What do you want?' will focus the client into the future in terms of defining what it is that he wants. The reply can be "I don't want," or "I want," or "I don't know what I want." These are the only three possible replies.

The first question is important because it is like the first move in chess, and to some extent it is going to set the tone and the direction of how the session will go. This quality of direction is very important because it will direct the client's attention— or he will direct our attention— to a particular location in his experience and to a particular orientation in time.

Whenever we ask a question, we are up to something. Questions are used to shape the nature of the interaction between us and the client. With our first question we do as little as possible to shape the environment. We want the client to deliver information to us as cleanly as possible. We do not impose a limited or a restricted and narrowed field of response. We may want to be unfocused to begin with.

The first bits of information the client delivers are going to be located somewhere in time and somewhere in experience. That is important. It will help to give us an idea of where the density of the client's experience is. We want the first questions to be vague enough to allow the client to begin to find his concern. Such questions do not have embedded metaphors or presuppositions about how the client should answer. Later on we may want to narrow the client's field of possible responses. If we narrow too early, we do not get the information that this client's responses are so scattered. (The important information may be contained in this function of scattering and not necessarily in the content that the client delivers.) The scattered effect may be the very thing that will take us into the nature and the depth of the problem. We are looking for some little clue which does not seem to fit. We take that and prise it open with our questions to enter into the matrix of the client's experience.

If a client is in a negative state and we want to do something to change it, we may use a polarity of that state: a positive response. To achieve this, we need to use our language carefully in shaping the resources so that we obtain an isomorphism that is opposite to the negative state. If the client has a feeling of *rough* and we ask him to go in and get something that is the opposite, 'smooth' for instance, but in fact the client's opposite is *calm*, we will not get the appropriate positive resource. The questions to access resources have to have this heuristic quality of discovery. If we phrase our sentences in direct injunctions, we will not reach this aspect of discovery, for our questions would narrow the field of response.

The client has a knot in the stomach and we want to get a positive resource that will do the opposite. We ask the client to get the affect, the sensations that he has when he has that knot, and to take that knot and give us the opposite words to it. Our language is clean when we are discovering what the client has, rather than telling him what he has or what he needs.

The second phase of intervention is an evolutionary process. We use language to surround the pathology so that it will loosen and become malleable. A client has a hard ball in the abdomen. If we were to say: 'Now see if you can break that ball up. See if you can smash it,' we would be giving a direct injunction based on the assumption that the ball has to smash. What if it has to grow? In this second phase of intervention we want to surround the ball with words so that the client can loosen it and find out the direction he has to go.

Therapist: 'And as you know about that ball, then take some time to discover what things could possibly happen so that the ball could be a little bit different.' This hints at the possibility that the ball could change. Client: "I think it could get smaller." Therapist: 'Take some more time and see just how it could get smaller.'

We are not telling the client what to do. By surrounding the symbol with our words, we give the client a narrow focus on the ball. We use the client's intuitive knowledge about the direction that can heal, and that helps shape the intervention. We facilitate the ball to begin to alter. Therapist: 'And how could that happen?' This language facilitates the process of change, the therapeutic process and the evolution of the symbol or metaphor.

Characteristics of clean questions. The therapist may want to orient the client to a specific experience which takes place at a specific time and place. Once the client is oriented, the therapist does not mix his tenses. The therapist directs the client *there then*: he does not require the client to comment on it. Clean questions also concentrate attention on the internal. The therapist wants the process to focus on the internal.

This use of clean questions takes the client inside his own experience. If the therapist has some doubt about the client's choice of time, and choice of event as well, the therapist creates a little matrix in each event. Because it is participatory therapy, the therapist then asks the client at what location he would like to do what he wants to do: at the father's house or the mother's house. We let the client decide.

This creates the opportunity for the client to discover what it is that he would like to do in the next phase. The therapist lets the client make his own decision. The therapist creates the context to enable the client to make his decision. Clean questions are participatory in the sense that the client is in control of his own therapy. The questions the therapist asks are shaped in such a way that the client makes the decisions about what to do, where to go next, and in what tense. The client's sense of responsibility removes the need for the therapist to be 'clever'.

Our work is permissive. It is the way of the flow of consciousness. In this it differs from Beck, who feels that it is very much the responsibility of the therapist to take the client where he needs to go. We do this by creating an environment in which the client can discover where it is that he needs to go. We do not know where exactly this particular client needs to go. We can make some guesses, but in doing so we are making an important distinction. If the therapist were very 'clever', he would tell the client what to do. He would have to deliver information to that client from outside, as a therapist. The quality of that information, and how it is integrated by that client, would be very different from what happens if we put our client into an experience and allow him to discover his information, from his experience, in his own way. The information evolves internally out of the client's experience. It is not introduced into the client's experience by the therapist.

Clean language always implies participatory experience between a client and a therapist. Questions are framed so that the client can answer them. The therapist has a responsibility to search for questions that the client can answer. When the therapist asks a question that the client cannot answer, it is up to the therapist to find another question. All the therapist's questions must relate to the client's experience. We ask questions that the client can answer; if he cannot, we have to change the question.

There is no given rule that says what a good question is or that the client can or must answer it. In clean language the therapist does not impose metaphors. Clean language has no metaphors, no embedded metaphors, and no hidden metaphors such as direction. What is up or what is down, what is on your mind suggests that a client has a mind and that there is indeed something on it. The client may in fact have a feeling, and the feeling may be in, not on it; or it may have nothing at all to do with the mind. That is why that question is not a clean question. It has that sense of a metaphor inherent in it.

A feeling has epistemology, a something else-ness, possibly in the stomach. Being a feeling, it may not be in the mind. The client says: "I walked through the door into the office." The therapist says: 'Did you have a reaction?' That is not clean because the therapist implies a reaction. Reaction is a loaded word. 'Did you experience something?' is cleaner. 'And then something happened?' is very clean. 'And what happened?' is clean as can be. Three words provide absolute economy.

The issue here is not so much the meaning of the word, but where the therapist's question focuses the client's attention. We want to direct the client's attention to this inner experience, to his inner process.

If we were to ask: 'And did you have a reaction?' we would create a split. The split would be that the client is here and now in the room with the therapist and the client would be directed to look back from this perspective because *did* means that it happened in the past. The client would have to look back into the past and tell us about it. That is the function of the word *did*. We want the client *not to have current reality* and to *transport him back* to that time of then as if he were *having then now*. The clean question will induce the physiology, and 'What happened?' facilitates this. That is different from: 'And did you have a reaction?' To answer this question, the client's perspective would have to shift to the *now* talking about *then* and the client would be dissociated. 'What happened?' associates the client and puts him back on the path. That is a fine but important difference.

'*Did* you have a reaction?' orients the client in two different time zones. 'What happened?' leaves the client in just the one zone. Because all the therapist's questions will have the same verb tense, they will all be oriented in the past. 'Did you have a reaction?' would induce the client to make a comment and to stay at the surface level. We would get descriptions partly in the matrix, but it would be difficult to deepen the significance.

Initially, we are talking to a client about a past event. Unless there is some specific reason for dissociating him, we would want to formulate clean questions with the purpose of having the client's process take him— transport him— back to the experience of his choice; the experience the client has a need to explore. Our clean questions facilitate a re-experiencing or reliving, an exploration and appreciation of the client's experience; in the right time zone, time-regressed. Clean questions also tend to produce vivid, colorful, fleeting, and startling images, metaphors, and symbols. These can be quite new to the client's conscious experience.

Tautology. We use tautology because it is almost unassailable. There is no way we can argue logically against tautological propositions such as: a circle is round, audible to the ear, look back in retrospect, or visible to the eye.

We can imagine a tautological continuum. A circle is a square would be at one end. Somewhere in the middle is: a circle is nice. At the other end: a circle is round. It is arguable that it is nice, and it is arguable that it is not. A shape that is like a hexagon is not really a circle, nor is it really a square, but it has properties of both. It can be said to resemble a circle or not. That is arguable, and along the continuum we have degrees of ambiguity.

People can differ in opinion about a statement. If the statement is disputable, it may set up wordy cognitions. A tautological statement is one that is highly defensible and almost impossible to argue against.

The opposite of a tautology is a statement which appears to be a total nonsense, being almost impossible to defend and very easily argued against. In the middle, for example, is a statement where it is as easy to find a number of arguments for as it is to find a number of arguments against. Clean questions can occupy an area from the middle of the continuum to as close to tautology as possible. We want to make statements that occupy this area. In other words, our statements have a high degree of conviction.

Dr. M.H. Erickson used a lot of these statements, and he might have said things like: 'And as you are sitting in your chair, breathing slowly, and I am talking to you, and comfort exists.' In doing so he would be making statements that were almost tautological and very hard to argue against. He would be saying the obvious.

To avoid the possibility of debate or conflict, the therapist should say things that are very easy for the client to agree with and very difficult for him to disagree with. In some cases Erickson did this by describing what was going on.

Our pattern is different from Erickson's. After describing all that we want a client to agree with, we do not want to create the *yes* set. One of the qualities of this therapy is to have a participatory process and if we ran *yes* sets we would presuppose that we know what a client wants to do. A lot of our work does not really involve trance. Often what we get from the client is an alpha state, a state of relaxation, a state of self-absorption or a state of reverie.

As the therapist delivers that information, these are not statements in which a client can create another matrix or another reality. The client is unlikely to enter into a cognitive or internal dialogue that would distract him from the experience the therapist is developing. We want to use a number of tautological statements to favor the process that will facilitate the client's entry into an alpha state, a process that will deny or help neutralize a discourse between client and therapist.

By using clean language, we are creating a hygienic environment in which we can keep the therapy inside the client's matrix. We further this by using reasonably tautological statements to get the client to go into or keep the client in the appropriate altered state, or to go to the appropriate position in his experience. Whether it is an altered state or not appears irrelevant. Clients know the where-ness, the it-ness, or the here-ness of it. The trance is totally incidental.

'And as you wonder about whether it is time to consider some of those experiences, it may be interesting to think about those experiences, and about what experience could be a (healing, helpful, useful) experience, and what experience could not be.'

When we send a client into his internal environment, the I-ness of the therapist should appear to cease to exist. Should the therapist speak of himself, he might split the client's reality because he creates the cognition that the client is where he is, and lets the client know that the therapist is present. A split reality is implied in that kind of statement. When the therapist says: 'As you listen to these words about tautologies,' the words are from the client's perspective. The therapist may be describing the client's process. The therapist is speaking in clean language. That is quite different from saying: 'And I want you to hear what I am saying about tautologies.'

The therapist can take himself out of it by talking about the client's experience rather than the therapist's activity. That way the therapist is *in* the client's experience. There is a presupposition that it is not quite clean when we say that the client *may*. This is disputable. The client may not want to listen. He could instead argue with the therapist about that.

We want to make statements that the client is not likely to think about, or want to argue against. We want to say things that are easy for the client to accept and that are connotative of his reality. In order to connote the client's reality, the therapist sometimes has to take a guess. The therapist speaks in a language that is quite careful. This language already contains the argument that that which is contained could also not be: 'So as you begin to know about this, it might be interesting to consider how it could be different, and could be different in such a way that the events become more acceptable to you.'

'And as you think about that time, *there then*, take some time to discover about what could happen, *there then*, that would be *different* in some way.' We want to allow the client to choose. That is why we say *different*. If we say desirable, or helpful, or even useful, we limit the client's choice of response.

A thirty year old woman has, as a child, been abused by her mother. She wants to go back to that moment, but as a thirty year old. She is going to let her anger out at the mother because she has been through therapy and has been taught now to get angry with the mother. We put her back into the memory. She goes back as a thirty year old woman, back to when she was six and her mother beat her. In the mind of the thirty year old she is now standing there as a thirty year old looking at her mother beating her up.

Cognitively, all she has wants is to get angry with her mother, and stop the latter beating her. This is where the epiphanic moment can occur. As she stands there, she looks and sees the hairs on the mother's legs, her socks rolled down, holes in her slippers, the dirty floor of the kitchen. She sees her brother stealing cookies while mother is not looking. She sees mother pulling her child's arm and beating her with a wooden spoon. At that moment, as she sees the mother's dishevelled look and unkempt hair, her anger subsides.

She wonders, and realizes that her mother was not equipped to have the kids that she had and it is a marvel that she survived. With that change in perspective, she no longer wants to be angry because she now understands her mother in a way she never understood before.

Resistance. The client's resistance is a product of the therapist's induction in defining the resistance. If the therapist asks a resistant question, he gets a resistant answer. It is not for the therapist to force a client to answer. It is for the therapist to change the question, to ask a question the client can answer. The asking of questions that therapists think are good questions will not get clients into the matrix, and is therefore not clean language. When the therapist asks a question, gets a funny answer, and asks the same question in a different form, he is at fault. He has not taken note of the information that the client has given.

We cannot define in advance the grammar, syntax or vocabulary of a clean question. A clean question is unique to each client. We can give general rules defining clean questions. Nonetheless, we have to discover which questions will fit which client. The therapist expects that some of his questions will be wrong and he does not expect an answer to them. Rather than wait for an answer, he asks other questions until he finds one that the client can answer readily. This is how the therapist enters into the client's matrix. Clean questions do not contain the therapist's presuppositions, attributions or characterizations. They do not convey the therapist's world.

Questions are asked with reference to a context that can include appostion of opposites or to the difference between two states, to assist in defining a state. If a client has difficulty in describing an event, say through being confused, the therapist goes to the opposite: 'Then how do you know when you are not confused?' When the client defines how he is when not confused, we can go back: 'And now what is the difference between when you are confused and when you are not confused?' When the client is unable to answer a question about one state, we can see if he can answer about the opposite.

Syllogisms. Syllogisms are usually embedded in the questions that we ask. Later on we will give some examples of how syllogisms are used. Basically the pattern is: premise A, premise B, and therefore C; major premise, minor premise. 'So if you have this particular feeling here, what would happen if you did not have that feeling, and if you did not have that feeling, would that be what you want?'

Relative and demonstrative pronouns. We use pronouns such as: 'You can take *that there* in *that* particular way.' Our use of pronouns may allow the client to personalize his own search for meaning and a process of closure can take place. Examples of pronouns used are: '*That can* happen in *those* particular ways so *that* it could be different.' We are not referring specifically to him, those, there, or you. We let the client personalize, rather than our restricting, the meaning of how he can take the statement.

Personal pronouns and time. When working in the past with memories, it is important to accurately and consistently address the different ages of the client. 'And what can *you* do?' refers to the client at his present age. 'And what can *he* do?' refers to the client at a younger age. 'And what could possibly happen *there then*, that could make a difference to him?' The question is clear and it increases the probability of change occurring. He as a child could change it; you as an adult could change it; his mother could change it; God could change it; an earthquake could change it. 'And what could *he* do to change it?' restricts the choice to an action by the child, who might have no resources in that situation. 'And what could *you* do to help him *there then*?' The adult goes back from now to help the boy then. This restricts the opportunity for help. The appropriate use of personal pronouns is a key element in locating the client in time.

Ambiguity. 'And what things could *happen* to those people there? And who might be able to go into there and change them?' Ambiguity allows the client to make multiple uses of meaning. One word can have many, many different meanings to him. The client can select his own meaning. The opposite of that is for the therapist to say many different words and the client can translate all those words to mean the same thing.

The clean questions are catalytic to the client's processing. They are necessary for the reaction to occur, for the change to occur. Clean questions do not participate actively as an ingredient. They favor an environment in which change can be facilitated.

2

The Matrix of Experience

Precis

The matrix is an artificial construct used as a teaching device and as a model of the client's psychological infrastructure. It helps the therapist plan and carry out the intervention. The matrix serves to expand the moment between stimulus and response. It is a representation of the non-conscious subjective experience; the client's internal reality that manifests itself in primary process language. This internal reality reveals its surprising content.

In cognitive therapy the client focuses on those thoughts and images that produce unnecessary discomfort or suffering or lead to self-defeating behavior. In our intervention we use clean language to evoke an inward mind set, memories, locus in a time or want set. We call this inward mind set the matrix.

The matrix occupies the ontological moment between Stimulus and Response, representing and containing not only the surface thoughts, automatic thoughts, and images, but also extends to pre-conscious and non-conscious functions.

The concept of matrix. The diagram which relates to the explanation of the matrix is an artificial construct used for teaching purposes, and by therapists to organize their thoughts. It is used as a representation of the mental process. This matrix is a useful fiction, a way in which we can examine the infrastructure of how the client constructs his world. The

matrix is a device that enables the therapist to use clean
language to freeze a moment in time, to stop the world and
examine the infrastructure of the client's internal experience.
The first objective in using the matrix is to help the therapist
to take the client's narrative words and translate them, within
the client's inner experience, into a living form of symbols and
metaphors. The matrix helps give structure to the therapist's
work. It is a device that helps to make sense of the client's
information and enables the therapist to structure the way he
asks questions. The matrix is a means of preserving and
protecting the information that is contained within the client's
inner experience.

In developing what lies within the client's moment in time,
the therapist needs to use a special language. This information
from the client's inner experience is not generally available in
terms of the normal cognitive constructs that we use in
everyday language. The client's information is rich in metaphors, imagery, and symbols. Clean language is the art, the
technique of eliciting what is in the client's matrix, and done in
the client's language, without the introduction by the therapist
of any characterization or other outside construct.

The therapist uses the concept of matrix to help him keep
his intervention within the client's mental set, so that his locus
in time, want set, sense channel, and internal language are
respected. The use of the concept of *matrix* enables the
therapist to facilitate the client's process and to plan and carry
out a precise intervention. By scrupulously staying within the
client's matrix, the therapist promotes the state of the client's
self-absorption, reverie, mini-trance or alpha state in which
therapeutic functions are facilitated.

In a co-operative and consenting process, the client discovers whether an evolution of his internal symbols, metaphors,
memories or semantic constructs will produce development in
a desired direction.

The content of matrix. On the surface, conscious level of his
matrix, the client perceives awareness of thoughts, memories,
and experiences. The client comments on his concerns,

whether past, present or future. We want to determine where in time the greatest density of the client's concerns is located. The therapist has to be very clear and very clean about the way he interrogates the client's process so that he does not impose presuppositions such as 'feel' or 'understand' upon the client.

The first level is what we call the descriptive level— the narrative level— in which the client relates her experience. It is a conscious level. It is here that the client describes her external experience. The external dialogue often contains metaphors and symbols— the clues to the inner process. "It happens when I see my mother. I tense up inside and avoid contact with her." The client first describes the external stimulus and then goes to the word *tense,* which is the first clue to the inner process. When the client describes, narrates or comments on her internal process, it is an external process. The client is talking about her inner experience and not physiologically living it. It is about the inner experience, and she is commenting on the process that is underneath.

The epistemological level. On the pre-conscious 'tip of the tongue' level of her matrix, the client experiences in response to the therapist's clean questions that probe her epistemological function: the memories, metaphors, internal symbols or semantic constructs that underlie her mind set or experience. These constructs enable the client to discover how she knows what she knows and to discover that she knows more than she thinks she knows.

The therapist takes a part of the dialogue about internal experience and extends the significance down to this epistemological level. This is where the client knows she knows something. We want to get the basis of that knowledge into the client's language. It can be physiological, such as a knot, a construct such as an external metaphor, or memories, or an idea in the language of semantics. A clue in the above example that leads to the epistemological level is the word tense: 'Tense, how?' "Tense in the guts like a fist." The fist will now be developed into a physiological form fully represented in the client's sensations. The symbol becomes an internal epistemological reference. That is how she knows she is tense. Many cases are satisfactorily resolved at this epistemological level.

The ontological level. From the non-conscious ontological level of her matrix, the client can consciously experience the nature of her belief that underlies, connects, associates or conditions her existential 'I am-ness'.

If we intervene to change fist, so that the response to her mother will alter, we may find that fist has a persistence and cannot be changed. This may be because fist has been a familiar experience in many different contexts and will not change as it is also related to other events. This is the clue that will lead to the ontological level. The ontology is the 'I am-ness'. It is how the client defines her reality, morals, beliefs, family, and societal rules, the nature of her being. The ontological level is like a great underground stream. It is the source that permeates many different epistemological experiences and has far-reaching implications. It is a common denominator of many experiences. A further metaphor or symbol has to be discovered to reach this level. It will have different qualities to fist and will usually be in a different order of reality. " I don't trust that I can change that and it will stay unchanged." The ontological clue is *trust.* If fist is to change, then the ontological criterion of trust needs to be satisfied first. Fist will not change unless the trust issue has been satisfied. *Trust* is now taken and extended down to establish an ontological metaphor: 'How do you know when you trust?' "I feel at peace." 'And when you are at peace, what's that like?' "It's like a drop of dew shining in the sky."

The ontological metaphor is the dewdrop. Dewdrop has to be present before the client will trust that fist can disappear. It may be that the client has had so many bad experiences with trusting that she does not know how to trust. Then the therapy takes a very different course. It is about trust and, most importantly, about ways to trust internal experience. This is how the ontological level interacts with the epistemological level.

The matrix diagram. Figure 1 is a graphic representation of

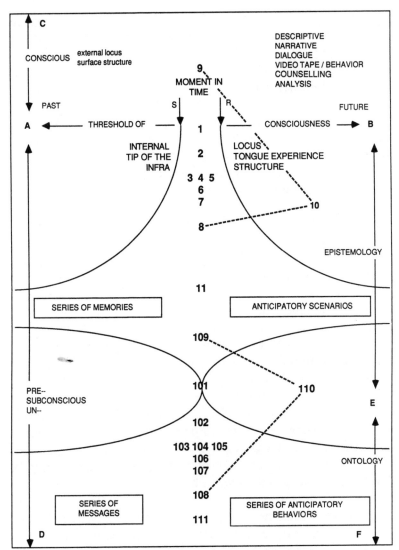

Fig. 1. — The matrix diagram. — A-B time line. A-C area of normal awareness. A-D area of non awareness. B-E area of epistemology. E-F area of ontology. S=stimulus. R=response. (1)-(11) epistemological questions. (101)-(111) ontological questions. See text.

a single matrix. The moment is located in external locus and in conscious awareness. The moment is manifested during the client's descriptive narrative of events. A word or phrase will give the first clue to its existence. The location along line A-B is important and great care must be taken in maintaining the congruence of verb tense. If the experience occurred in the past, all questions address that moment. If a question is asked in the present (such as: 'How do you feel now?') the client will be pulled out of the matrix and experience an uncomfortable split in time. Area A-D represents the other than conscious levels of experience. The infrastructure of non-conscious information processing is located in this area. The first non-conscious level, Area B-E, is the epistemological level. Here the client discovers how he knows that he knows. The questions tend to induce a naturalistic trance facilitated by the search for internal knowledge.

Epistemological questions 1-11. 1. 'And when you have tight, where do you have tight?' 2. 'And when you have tight in your stomach, where in your stomach do you have tight?' (Gives location to the experience of the feeling.) 3. 'And when the tight is in the pit of your stomach, what is it like?' (Simile: "It's like a fist.") 4. 'And when the fist is in the pit of your stomach, what size is it?' 5,6. Shape, color, temperature, texture. (Develops the sensory modalities of the fist and gives it form and experiential reality.) 7,8. 'And when the big, rough, cold fist is in your stomach, does it have any movement?' 9. 'And when you have fist, what happens?' (Moves client out of matrix and links to external behavioral reality. Checks that fist is related to behavior, thought, or feeling.) 10. 'When you see your mother, you have this fist in your stomach that goes to your heart and this makes you avoid her.' (Confirms the connection between fist and external behavior. Question induces the client back into the matrix.) 11.'And take some time and see if you can discover any more qualities about that fist, and all the times when it may have been useful.' (Deepens and develops the integrity of fist by adding detail.) Fist becomes the epistemological knowledge form.

At this level fist can be used to go back in the past. It allows access to a series of significant memories associated with fist. Anticipatory scenarios are memories in the future associated with fist. This process assembles the experience of past, present, and future. From this procedure the therapist determines the greatest density of feeling.

Is the density of feeling in memories, in present physiology of fist, in semantic constructs or in future anticipatory scenarios? If this process does not lead to a satisfactory resolution of fist, and an issue such as *trust* stops fist from changing, this is the first clue that leads to the ontological level: "I don't trust that I can change fist and that it will stay changed."

Ontological questions 101-111. 101. 'And when you don't trust, how do you know you don't trust?' (Takes trust and determines how the client knows that she does not trust. The issue of trust prevents the fist from changing.) 102-108. Establish the metaphor or symbol for trust at the ontological level: 102. 'And when you just know you don't trust, how do you know that?' 103. 'And when you know in your head that you don't trust, where about in your head do you know that?' 104. 'And when you have that feeling at the front of your head, what is that like?' (Simile: "It's like a hollow that has been left by a dewdrop.") 105-106. Establish shape, color, temperature, texture. 107. Establishes movement. 108. 'And what is the difference between when you don't have dewdrop and when you do?' (Establishes the difference.) 109. 'And when you don't have dewdrop, that's how you know you don't trust. And when you don't trust, then fist cannot change.' (Checks that dewdrop is related to fist and that this relationship makes sense to client.) 110. 'And if fist is to change, then dewdrop will need to be present.' (Connects fist to dewdrop.) 111. 'And take a little time to know about when you don't have dewdrop, and about all the things that would have to happen so that dewdrop could be there in just the way dewdrop needs to be there to know about trust.' (Develops details of dewdrop.)

The series of messages are past experiences of how trust was established or not established. The series of anticipatory behaviors establish the future implications of trusting or not trusting.

The objective is to create a therapeutic environment in which dewdrop is present. The client then knows she can trust. When this occurs, the fist in epistemology can now change because the criterion of trust has been formed. We expect this change (creating dewdrop) in the internal ontological infrastructure to produce a change in the epistemological fist.

The questions, with the exception of 9., facilitate a naturalistic trance as the client keeps to her internal experience. The process in the matrix is facilitated by the therapist. This is accomplished by the therapist using language that resonates with the client's internal process. These language forms, such as fist or dewdrop, are constructed realities, fragile and easily destroyed by cognitive questions. Coherence in the matrix is maintained by directing the therapist's questions to the precise location in the body of fist or dewdrop and maintaining the exact orientation in time. Violating the co-ordinates of time or place destroys the delicate fabric of the matrical experience. The questions extend the significance down into the internal experience. They are synchronic: everything occurs at the same moment in time. Ordinarily, therapeutic questions tend to be diachronic, in that the client gives information across time. Extending the significance down causes the client to go internal and maintain the coherence with her internal experience.

Normal therapeutic questions gather information from the client. Such questions allow the therapist to share and understand the client's experience and possibly interpret it. Clean questions access memories, metaphors, symbols, and semantic constructs in the client's internal reality. The client understands her processes experientially. The therapist may not need to know the contents of the client's process.

We establish in which of the four languages the client represents her experience. The therapist's clean questions act like a lens that focuses the client's attention on the key elements of the internal sequence. The internal sequence may have a variety of elements that are linked together. A given stimulus, Mother for example, elicits a memory flash back of mother scolding; red flushing in the face; fist in stomach; dizziness in the head; external flight. Using words like 'imagine' or 'visualize' restricts the ability of the client to respond, and thereby robs the response of its power. These words may also dissociate the client from her experiential base, as they induce a visual descriptive response.

Healing environment. The matrix helps to constellate both the negative experience of the client's pathology (fist) and the positive resources that can heal within the client's own experiences. The matrix provides a setting in which the therapist can alter the environment around a particular element of pathology (fist). The therapist utilizes the client's intuitive knowledge, the intuitive healing ability, first. If this is not effective, the therapist can introduce external resources such as cognitive knowledge or behavioral or family intervention.

Giving form. The matrix provides an environment in which words that narrate experience can be translated into an inner experiential form. The word anxiety is translated into the symbol fist. The form (fist) contains more detailed knowledge than the original descriptive word (anxious). This new knowledge, previously unavailable to the client, is accessed by developing fist.

Density. The greatest density within the matrix exists around the content that is most intensely experienced. The therapist asks questions that enable the client to decide which element in the matrix represents the most intense experience of the pathology: is it flash back, knot in stomach, beating heart or sweating? The client determines inside the matrix that the beating heart is the worst, most intense element. If the beating heart could be calmed, the rest would not matter so much. The intervention, therefore, is first focused on the beating heart. We may attend to knot in stomach and flash back later.

Locus in time. The therapist's questions serve to locate a particular moment in time. Most questions will be in the near past or distant past. The therapist must be clear as to the particular moment addressed by his question: 'What are you feeling?' (present/past/future) 'What are you feeling now?' (present) 'What are you feeling now about that?' (in the present moment about past moment) 'What did you feel?' (past and present) 'What did you feel then?' (past).

Changing the question's tense will locate the client in time. There is great flexibility in the matrix, and memories, people, and resources can be transported to past and future times. Time is stopped and extended down in the matrix and then is extended laterally into the past or future.

A fifty year old client was molested by her uncle at the age of three. In her memory she wanted her mother to come and help her. Her mother had died when the client was two. The phrasing of the question can transport resources over time: 'And what could a mother who is dead do for her little girl when those things are being done by that uncle?' White lights descend, enter the memory, and remove the fear. A dead mother can send that white light to heal her daughter. This is an example of flexibility in time and place that can occur when the client is fully invested in the matrix. This can only occur in the matrix, in an internal state. Resources can be taken from the present and future to the past: 'And the things you know now, and the knowledge you know now, how could that go back to then and change then so that then could be different?'

Reality check. When the elements in the matrix have been formatted, the therapist asks the client about their implications for external reality. This ensures that the selected elements of the matrix relate to the behavioral aspect of the presenting problem: 'If the element fist were to change in some way, would this give you what you want and enable you to change your behavior in some way?' The therapist helps the client to change fist in the matrix. When fist changes, the behavior will change. The client knows intuitively that this connection makes sense. This reality test can be made before the intervention and increases the probability of success. Another reality test is made after the intervention to determine if changing fist *in matrix* will change the behavior.

In the process of constructing the presenting matrix, the therapist can map out the opposite, the antithesis; he can construct that as well and use it in an intervention later on.

Does the client attend more to the external phenomena or the internal reality? Where in time is the client focusing his attention? Is he more present-oriented, past-oriented or future-oriented? Where in time does the density of the pathology lie? Most often, one of the four languages is the primary medium in which the message is delivered. The therapist discovers the particular language in order to operate in it.

We use what is there in the client to heal himself, as opposed to an intervention in which the therapist introduces outside factors such as knowledge or behavioral or cognitive activity. The first object is to find ways of altering even a syntactical structure of that particular language in the matrix in order to create an environment in which healing can occur. The matrix provides a vehicle in which the therapist can alter the environment around a particular item of pathology. This can assist the client, with minimal intervention, to discover how it is that he can heal. The therapist first utilizes the client's intuitive knowledge, his intuitive healing ability.

One use of the matrix is to take the client's knowledge and to put it into a live form. Symbols and metaphors help to make this knowledge alive, rather than just putting it into words. It may be that once the therapist has established a matrix there may not be much that he can do about it. He cannot devise a further intervention. The therapist should make this clear. The client now has information and knowledge he did not possess before. Putting it into a form and making that knowledge come to life can be healing in and of itself. Now the client has an experiential knowledge of his own process and a framework within which to organize that knowledge. For the client who is confusing or confused, the therapist can have him put a structure to the complaint. The client can now see the mechanism that operates in the metaphor of his confusion. This knowledge can make that confusion bearable.

Each matrix is constructed in each moment of time, right through the client's history. The significant events in a history to do with the current matrix show up as denser or stronger points. The experiences that have occurred in the near past will be impacted by events that occurred before that, will meet at this particular matrix, and will also come forward to the present, which, in turn, will influence this current matrix. Events in the past come forward and influence this event that is in the here and now. Other events or histories or the ontology come forward and extend into the future, so that the future is also affected by these events. The future is partly made up of projections from the present. From this matrix extend projections which go forward into the future to construct events and other matrices of what may be. Elements from the past go right through. There is a feedback loop in which constructs of the future come back in the same way that events from the past can haunt the client in the present. These constructs from the future can also come back and enter into this current matrix. In other words, it can haunt from the future.

This can be part of the structure of anticipatory anxiety. It can motivate from the future, because these forces can be every bit as positive or as negative, and every bit as significant as things from the past. The current state of psychotherapy is about uncovering things and making conscious the processes of the present and past. We have little experience in orchestrating ways in which the future comes back to manifest itself in the present.

In some other cultures there is value in the past, in terms of the mythologies— our ancestors— and there is also value in the future, in terms of gods or beliefs or even fears and taboos. These beliefs are about things that will happen in the future if this good or bad thing is done in the present. The good deed in the present has value in some types of worship, as can an activity like honoring the ancestors. Honoring ancestors is about things from the past coming to the present and extending into the future.

There is dual feedback into the matrix. When working in the matrix there is no limitation to going up or down, or backward or forward, in time. Time is not a linear dimension when one is inside the matrix. When one extends out along a time line, it moves forward in one direction only, but the matrix is not bound by time-space limitations. The extended matrix is like a world-view: it is a telescopic view of the whole history of the client's life and his expectation of living again in the future.

The therapist decides where the matrix fits and which matrix he is stopping at what point; freeze-framing to examine the internal infrastructure of the client's experience. Critical to this process is where along the time line the therapist focuses his questions in order to freeze that moment. One second either side will give the therapist an entirely different matrix, so a macro view helps the therapist in the initial phase of gathering information. This phase is more externally oriented, enabling the therapist to focus on a particular point. Then the relationship between that point and other points is constellated so that as the therapist goes into the matrix, he knows where he is extending down or laterally in time. We know what events in the external world correlate with a particular element in the matrix. An overview of the extended matrix is useful in ⁺erms of deciding where in the client's pathology the therapist is going to take the slice and enter the matrix. The therapist might choose several different matrices that he may decide to integrate later.

When the client is oriented in his past, he is not who he is now. If the client is thirty years old now in the present and a seven year old in the past, what the therapist may find is that the seven year old boy cannot do or say what is needed. He has the limitations of a seven year old boy. The therapist needs to be aware that it may take somebody in the past or another resource to do it, because it is impossible for that seven year old to do it. Either the therapist speaks for the client or somebody who was there can speak for him or some magical animal speaks for him.

'And what could possibly happen that could make a difference *there then* for him?' That is very clean. That allows him *there* to make the difference, him *now* to make the difference, something else to make the difference, God to make the difference, Mother to come in and make the difference; allowing all those possibilities without directing. The word 'allow' means that somebody has to give permission now. Is it the seven year old who gives permission, or the thirty year old who gives permission? And what does he need permission for anyway? The three words 'Can you allow?' are reasonably clean, but they contain many loaded presuppositions.

It is *there then*, not there *and* then because the *and* splits the reality. If he says *there then*, there is no mistaking that *there then* refers to the matrix: 'And what could happen *there then* that could make a difference in some way so that it could be different?' That is huge, wide permission and it does not limit the client. It is completely clean. When the therapist gives that specific injunction, it guides the client into that portion of the matrix. The therapist can surround each element in the matrix because he can extend it into the past, present, and future. The therapist directs the client to the past: 'And take some time to discover what could happen *there then* that could be different, and as you do that it might be interesting to think about....' The therapist has directed the client there, and is going to leave him there to think about it surrounded with these ideas. The client does not have to do any of these things, but the therapist is going to surround that matrix, extend it into the present: 'And to think about the knowledge that you have now and how you can take that knowledge now back to then. And you can think about the people that you had then and how they might be able to do something then so that it could be different. And know about what things could happen just before then, that if those things happened then, again it would have been different. And it is interesting to think about those things then that could make then different, or about the knowledge that you know now and the people that you know now and about how those could go back to then and assist you in some way so then could be different. So take a little time to discover about what could happen that could be different.'

The client is in the matrix, he is part of the past and the therapist surrounds him with these possibilities, these resources. As the therapist surrounds him, bathes him, in that minute he is changing the environment around the client. He introduces things from the now to go back and reactivates people that were right there at that time. The therapist asks what could happen just before this moment that could have prevented it. And the client did not prevent it. And all this time he thought it was his father. This additional information, not available before, is the straw that breaks the camel's back. That is the epiphanic moment,* that is the thing that makes it differ. The therapist is searching for possibly that one thing, that piece of information, and, suddenly, the whole perspective changes and the client can be left in a profound trance.

The piece of information, from the matrix at age seven, has to go forward to now. The client now has a dissonance in all his memories after seven and in all the matrices to do with his father. It is disconcerting when that happens because it takes some time for the whole history to adjust. The generative change occurs at the ontological level. Now that the client has found out about his father, that is the element that sweeps up through the system. It '…can take some time' to work through the system. Often that is all the therapist needs to do and the matrix will itself change. It can be just a matter of a few days.

One could conceivably finish the whole intervention in the same session by going through all the relevant memories of the father, remaking the epistemology of the father. That way the client knows it is complete: he has had the new mental step about his father established. The old one has now gone and this new one is there and the therapist has facilitated this by moving the client through it at an epistemological level. We do not recommend this. The dreams, and all these thoughts, will start coming to mind. The client will have to restructure his experience and cognitions about his father in the natural course of events in time and dreams. Alternatively the therapist might want to restructure a number of matrices relating to

---

*For definition see footnote,Chapter 3 p. 56

a particular person and to a particular event right there at the session or a series of sessions.

We also like, as much as possible, to let the client heal himself without the therapist. The client may get stuck on one or two items, requiring the therapist to prod those memories. The therapist knows that it is done, when it is done, or that more work is needed. The epistemology of the father is, "Like this hand with steel gloves on." After the change, "These gloves have now gone to chain-mail," and, "The rod has now turned into the branch of a tree that bends," and that is better. But the client does not like the rod, and the hand is still very heavy. The therapist might take the client through memories and continue until the client has just his father's hand, which he wants. It comes out that, "Yes, that is the hand of my father. When my father was my age, thirty years old, I remember he had this scar. He had very strong hands. Now that is his hand, it is not this steely one any longer, and in his hand he has a tree that has now turned into this toy. He brought me a little wooden toy, and it has turned into this wooden toy, and he is holding it in his hand and that is how I would like to remember him."

Directionality. As the client goes down the matrix, extending its significance, we may meet greater resistance. The therapist needs skillful questions to extend the significance down, because a natural tendency, particularly at the interface between the external level and the internal level, is to go laterally. Going laterally at the external level would be going into the past or going into the future, or talking about the things that happened after the response. The client naturally gives much internal information. The therapist wants to freeze a moment in time to go down into the matrix. The therapist also wants a synoptic view. In a synoptic view we see varying levels of reality and how they interact. This is what going down in the matrix achieves. At the epistemological level, and the ontological level, the therapist can also go laterally. Once the therapist has the client in his epistemology, he keeps him there by keeping everything of the future or the past at the epistemological level. The therapist uses that epistemology to transport the client over time and does not wish him to surface to an external view.

The therapist may want to check that the epistemology makes sense in the real world: 'So you have this knot in your stomach that is red like fire, and when you have this knot in the stomach does this mean...?' That question translates into external reality: 'Does this mean that you then cannot face your father?' and the client answers "Yes," and then the therapist puts the client back into epistemology. What the therapist does is a quick check and return, introducing the client back into matrix by repeating at the epistemological level: 'So when you have that red knot, is that the thing that prevents you from having your chat with your father, or is there something else?'

A therapist could question: 'So when you are going to see your father again, do you think that will happen?' That question would take the client right out of the matrix and leave him out. A better formulation is: 'So take some time to think about that red knot, and about a time in the future when you may see your father, and is there anything you might do to change that red knot so that it could be different?' That question should keep the client at the epistemological level.

The therapist bears in mind at what level he is asking questions so that he connotes the client's reality by leaving him at the current level. It is disruptive to change and switch levels abruptly: the therapist can intrude briefly, but if he stays too long on a question he will pull the client back out to another way of thinking.

The epistemological and the ontological levels are indicative of altered states. When the client is at those levels, he is in trance. The client comes out of the trance when he meta-comments about his experience at the first level, or when he discourses about the external happening. The ontological level is a field created by the presence of all the experience that would be represented by the sum total of the different interrelated matrices. When asking the questions, it is best to bear in mind that the questions will probably direct the client's focus of attention to a particular level at which he is going to answer. The question needs to be constructed so that it maintains the process at the client's level, that is, the level that he last answered from.

When the client is in epistemological level, we may want to arrive at the symbol, at the representation of the central issue of his state. We do not know how we are going to get there. We surround the matrix and once we get in the epistemological level, we can wait there, allowing the client to be surrounded by new ways of experiencing these events. We are waiting for something to distill; something which will drop the client into the ontological level, where there will be a new insight or where there will be a spontaneous experiential change or where the perspectives will be altered.

In this loosening up, because of the dimensional aspects of a matrix, it matters where forms are in relation to other structures so that by moving metaphors and symbols, juxta-positioning these forms, integrating them, changing sequences, the therapist can alter the nature of the contents that are in the matrix. Once the therapist alters the position of an element relative to another, he induces change.

When the therapist goes for the opposite in a matrix, he is spatially separating these symbolic forms in the client's experience and, when he moves to synthesis or integration, he spatially moves one symbol into, onto or around the other. This mechanical moving of forms within the client's mind or experience or body is useful in performing interventions in the matrix. These language forms, metaphors, and symbols contain discreet bits of knowledge and information not ordinarily available to the client. When the client is at the epistemological level, he is likely to answer in terms of epistemology. Does the client go external? Or does he go internal? That is important information, and to obtain this is one of the uses of asking ambiguous questions.

The therapist would normally want to direct the sentence or the question to where the last answer came from. This requires maintaining congruence with the client's answer and not with the therapist's sense of congruency, or where he wants to take the client. The therapist keeps going until the client's attention is fixed.

'You are somewhere now. When you tense up, what is that like?' "It is like a wrench is inside me tying me up." 'And what is that wrench like?' "The wrench is like a ball, a tennis ball, a compacted tennis ball." So here we have a knot, to a wrench, to a tennis ball. The therapist keeps following this down and it does not matter that a wrench is mentioned or a knot. What matters is where it ends up, because this is a sculpted reality and only the end product is important. The client knows retrospectively that the compacted tennis ball really is it. It is the *it-ness* of his pathology, and the wrench and knot are just transitional states in which the client could develop his very particular, unique, and idiosyncratic language.

Changing the relationship of forms, bringing one symbol or metaphor to interact with the other, can directly alter these elements. This is true of metaphors, symbols, memories, and even the words expressing the client's experience. The therapist can move these items about. He can move a particular symbol by bringing it to a higher matrix, or he can drop it into a lower matrix, or he could take it to a future level, or take it back to a past level. He can change certain aspects of a symbol, changing such things as the direction of its travel, the direction of its spin, changing its power, its size, its texture.

Changing the syntax, the order of sentences, or words, or punctuating differently can alter the meaning. The same operation can be performed within each of the four languages. We need not necessarily alter the meaning directly, or change the memory of events, and yet we can punctuate the meaning of that event quite differently.

Clients are more intent on maintaining energy in what they believe, or what they think is true, than in the qualities that have to do with punctuation or syntax. As long as the client can have those words there, the therapist can put an apostrophe, or question mark, here and the client will allow that change, and of course what happens is that a tiny alteration, punctuation or other modality changes the nature of the meaning or the sense of the client's construct.

The therapist keeps the matrix in his head to help give structure to his work. It is primarily a vehicle to make sense of the information that the client gives and that enables the therapist to structure the way he asks questions. For the client it is simply a fiction, because when working within the matrix of his experience, he does not need to know it. He is living it, and it is there. The therapist may wish to give some examples and talk about a matrix at the beginning of an intervention so that the client understands what he is doing. Often, particularly in going to the epistemological level, the client will report he never felt or experienced these phenomena. It is part of an experience that is hallucinatory by nature.

Ordinarily, what the client wants is not to have what he has got. After the intervention the therapist may want to inform the client and explain what he did so that the client can make sense of it. While he is in this matrix, the client normally does not care a great deal about what the therapist is doing. The client's attention is focused inward and the therapist is not really there.

The Want Frame

Precis

The want frame utilizes the client's energy in the direction of his want. This avoids resistance and gives direction to the healing. Every twist and turn, every suggestion in the intervention is related to the want. The client feels validated and has a new and experiential way of knowing what he wants and what he does not want. The client discovers the metaphors that tell him how he knows what he wants.

Establishing a want. It is important to pre-empt therapeutic resistance. This technique is a way of producing an environment around the client's experience, in which he can discover for himself experientially *in matrix* what it is that he wants. We evoke that environment by moving experience over time. It is not so much the meaning of the words, or the understanding that is used, but a time line in which experience is sorted, experience is grouped, compared, and contrasted.

In order that a client knows what he wants, he has to have some ideas about what it is like. The client needs to conceive in the future and, if he is not future-oriented, this is more difficult. If the client is not future-oriented, he is most likely past-oriented. This technique serves to organize past experience so the client can discover in the past how he knows what he wanted and then translate that want into the future. In doing this the client can have some experience of knowing in the present what it is that he wants in the future. When a client does not know what he wants, one of the things he is often sure of is that he does not want what he has now.

Moving constructs in time. "Nothing is the way I want it." The client knows that what he has now he does not want. We are going to sequence this in time, using time as a base: 'How long have you had what you have got now?' "Well, it has been six years." 'So for six years you have not had what you want because you have had what you have got now?' "Yes." 'So then something happened in the six years which gave you what you have got?' "Yes."

Now we have a period of time established and we call it *the six years*. We know that for *six years* the client had this 'whatever it is' that he does not want. This concept is going to become the pivotal point. What we establish here is a concept, some construct in the future that would be like what he wants. It is called a telos; a pie in the sky, Garden of Eden, or some future happy time: when my ship comes in, the country cottage, living happily ever after, a purpose, an aim in life.

At the moment the client often does not have the ability to put it into words— often he does not even know what it is— and we are going to help produce a structure to that future reality by using a path. In six years he has not had what he wants. Going back before six years, we ask an important question: 'So before *six years*, did you have what you wanted then?' Now we establish: 'Did something happen here? Did you have what you wanted then? Were things okay and then *six years* happened and then you lost it?' If the answer to that is yes, we ask a question to establish the idea that some of what the client wants in the future could be like what he had before. We are setting up an experience, helping him, teaching him to recognize what he wants through something good he had before.

Orienting thoughts in time. We want the client to take a wider view and ask about the beginning of the time that this unwanted thought existed. This may serve to orient the client to the possibility that there was a time that existed before, a time when his complaint was not there. When we do that, we have the opportunity of orienting to three different times: *before thought, at thought* or *after thought.*

Before thought orients the client to a time preceding this experience: 'Has there ever been a time in which you did not think the world was not the way you wanted it to be?'

At thought orients the client right to the first experience: 'Can you remember the first time at which you knew or the first time that something happened that enabled you to make that statement?'

After thought covers the ground between thought and now. This pertains to how the thought experience developed: 'What things that happened in your life made it possible for you to say something like that?'

These three questions orient the client towards confirming what that statement is. As the client goes back and relates the development, we are not casting any doubt, we are seeking historically for the client to give us information about how that statement could be true. An interesting paradox can occur as he replies, particularly to the first question, about times before this thought occurred.

The want frame can, in and of itself, be an intervention and all that is needed. It also can be the first part of gathering information. The importance of the want frame is that, first, it orients the client into the future and it orients him to the nature of *solutions* rather than the nature of problems. Second, the want frame gives us a direction in which to orient the client to best heal himself and it helps establish, by that direction, the line of least resistance. The want frame actively enlists the client's energy and channels that energy towards that particular outcome.

When establishing the particular want, everything that occurs in therapy thereafter is related and aligned in the same direction as that want. Even though the therapist may wish to achieve something else in therapy than what is stated in the client's want, he goes down that want frame path first. This is where the energy lies. Once we have gone down there, we can make a change in direction and go tangentially to the want.

Regardless of the situation, the therapist needs to know what it is that the client wants. Everything we do is going to have the same direction as that want. Every intervention with its tangential is going to relate to the client's want. The therapist, therefore, may not have to oppose any energy. He does not have to help the client to try to understand. The therapist has a direction in which his intervention is going and he is less likely to meet any resistance. Some questions that help establish the want frame are: 'What is it that you want?' 'Is there something you would like?' 'Are there any things you might want different in any way?' 'What is it that you want that could be different in some way and that being different in some way might be useful to help you get what you want?'

Basic technology of want. At the very beginning of a therapeutic interview the simple question, 'What do you want?' is *the* question to ask. This question can be asked in a number of different ways.

When we ask, 'What do you want?' we can get a big answer: "Well, what I want is love." It may take us some time to get that down to some specifics. Another question which is sometimes acceptable is (and we may ask this one later on): 'What do you want that might happen here?' That question takes us away from the big picture and puts us into something more practical. It is something that might be achievable in the session on a doable basis.

If a client has no conception of a want that is doable and achievable in this hour, then he is not going to be able to answer that question. We then have to go to the bigger picture of what he wants. If he can answer it, that is good. If he cannot, and the want cannot be contained in a simple statement, we do not think we should force the client into formulating his want in this manner.

When we start off with, 'What do you want?' there are only three possible answers: the client can say what it is he wants; he can say what he does not want; he can state that he does not know. Each of these three answers is to be valued equally. There is as much value in what the client does *not* want and does *not* know as in very clearly and very simply elucidating what it is he does want.

In the want frame we can make use of whatever a client gives us. We may have to put it into a different form before we can make a useful therapeutic contribution. We help the client discover how it is that he knows what he wants.

The main focus is on whatever the client gives us. We will value and use that information to plan the intervention. Let us take the first case, where the client states positively what he wants. First we define what language the want is in. The client says: "I want happiness." To define that want, we find out what his happiness is like. We want to determine what language the client uses to deliver the information about his want. Is it in a symbol or in a metaphor? Is it semantic or is it behavioral? Is the happiness internally defined in such a way as: "I just want to feel happy," or is it intermingled with some external factor?

Client: "I want self-confidence." 'So when you have self-confidence, what is that like? How do you know that you know that you want to be self-confident?' And the client says, "I just know that is what I want." It is reasonably easy to get this want into a form: 'How long have you known you have wanted that?' and: 'Has there been a time when you knew you did not want that and wanted something else?' By asking these questions we are going to extend the significance down to getting an epistemology for that want. We want to discover the internal physiological symbol. Once the client has established his symbol, we no longer talk about self-confidence.

A basic objective in working with the want frame is to shape and form the want into something that may be doable or achievable in therapy. We test, form, and shape the want so that it is doable. It may turn out that just doing this may be the therapeutic outcome itself. Initially we are not even concerned about what might be a desirable objective for the client. We establish and test whether the want is a strongly held belief. Can it be altered or made malleable? Are there any alternatives? When we have that information, we plan an intervention which will help achieve what it is that the client wants.

At this initial phase we are concerned with putting the want into a form and testing its validity. For some clients it might take one minute to do this. For other clients, who are not sure what they want and do not have much conviction about it, it may be easy to change their want. It is worthwhile to spend time negotiating the want and testing it so that we establish a firm direction in which to focus our intervention. In this preparatory phase we flesh out the want and test its integrity.

Epistemology of the want. The want frame is an important key to powerful, elegant therapy because: 1. It clearly establishes the want; 2. It establishes it in a way the client never knew before. It gets right into the client's epistemology; 3. Every twist and turn, every suggestion in the intervention is always directly related to the want; 4. In doing this we pre-empt resistance because we are not guessing at what the client wants. We utilize the client's energy in the direction of his want and the intervention is shaped and framed in terms of the client's expressed want. Whether we go into memories, symbols or metaphors, each intervention is always related back to the original want.

We keep testing, making sure that this is still what the client really wants. Used in this way the want frame pre-empts resistance and enlists the client in the participatory process. We need to formulate our interventions constantly in terms of the stated want.

Some therapists get a kind of a want frame when they make a contract with the client. The want frame is then part of the contract: 'We are working here together in order to get you this thing that you want.' That gives the client a social or cognitive process about what he wants. When we get to the epistemology, it can be what the client really wants at a gut level: 'So you want to stop smoking?' "Yeah, it is for my health." However, when we establish the epistemology ('so when you smoke, you feel calm and floating on a cloud; when you do not smoke, you are all irritated.') that is different. Floating on a cloud is a better, more desired state than being irritated and jumpy, even though verbally the client says he wants to quit.

We also use the want frame to go into the future: 'If you did get what you want, how could you know that?' We want the answer established on two different levels. First we establish it internally: "I would have this floating cloud. I would feel different inside. I would feel warm and that is how I would know." Then we establish it on a behavioral level: "Well, I would be able to enjoy doing all these things."

We establish the criteria by which the client will recognize the goal: 'How will you know the therapy has been successful? How will you know you have gotten what you want?' Many therapists ask this sort of question. That is also part of their contract-making. However, it is usually not as probing as our method: "Well, sure, my cloud will have a silver lining, that is all. It will not be black like this, it will be light and fluffy."

Establishing the client's want is powerful therapy. The client can go out with the knowledge of what he wants and have that confirmation inside himself. He can return to his old milieu, the same environment, the same life and he can survive all that much better because he has a new confidence.

Now the client knows *this I want* and *that I do not want.* Sometimes it suffices to give assertion training: to teach the client that he is entitled to *want what he wants, to not want what he does not want* and to tell people what he wants and does not want. The only reason he needs to give is to say *I want it* because *I want it* and *I do not want it* because *I do not want it.* When he is talking to people, he does not have to provide justification for it.

We have straightened out some of the client's internal chaos. He can exist better in the world if the chaos is external, and his internal chaos is now limited. Often when the client does not know what he wants, he is in a crazy environment where he is getting schizophrenogenic messages.

Our method is an evolutionary process, and in an evolutionary process we work with the material that is there. We alter the internal environment so that the want will mutate or evolve into a more useful, a more doable, want. This is the purpose of valuing the want that the client brings. We go inside the matrix of the client's experience to work with the structure of how it is that he knows, how it is that he wants that want. Working with that structure we can alter the way in which he wants things without necessarily having to directly challenge his particular want. It does not matter how vaguely a client states his want. There is always something that we can do to protect the integrity of that want until we can get at the basis, at the epistemology.

Whatever the client says, whether it is formulated in the negative or the positive, or if the client first presents his information about something that he does not want, it is not at this stage that we tell him that he cannot want what he wants. That want may be a very real, valuable part of the client's experience, and for the therapist to try and reshape it immediately could simply destroy the matrix. It does not matter how illogical or how much against the therapeutic intuition that want is. The therapist values that want because that is the language of the client's experience. It is easy, later on, to construct the counter example of that want to obtain the opposite matrix, which is something more positive when the client is not giving the positive want. It is one thing to talk the client out of an idea which is at an external reality level. It is an entirely different matter to let him have his want, and value his want, and change his want at an epistemological and an ontological level. Once it is changed in the infrastructure, it is not likely to come back again.

The purpose in the want frame is to get at a client's actual knowing, at a level that operates below the structure of the details and narrative about the components that make up the conflict. The want frame will either challenge what a client wants and give his want an integrity, or it will assist in developing what the client wants. When the client knows what he does not want, we also develop what he does want. We thereby facilitate an evolutionary process from what he does not want into something that he might want.

Ontology. Now we move into another sequence of events which is about *trust.* It is not about knowing: "When I do know something, how can I trust I know that?"

We find that as a child this client knew what he knew and he was confident, and then this event happened. From that time on he no longer really knew. There was always some doubt and then gradually it got worse and worse. What we do is to restructure the memories of the event so that the client knows how to trust because sometime in this matrix of trust there were things that the client did that turned out so badly that he can no longer trust his own judgement. We examine those experiences, perhaps ask the client to restructure them, and modify the voice in the head that doubts.

In dealing with this aspect of a client, we are not actually dealing with the event as such. We are helping to build up in this client a way of knowing how he knows something, so that he has some way to know: "That is what I want." We help the client develop some skills and a degree of confidence in being able to know what he wants and to have some sense of trust about that. It happens that in giving the client a way of knowing how to know, some of the presenting problems will resolve. Now the client has a new operational metaphor.

The object of this is to give the client a way of experientially knowing what it is that he wants. With a well-formed want we may be able to do something therapeutically. Here the objective of the want set is to test the integrity of the client's want and to give him the opportunity of experiencing that want in a different way.

Some external and environmental realities are impossible to alter. Clients may have to live with them, and yet we can still re-establish the integrity of the knowledge base. It is right and proper not to put up with being beaten. The feeling of revulsion at being beaten can be subjugated by social pressures. We can enhance a feeling that the client has. We give confirmation to a want that is real. The priority of what he wants within himself is re-established. Helping the client with this difficulty may enable him to go out into a hostile environment and survive with his integrity intact.

Undoable want. It is better to go down the want pathway and explore the undoable want completely until we get to the end and possibly extinguish that want. Then we can explore a more realistic want. When there are a number of different wants and the client does not know what he wants, we get the *in matrix* experience of having that want, which may help extinguish that want.

"I still want to be loved by him, I still want him to love me." If we fail to connote that, the elasticity remains and whatever we might negotiate after that will to some extent be undermined by the fact that the client still has this other want at the back of her mind.

To trace a want down its particular pathway, to get to an impasse and then to leave the way open because it becomes pregnant with possibilities, is part of facilitating the epiphanic moment:* 'You want to kill that man or you want to commit suicide. Okay, how would you commit suicide, what would happen inside when you get to the point when you actually commit suicide?'

The client gets down to the end of this box canyon. There is no way out. She is trapped within it. She may make a quantum leap out onto another pathway which will constellate a different want. We may not logically be able to get out of the client's want, but as we connote and extend it, we are seeking a conversion experience when the want transforms into something else. Should we try to ignore, or not pay appropriate homage to, that want, it may return later and interfere with a good outcome.

Don't know. The client can respond: "I do not know." At this moment he does not know what he wants. If we ask or cajole the client into proffering some information at a linguistic level, we are likely to get some more of the same. When the client does not know, we put the not knowing into a form. The fact that he does not know is important. This is part of the presenting problem. If we ignore it or try to get around it, we miss valuable

---

*An epiphanic moment is the instance when the client is confronted with the stark reality of a common, ordinary, everyday occurrence, and in that confrontation something happens that causes the client to alter his point of view.

information that can contribute to a well-formed outcome. It is no accident that this client does not know what he wants.

We give the client an experiential way *in matrix* of knowing what the want is in metaphorical or symbolic language. From metaphor or symbol we want to translate it into the real world and see what would have to happen in order for the client to get what he wants: 'Is what you want what you have got now?' "No, I do not want what I have go now." 'What do you want?' "I do not know." 'Is what you have go now what you want?' "No, it is not." Now a simple linguistic switch: 'What you *do know* is that you *do not want* what you have got now.' Now we know what he does not want and we get that defined in solid form, together with its polarity.

Testing the want. We are valuing that want in the past, present, and future, as well as building up a profile of that want and examining the behavioral components and what the client's expectations are. We also examine what the client has done in order to fulfill that want. How many things has he done in the past when he thought that that want was going to be fulfilled? What is important is the deep structure of that want, which is how the client knows he wants it. When he obtains what he wants, how does he recognize it? In the past when that had happened, when did he first recognize that this was what he wanted? At what moment was there a dissonance between his internal epistemology and the actual behavior?

If the client says it with words, that is one thing. He may cognitively be able to tell us what he 'wants', but, by putting him inside the matrix and getting the epistemology, we assist the client to experientially *in matrix* verify what he really wants. The problem with asking the client what he really wants is that so often we get a cognitive, social response and this can often be at odds with his epistemology, his experiential way of knowing his want. We are providing an environment for testing the integrity of the want: if it stands firm, it is a solid want.

This intervention is to help the client get what he wants. The purpose of the operation is to test the integrity of the want, check that it stands up, is well-formed, and see that it is something doable.

The intervention connotes reality, it does not destroy the want. It may very gently evolve the want into something different. Sometimes the client responds by defining what he does not want. This is stated in the negative and we use that information also.

We take what the client does *not* want and use that to get a sharper definition of what he *does* want. One way of doing that is to find out: 'Is what you do not want what you have got now? How long have you had what you do not want?' We bind that in time and we define what he does not want so that we can enter into the matrix: 'What you do not want is what you have got now. And what is it like? How do you know you know you do not want what you have?' What we are getting at is the internal language that describes the want.

When we ask: 'Is this the same feeling or a different feeling? How long have you wanted that?' we also undermine that want, because as we interrogate a want it will either become prominent or transform into something else. We are casting aspersions upon it and we are giving the client the experience of exploring: "Is that want what I really want, or could it possibly be something else?" When the client says he wants something, it may only be symbolic. By going into the epistemology and ontology with these techniques, the client develops a new knowledge of his want.

Faulty want. The client wants his father not to have left home, and that is all he wants. He wants things to have been different. But his wants are actually nearly impossible to realize. The father cannot come back, he has remarried now; or, "I want my husband to love, me, and he has gone off with another woman." These are all wants that are generally acknowledged as being outside the client's control. These are the should-have-been, could-have-been, would-have-been, and so forth. We generally do not want to change any of those. If we say: 'You cannot have a should,' or, 'You cannot have this could,' or, 'That is wishful thinking, these wants that you are talking about,' in response to the client's statements of: "If things had only been different," or "If I had only stayed in school," we would be taking something away from him. Our approach allows the client to experience his want internally, in the expectation that it may evolve.

There is also the same structure of wants in the future: "If I ever see him again, I am so angry, I want to kill him." This is a future want. Now, some therapists would perhaps talk that client out of those wants or change to other wants which are within the client's control. When a therapist does that, he does it at a superficial level. If the therapist deepens the significance about that want and works in its matrix of experience with the epistemology, he has a much better chance of significantly altering that client's experience and changing his life. The client may agree with the therapist at a cognitive level that this is a silly want. However, he still wants that want because it is experientially based. In handling each want the therapist may put the client into the matrix to create an environment which will favor the epiphanic moment.

The client wants to commit suicide. By talking him into the epistemological level, where that feeling is now, we often find a metaphorical component external to the body. It is *like* his life: there is no future, it is all pitch-black. He is covered in this blackness, he cannot see any light. By putting the client into that experience at that level, then constructing memories in the future about how he would go about committing suicide and examining it in excruciating detail, the therapist tackles it at the behavioral *in matrix* level of exactly what the client is going to do, and also at a metaphorical level of what will change. "It is like the end of a bridge and as I come closer, the more I get feelings of wanting to suicide, the closer I come to walking off the end of this bridge and the bridge just drops into this deep hole." The client begins to walk that bridge and to get closer and closer to the end. As he gets closer, the anxiety increases. All this is done internally. Just as the client is about to step off into the blackness, he finds that there is something there, the bridge does not just end. As the client gets closer, the blackness begins to turn to gray and he can actually see that there is something on the other side.

In this case we have validated the want to commit suicide and extended the client experientially *in matrix*, in detail of what he would do: every breath, every step, every movement, until the client reaches a point where that reality or the fear of that reality can no longer hold the same balance. Dr. Carl Whittaker talks about this in terms of extending the thing until it loses its elasticity. Erickson would perform a similar operation in terms of some of his tasking, describing the task in greatest detail.

Ours is a way of doing that inside a matrix. It is a lot safer than doing it behaviorally. We do not talk the client out of what he wants, but, in fact, paradoxically give him what he wants experientially *in matrix*. What we are seeking is this epiphanic moment, the moment when somehow, suddenly, the elasticity of that pathology snaps, collapses, and is now no longer available to the client in the same way. The pathology loses its obsessiveness and desire. 'Everything' has changed and it is one of these changes that occurs in a moment; it is not something that is likely to occur in a logical, well thought out manner.

The client wants to kill her ex-lover because her hurt is so strong. The therapist establishes the anatomy of the hurt: "My heart has been stabbed with a stiletto and it is bleeding buckets of blood. If I kill him or hurt him in some way, then my heart will stop bleeding." The therapist takes the client through her images and relates everything to the heart because that is what the client wants. She wants her heart to stop bleeding. One way of doing that is to kill the lover. The therapist projects the want into the future: 'How would you kill him? Where would you kill him? Would you kill him with a knife and stab him through the heart? Okay, so you get the knife in your hand and put that right over his heart and put it in.' At that point the therapist can go into the future: 'All right, so let us go into the future one second after you have stabbed him and look at the consequences. You are just pulling your hand off the knife. What would you do and what would you feel? What would you do two seconds later? And as you turned around and walked away, would he make a sound? Would he say something? Would he kick, would he scream? And as you look at him there on the floor, what would you do? Would you call the police? Would you run away and would they chase you? How would you plan for that?' The therapist tests: 'And what would happen to your heart, would it stop bleeding?' "Yes, it would stop bleeding." 'And is that what you want, your heart to stop bleeding?' "Well, although it has stopped bleeding, it has got this terrible big gash and scar and now that I see that I do not want that scar there, I want it healed." 'So if you kill him then, will that make it heal?' "No, it will make it stop bleeding, yes." 'Okay, what will it take to make it heal? What would you need to do to make this heart so that it would heal?' "Well, I would need to really tell him what I thought of him." At this point, if it is doable, the therapist could say: 'Can you make a behavioral plan to do that?' If it is not doable behaviorally, the therapist can take the client back through the memories; collate the memories of when this heart was wounded and facilitate the client's construction of memories which will potentially heal the heart. We are using the client's want. We are valuing the want no matter how it appears.

When the client is in the matrix, we can go into the future or the past; we can also go to the opposite of what the client really wants. We enter into another world with a wide range of possibilities about how this client can heal; a range that is not available in external reality or in the first order of the descriptive reality of the matrix. If a want is not doable, whatever the therapist does, it has to change the epistemology of that want. If that comes down to: "I want my heart to be healed," and the therapist has the client produce an image of the killing, and the heart does not heal, the fantasy has been wasted. "I really wanted to kill him for doing what he did to me." We put that into a form: 'So what was the strongest moment when you really wanted to kill him?' "Well, it was when he said it was always just an affair." 'So you really wanted to kill him. How did you know you really wanted to kill him?' "Well, I was so enraged." 'And where were you enraged?' "Well, I was shaking." 'And when you were shaking and enraged, whereabouts was that?'

It is difficult to decathect the client's anger. We do not let go of things, things let go of us. The want is contained within the client's internal matrix of experience, and the object of this intervention is to end up with a serviceable want. What is unique about this client's epistemology, her unique way of knowing or not knowing what she wants? And what is it that creates the conflict situation for her? We think the answer lies in the client's epistemology. The purpose is to get to the client's knowing at a level that operates below the structure of the details and narrative of the components that make up the conflict.

We examine the possibility of other wants. When the intervention is successful in this way, the original want is no longer there; it has now evolved into something else, which is what we strive to achieve. Particularly if there is obsessiveness in the want, and the client has wanted this for a long time, we redirect the energy so that the hate might conceivably evolve into a metaphorical behavior.

4

Operations, Procedures, and Interventions

Precis

These operations, procedures, and interventions have a goodness of fit through the client's own experience. The client maintains his state of self-absorption and attention. He responds readily, if somewhat slowly, to the therapist's questions. The client has a sense that the intervention will succeed. The client's cognitions, emotions, and behavior are altered in a lasting and generalizing way. These operations are generic examples. Each therapy develops in its own spontaneous way.

Operations and procedures. Restructuring memories, metaphors, symbols, and semantic contents are our major interventions. These interventions are made up of operations and procedures. The procedures are made by combining a number of operations.

Formatting. The most common operations are: formatting the client's complaints into a specific memory, metaphor, symbol or detailed semantic construct; establishing the want frame and its immediate internal antecedents and sequelae. Sequencing of the underlying forms, and external events, is also frequently practiced.

The essence of formatting consists of putting the client's presenting complaint, the client's words, into a visual, feeling/ physiological, conceptual or word form. This underlying form is, stands for, or represents the unwanted memory, feeling, thought or behavior: 'The physiological process *is* the emotion.'

Dissociation. Freezing a moment in time and formatting are important operations that help facilitate the process of dissociation. The six most commonly used modalities favoring dissociation are set out, together with appropriate wording, in Table 2 (see p. 65).

Interventions. Each of the four client languages has its own interventions. We practice fourteen major interventions and these interventions are listed and summarized in Table 5 (see pp. 92, 93). The table summarizes three interventions on memories, six interventions on symbols, three on metaphors, one for semantic constructs, and the alternate symbolic intervention that can be applied to certain cases, presenting in the language of memories, metaphors or symbols.

Symbols. During the design phase of an intervention, we have to be open-minded as to what might be the most useful intervention for this client, at this moment, and how we can integrate the different languages. First we look for symbols, because some clients speak in the language of internal symbols. When a client presents with a feeling, or he uses any type of feeling word (that is, a descriptive word as in: "I am depressed," "I am unhappy," or "I get nervous."), what we do, when possible, is to have this take on another form. The experience is described by that feeling word. We want to see if it will take on the language of symbols. We take the experience out of words and put it into a physiological symbol that will be located in the body, for example: 'When you feel anxious, how do you know you are anxious?' And the client might reply: "Well, I just feel, I get all tense." 'And where do you get tense?' "In my chest." 'Where in your chest?' "In my throat." 'And it is like what?' "It is like a fist." Rather than let the client talk about

TABLE 2

Table of Common Operations

Operation	Description
Formatting	Client's words into underlying form

Presenting complaint

Memory	Vietnam	looking into child's eyes
Metaphor	depression	black cloud around head
Symbol	anxious	red knotted ball in stomach
Semantic construct	incompatible	she disagrees with me and is immature
Want	I want I don't want	I don't know

Therapist's questions / injunctions

Operation	Description
Sequencing	'And what happens just before and just after you get fist?' Obtaining details of client's internal processes and procedures.
Freeze moment in time	'When that happened, *there then,* what happened?'
Extend significance down into epistemology entering matrix	'And when you have that feeling where do you have it?' size, shape, qualities, movement, simile
Assemble memories	'When was the last time you had fist? First time, most intense times?'
Rank in affective order	'Put those memories in order of intensity.'
Dissociation visual	'And can you see that from a different point of view, different angle, from up or down?'
voice	Rhythm and flow of therapist's voice envelops client: 'And thinking about all those things and how they happened.'
time	'And knowing about what happened *there then.*'
feeling	'And knowing about what that felt like *there then.*'
space	'And knowing about all that happened there.'
adult / child	'And what can that little girl tell you that she needs you to know?'
Naming internal state	'And as you know about that fist, what would be just the perfect name to call that fist?' "Father's fist."
Relate symbol externally	'When you have father's fist, what does that mean?' (external) 'If you do not have father's fist, would this get you what you want?' (connecting internal with external)
Orientate to future solution	'What do you want? If you got it what would it be like? How would you know when you got it?

the word 'anxiety', the significance is extended down into the matrix, to the epistemological level, where it is given a form. Now, instead of anxiety, we can talk about when the client has this fist; the client's personal idiosyncratic language of that symbol.

What can we do to plan an intervention with this physiological symbol? First we want to relate this fist, this symbol, to the client's external reality. Is the presence of this fist the signal that lets the client know he has the anxiety? When he has fist, does he exhibit certain behaviors? Are there some he is not able to do? We want to make sure that there is a strong link between this internal experience of a fist and the desired objective or goal that the client wants to achieve. The client reports that, "When I have fist on my throat, I just cannot get myself to walk into the store." To make the external connection, the therapist sends the client inside the matrix with a question: 'Now if you did not have fist, would you then be able to go into the store?' If the client replies "Yes" then we have got the solid link, the syllogism. If we alter fist, or in the absence of fist, the client can go into the store. It is a simple syllogism: when I have fist, I cannot go into the store; when I do not have fist, I can go into the store; if I learn to alter, dissolve or take away the fist, I will be able to go into the store at will— comfortably, without fist.

Now, rather than doing a behavioral intervention at an external level of educating the client to go into the store, we assume that if we can alter the internal reality or presence of this fist, the client may well be able to do the behavior. The client can sometimes suggest that before he leaves the session. It will be important that he knows that he can accomplish it, even though he has not performed directly yet. At this moment he knows that he cannot go into the store without his getting *fist*. The intervention now focuses internally on ways in which that fist can be different.

In the presence of fist, we ask the client to name the sensations that he has when he has fist. It might, for example, be: "It is tense, tight, and hot." The client's fist has three qualities that give those particular sensations. We set up another set of physiological symbols that will be the opposite.

We move from this symbolic fist level and use these three names at a linguistic level. We have translated fist into the three words, and we can use those three words instead of the fist for the moment. Now we want to get the opposite words. They may be to feel soft, relaxed, and cool. The three words have got to be exact opposites. These are idiosyncratic opposites. They can be dictionary definitions, but not necessarily so.

We want to translate those three positive, affective words, the idiosyncratic opposites, into a symbolic internal physiological form, analogous to fist. We can do this by going through memories. We ask the client to think of a time when he had 'relaxed'; to feel the feelings of the time when he relaxed. As he does that, we see if he can develop a symbol or an image that would give him exactly the same feeling. The words we use to invite the client to do this might be: 'Now take some time to think of a time when you had relaxed and you had relaxed very comfortably. When you can feel the feelings of being relaxed, just see how you can develop a symbol or an image from out of that time that represents that feeling of relaxed, so that when you look at that, you can know that feeling of relaxed. Then just put that up there in your head.'

Using the same pattern, we go ahead and do the next word, putting the first and second 'opposite' symbols together, and similarly for the third word, so that we end up with perhaps three opposite symbols.

Now we have these three opposite symbols (for example, a symbol for relaxed might be a beach, for soft might be a cloud, and for cool might be the water). These combine and now they are in the same type of *form* as the fist we originally started with. We want to test the symbols to see which is strongest. We get the client to enhance the feelings associated with the new positive symbols and find out which is stronger: the fist or the three positive symbols. If the fist is stronger, we go through the same pattern again, adding more symbols until the client knows that the new symbols are stronger. When he has made them stronger, we can invite the client to introduce those symbols into the fist. We might say it like this: 'When you are

TABLE 3

Table of Frequent Symbols

Presenting symbol complaint	Location	Qualities / function	Transformed symbol
Knot anxiety, depr.	stomach, gut	black, tight, hot	cool, meandering stream
Ball fear	stomach, chest, breast	hard, round, moves	warm, yellow sun
Rock anxiety, depr.	stomach, chest	hard, cold, heavy	soft cloud

Fist
    depr., anxiety,
    relationship
	stomach,
	throat, chest
		hard, tense,
		grasping
			soft, open
			hand, book

Weight depression	shoulders, chest	heavy, leaden	crumble

Hole
    loss, abuse, depr.
    anxiety
	stomach,
	heart, head
		black, empty,
		bottomless
			forest,
			lake

Knife
    abuse, loss,
    desertion
	heart, back,
	abdomen,
	genitals
		sharp, shiny,
		hard
			flower,
			shield

Blank
    confusion, anger,
    panic
	behind eyes,
	in front of
	eyes
		blurred
		screen
			picture
			slides,
			computer screen

sure that the symbols are stronger than the fist, just bring those down into the fist and let them do what they need to do.' We seek to have these symbols transform that fist into something else. There are a number of things that might happen. The procedure may completely *dissolve* the fist and the fist will no longer be there. More probably the symbols will come in and occupy the place of the fist, and that is primarily what we aim for. This way we *replace* the negative physiology with a positive one. Another possibility, if the symbols go in, is that they may combine with the fist and alter both forms. That is not as good as the replacement of symbols. The last possibility is that the positive symbols will come down into the fist, nothing much will happen and the symbols will go away, while the fist remains. That is not a successful procedure.

The next phase is to test whether this has been a successful procedure or not. First we have the client check to make sure that the fist is no longer present. Then we ask the client to go back to times in the past when he had that feeling of *fist*, think of those times and see if he can get *fist* back. As he does that we ask him to use his new positive symbols to alter *fist*. If it has been a successful intervention, the client will be able to do that and the fist will not come back. That is how the intervention is tested in the past.

We now attend to the future. In cases of anticipatory anxiety, we have the client go into the future and construct some memories in the future, writing some scenarios in which he knows that going on to certain doorways, certain places, he will get *fist* back. As he does that, he takes those symbols and the new learning to give him what he needs to have. We ask the client to run more scenarios in the future. If the fist does not manifest itself, it is a successful procedure.

The therapist lets the client take some time to make the change. The client learns how to use the skill with his beach and how the beach can depotentiate, can neutralize any semblance of a fist. When that has happened successfully and the client cannot get the fist back, the therapist knows that he has carried out a successful internal procedure. It just remains to set up a simple behavioral task in which this can be validated. It is best to check within the client's epistemology, that he knows right there, before he leaves, that he can now do this behavior because *fist* is absent. Sometimes, with clients who already have successful memories, the therapist might construct a simple behavioral task with the client and let the latter tell him what he would want to do that would satisfy his criterion for a successful intervention.

The therapist gives the client the time he needs and allows him to do the things he needs to do. Then the therapist asks: 'Let me know if you are satisfied with that. What else needs to be done? Are you sure you are satisfied?' If the client says the symbols are not stronger than the fist, then we go back, get more symbols, and go through the procedure again.

When dealing with symbols and metaphors, and we are within this internal language of the client, there are two primary aspects that concern us in this internal world. Externally, the meaning of words is of the utmost importance. In the internal language the first important consideration is difference: what is different and what is similar between different moments, between different internal states, between different symbols, between different feelings, and the difference between when you go to walk through a door and you get a fear and when you do not get a fear of walking through a different door. Symbols help us to quantify and qualify this language of similarity or difference.

The second aspect is the relationships or sequencing of specialness, geography, and topology of how one element is relating to another within the matrix. An intervention can consist of altering the relationship of one element to another. The fabric of that relationship is contained within the symbol, within the metaphor, whereas that is not often the case with a semantic construct. It is relationships that we are examining when we are altering patterns within a metaphor or when we are, as in the previous example, using interaction between symbols. The relationship between different symbols is what is important, as is their juxtaposition to each other so that the therapist can use some symbols— physiological symbols— to drive out other physiological symbols that have been made manifest.

These symbols carry more than just meaning and this is why it is so important that they *not* be translated into external meaning, as this takes them out of the matrix. It is different from the usual context. We do not want to analyze or to interpret what this fist means. The meaning that we would ascribe to it is not necessarily the client's. The client's fist is the client's and it is fists all the way down. Immediately the therapist tries to attribute a meaning outside of that, he is no longer dealing with the symbol and it loses its psychological power. Using our method the client may get retrospective insight, and that is the best kind of insight. Insight occurs retrospectively. Our kind of change is taking place on an experiential inner level. Relationship of elements is a common thread that runs through the fabric of this therapy.

The purpose is to make these symbols isomorphic with the original presenting problem and then to integrate them. That is the dialectic that the therapist evokes. At the linguistic level, it is necessary to provide a precise and quality group of symbols that will do the job. The relationship between those derived symbols and the originals will be as opposites and they will have the right amount of psychological power and meaning in order to change the original presenting pathology.

Later we will see that the presenting problem can be a physiological symbol based on the body. It can be a particular memory and we can make a symbolic intervention on a memory. It can be a myth or a metaphor external to the body, and it can be a semantic construct in which the therapist wants to intervene on a semantic structure. This is a common pattern in our work and will give a great deal of internal precision to change *whatever* the presenting language form is.

There is a shortened version of symbolic intervention. We put the presenting complaint into a form that is, say, physiological: a particular knot. The therapist simply asks quite directly for the naming of the sensation. It is quite important, however, to name that sensation and get just the right name. It has to have a sensate name so that: "There is this knot in the stomach and it feels tight and cold." Therapist: 'Now, what would be the opposite feeling that you could have?' We give the client a chance to get the opposite feeling. The therapist has the client put the knot in the stomach in the one hand and then put an opposite symbol in the other hand. We take some time to build up that new positive symbol until it is physiologically stronger. Once the therapist and the client are sure that the hand with the positive symbol is stronger, with a simple instruction to integrate, the client can just bring the hands together and that brings the opposite symbols together.

That is a very shortened version. For a strong piece of pathology, something that has been invasive for the client, it is unlikely to work. There is too much there for just simple words to construct something that will be strong enough on the opposite side.

With many people, negative experiences and displeasures tend to be stronger, more powerful, more intense, heavier than pleasures. We are all familiar with the negative body symbols like knots, lumps, blocks of ice, and like a knife stuck in there, or searing flame, or balls of molten lead; all heavy, hot, cold sharp, painful things. The most important quality of the positive opposites is that they have to be isomorphically opposite to the negative symbols. That is why we get the negative symbol established first.

A dagger could be cold, hard steel and if the client opposes it with a symbol such as a baby, a baby and a dagger are brought together. It is unlikely that the baby, even for a woman who is very child-oriented, is going to be strong enough to weaken that dagger. There is no certainty: it is steel and flesh. We might end up with a slab of baby. That is not a workable outcome. Particularly when we are dealing with psychotic phenomena, the evil forms— the negative symbols— are going to be very evil and the good in the client is going to be very innocent. When innocence and evil come together, the evil is likely to win.

The therapist cannot know the outcome in advance. All he can do is ask the client to go through it again and see if he can find additional and stronger positive symbols. With the injunction to integrate, the therapist also gives the client permission *not* to integrate the symbols. The client can see if it is possible and surprising things can happen if it is a very powerful image of a baby. A believer might have the Christ child and the aura. This can bring some real power, and the aura surrounding *that baby*, when it comes to the dagger, can melt that dagger. The dagger melts as it integrates. A supernatural baby is required to do this job.

Symbols of nature, such as flowers, trees, and water, can often be important. It is best not to make any leading judgements, as are made with guided imagery: thinking of a peaceful scene, being by the ocean with the waves lapping, is not necessarily relaxing. If a client is afraid of water, the therapist creates a worse state. Let the client obtain the symbols. If they do not work, the client may search and find others. If that does not work, the therapist moves to another intervention because in this case it may not be possible, at this time, to change the internal experience with other internal experiences.

There are some people who lead such impoverished lives that they do not have positive resources in their experience that are strong enough to counteract the unwanted feeling. Such clients have to search the possibilities of the future and orient to their own future constructs. Another alternative is to break up the presenting pathology into very small, doable bits. Make the smallest change that is possible in one small section and treat the syndrome like a mosaic, changing one piece at a time. If there is nothing positive at all in the client's experience, the therapist can either fabricate a resource or make one present in the past. If the therapist cannot do that for the client, he may be able to introduce people into the matrix that can.

When negative symbols are tenacious, the therapist may decide to import external resources in the form of people or spiritual symbols. Very fixed negative symbols may continue to resist. The therapist determines what external items can be altered, what types of behavioral changes or environmental changes would need to be evoked in the mind. The therapist uses aspects of the negative symbol as a referential index to the nature of external changes that may usefully be made. The client confronts his father and when he has done that the therapist checks whether that knot got bigger or smaller, and what size it is now. The therapist uses this negative symbol as a reference, a gauge, to determine the degree of success that he is having with an external behavioral intervention. Does the internal physiology change? This is a referential index; it is an internal reference as to the progress that is made in therapy. The knife can be getting warmer, smaller, less shiny, softer, and so on.

The client is given physical things to do in external reality. Changes in the symbol are used as a means of validating the effectiveness of the therapy. The next time the client comes in, he has a reference point against which he can sense whether the work is successful or not. If the dagger has become smaller, less shiny, and is becoming like plastic, the therapy is going in the right direction. If the dagger is exactly the same, little has been accomplished. If it has got bigger, harder, and colder, that particular intervention may be harmful to the client. Before working at the behavioral level, the therapist has the opportunity of using that referential index as a means of deciding which behavioral intervention he would like to employ.

A client has a confrontation with her father. Every time she goes to see him or speak to him, she gets a gray ball in her left breast. This ball is hard, like old stringy leather. The therapist is unable to cause any internal changes that will make this ball dissipate. In this event, the therapist wants to determine what he can do externally. The therapist would like to find an external behavioral task that is linked to the symbol. Rather than being clever by coming up with one, the therapist lets the client decide on a good behavioral task. The therapist may want to take that a step further, should the client have no skill in setting such a task herself.

When teaching the client a new skill, internally, *in matrix*, it is also tested in the office. The therapist sets it up and gives the client the choice of three behavioral tasks. There may be a need to set some patterns first. The therapist might say that here are a number of possible procedures to be carried out. Number one is: you will arrange to have dinner with your father and do this, and this, and this. Number two is that we will possibly bring your whole family, your mother and your father, in here and we will have a family session together. Number three will be to write your father a letter. Then the therapist goes over each of these tasks in great detail, and gives the client another two choices. The therapist has the client go to the future in the context of how she might formulate her own intervention.

'Now take one, two, and three and go into the future. Construct some scenarios, some memories in the future, and when you have done those three, think of maybe one or two others yourself and go through each one very, very thoroughly. Take all the time you need, and as you go through each one, then notice that leather ball and see which of those particular things you may be able to do that would alter that leather ball, or would affect the nature of the leather ball.' That leather ball may have altered in some way. We let the client come back and say which scenario seemed to alter it.

The client may not like the scenario which seemed to have a desired effect. The client goes internal to select an intervention. That has a greater chance of success than the therapist deciding which is the best intervention. This gives the client a way of deciding. She does not have to do it 'intellectually'. All she has to do is watch this leather ball and see how this ball reacts. That is what the therapist tells her. That is the benefit of using the physiological symbol as an epistemological indicator, a measuring device. There may be little resistance to doing the behavioral intervention because once the client has run through it in the matrix, she can often do it successfully on the outside.

Should the symbolic intervention and the use of the symbols not succeed, the therapist can continue outside of the matrix in a behavioral intervention and use what the client has done in the matrix as a way of measuring the success of the behavioral intervention. Before the therapist does that, he may also introduce other resources into the matrix. He may bring people from outside into the matrix. The general pattern of the intervention is to put the physiology into a symbolic form and find an element that is already inside the matrix to alter the symbol. If unsuccessful, the therapist goes outside the matrix and sees what knowledge, information, people, and resources he can introduce into the matrix from the client's other matrices, or even from the therapist himself, if necessary. This time the therapist may try many things that might go in there, because the matrix is well defended and the therapist is striving to put in a resource.

The therapist might convey a metaphor, he might tell the client a story, he might give the client some straight facts and couch them in words that will deliver the facts right through that matrix in a way that will go in and alter the symbol. The information and the way the therapist delivers his words are designed to use the client's experience directly. As the therapist talks to the client, it is with the expectation of those words going in and affecting the client in some way to change the client in the experience of her symbol.

The therapist may have to deliver resources from the outside. Having done all he can to change internal experience, and there being no change, the therapist goes to the outside, changes things externally and behaviorally, and goes into the matrix just to check. When we say externally and behaviorally, we are still talking within the office. We are not yet sending the client to visit her father. This time the therapist tests internals to establish which external behavior to select and sends the client to do her task outside, in the real world.

Metaphors. Metaphors are used by a client to express complaints. The constructs are external to his body: "A cloud hanging over me," "A wall around me," "I am at the bottom of a well." There is a continuum between symbols and metaphors because some metaphors may penetrate the body, so in a certain sense they are interchangeable. Certain metaphors go towards semantic constructs, to ideas, to parables, to mythologies that are close to the metaphors, but involve more of a story or parable content.

As the client narrates, we are looking for a word or a phrase in which the metaphor is already embedded. Many of the

TABLE 4

Table of Frequent Metaphors

Presenting metaphor complaint	Location	Qualities/function	Transformed metaphor
Cloud depression	around head	black, cold, thick	white cloud, bird
Wall anger, abuse, trauma, relation.	front, around, between	brick, thick, tall	road, pebbles, house
Tunnel depr., abuse	in front	dark, long, slippery	private garden, green pastures, rebirth
Hole, Pit, Well depression, abuse	surround, in	deep, slippery, dark	steps, meadow
Drowning depr., relation	all around	water, dark, whirlpool	rock under feet, island
Slippery slope anxiety, trauma	under, front	wet, hard	sandy path, steps, beach
Cage relationship	all around	iron, bird cage	amulet around bird
Carousel confusion, panic	front of eyes, around head	spins like top, blurry	record disc, cassette tape
Tracks confusion, depr., anxiety	in front	criss-crossed, too many	forest path
Shield abuse, relation	on chest	black, heavy, metal	light, lucite ring
Blown about anxiety	all around	intermittent	reed, sail
Voices	outside head	evil, enemy, destructive	wise voice

constructs of our languages contain this type of embedded or hidden metaphor that is already implicit in the choice of a word that the client uses. Formatting may involve giving form to that word and mapping it out in its integral form (the entire metaphor not just that word). When the client says: "My mind *draws* a blank," that is different from a mind *going* blank or "I *feel* a blank." There is a hidden mechanism that operates within the structure and that is another important aspect of the metaphor. It not only has a structure— a blank can be such a structure— but also a mechanism. The mechanism in this case is the *drawing* of a blank. Another metaphor which *goes* blank has a different direction, a different sequencing for that blankness to occur. Feeling a blank has a different mechanism yet again. These metaphors are very specific and quite different.

We have to give the metaphor form and we do this by taking the small details that we get and extending the significance down, so that the client can put it into other words, can deepen the experience. The client can possibly put the metaphor into a visual or a feeling form and get a structure in place that allows us to specify exactly where the blank or cloud is, or how big it is, and relate all this to the context of time or stimulus. 'When does it occur? Who does it occur with? What makes it occur? What makes it go away? Where or when does it never occur?' We are looking for the supporting elements that go on to embed this metaphor in this client's experience. The structure and the function of the metaphor are going to be important in terms of how we are going to make an intervention. The two are interdependent.

Going inside the metaphor. A metaphor is often a representation of a great depth of pathology and we want to give it the attention it is due. Often metaphors are the means by which clients make sense of their world. Metaphors help structure reality. One client will make sense by using a computer model that he has in his head. Another client will make connections with wires, or will take on the metaphor of an office: he has a filing system in his head.

Metaphors will often come from inside the client's head. This is different from a symbol or a metaphor which is interchangeable within the client's head. Either could be in his head or external to it, and we observe how it functions. If it is in large part a *functioning mechanism*, it is better to treat it as a metaphor rather than as a symbol.

"I have this tape in my head that goes round and round." We treat that as a metaphor. Whereas, "I have a headache, like a molten rock in my head" is treated as a symbol because a molten rock is very physiological by nature and it would have more in common with a symbol than a metaphor.

To give the metaphor form, we first give it form in terms of structure: 'Where is the blank? Is it round? Is it square? Is it oblong? Is the blank in front of your mind, behind your mind; is it in front of your eyes, or inside your head?' As we are getting structure, we also develop a function. We tie structure and function together by asking functional questions: 'When the blank comes, where does it come from? Does it come from the middle of your head, from the side? Does it come laterally or vertically? What sort of direction does this blank have? Under what conditions does it come? What needs to be present for that metaphor to come? What stimuli will help make it go?' In other words: 'What impacts upon it to change? Which features go first, so when your mind starts to go clear or become clear, does it change from a square and begin to be round and soft, or does it shrink? Or does it seem to move into the distance?'

Later, when we make the intervention, we want the client to improve on both the structure and the functional aspects of the metaphor. The object may not always be to change the metaphor completely so as to stop the client having a blank mind. We may just alter something in the function of the blank. The client can have a blank but, when he has it, we let it come in stages, so the mind just goes blank slowly, so he has a degree of control on the amount of blankness rather than the mind just switching directly to blank. In this operation we are not changing the metaphor or anything about the structure of the metaphor, we are changing the function.

Altering the structure of a metaphor may involve a whole restructuring of the metaphor into a totally different metaphor. The client has a cloud, and the problem with the cloud is that it hangs over everything the client does, and keeps raining on his parade. The function of the cloud is to get blown about by every ill wind. As the client evolves, both the function and the structure of that metaphor, the cloud transforms into an eagle. The eagle can fly and it can make use of the wind to gain height and to see. That is changing both structure and function.

If this cloud is a black cloud, the function may alter. The cloud becomes surrounded by mountains, which will create air currents that are favorable to the cloud and can protect the cloud. The cloud remains a cloud. We have helped the client evolve some control over how that cloud functions. We have not altered the cloud.

Formatting the metaphor. In mapping out the metaphor, for the first time the client discovers his metaphor and realizes that this is his own personal metaphor. We can leave that to work inside the client's experience; just making it known and putting it in that form may in fact be sufficient intervention. The client can understand more of his behavior and many of the things that he does because he now has a way of making sense of it.

Exposing and putting the metaphor into a form is the simplest type of intervention. We are not introducing any foreign content. We are using clean language, asking questions of a descriptive nature. The client gets this new way of characterizing his experience. Now he discovers a series of tapes that he has in his head. We are allowing the client the opportunity to find out what he can discover himself. There is much value in doing that without being a clever therapist and striving to interpret. We do not interpret a metaphor. By asking questions around and about it, we can help develop or increase the opportunities for the clients to discover.

In the second part of an intervention, we get more actively involved in exploring, or in creating opportunities for the client to discover more information. We surround that metaphor with questions, with a few observations that are always very tentative: 'So take some time to think about those screens and how that screen protects you, and just go back through your history, about times when you had *screen* and find out about times when *screen* was useful; and about times when *screen* was not so useful. As you do that, it might be interesting to wonder about the usefulness of *screen* now and about what things could be different about that *screen* that would in some way seem to be more useful than the way that *screen* is. So think about those things and take some time to learn about all those properties of *screen* that you did not really know before.'

Here we are surrounding the screen. We are not doing anything to it. We are just using the words to provide an environment around that screen so the client can interrogate his own process. We have now reified the screen: it becomes real and alive inside the client's experience, and away from words. This is important for the power of the metaphor. We want the client to enter into the metaphor and allow the cognitions to happen retrospectively.

The client goes on to explore, to examine, to discover the qualities of his screen. There is value in assisting the client to get to know the qualities of his metaphor. We assist the client to learn about the function of his metaphor. If this screen is made of wire mesh then, as we give information to the client, we can start talking about the generic properties of the metaphor. The client's metaphor is specific. We do not know all the features of the metaphor, nor does the client. by relating the generic qualities, we can help the client shape the specifics of his metaphor.

'It is interesting to think about *screen*, and what that *screen* is made of, and about just what colors that wire would be, and about what size would the holes be, and would the holes be square or diamond-shaped, or could they be another pattern, and just how thick would that material be? Would it seem to be a wire screen, or a plastic screen, or some other material. And about those holes: are those holes even all the way through that screen, or are some bigger than others? And what does that screen stop? What things will that screen keep out and what things will it keep in? Screens work in both directions, and what things can get through those holes and what things get stopped?'

We talk about the properties of the holes and of the material, and about shape, and, 'Whereabouts is that screen, and who is on one side and who is on the other, and what things does it keep from coming through? And can some things come around the screen? Is the screen moveable, can it be put up or taken down, or do you always have to have a screen?'

This is talking about the generic properties of the screen and that will help to give it form. There is not one statement or allusion to the *screen* being bad or good or anything like that. We are talking about generic properties of screens. The client will take in those questions. In responding to those questions, an alteration is induced because, in response to wondering about the generic properties of screens, the client begins to question the properties of his screen. This is a gentle way of creating an environment around the screen, which may perform two functions: it may elicit more and more detail about it, or it may loosen and make more malleable the properties of this screen so that the client could change some of the properties, such as the hole size, or the constituent material, or the weight of the screen. The screen holes may have become so large now that everything gets through and the client discovers that somehow he has got to reduce the size of the screen, or else he needs to substitute a transparent solid screen because it has got too cold and the chill winds blow through.

If the client had a glass screen or a special plastic screen, that would stop those chill winds blowing through. We may get a combination of plastic and wire so the client can get the qualities of both. This is a way of helping the client discover the unique properties of his screen. As he discovers them, he is able to make these changes, and make them himself.

These are some ways of working with a metaphor. Through this approach we can help bring more and more detail, and focus right into the minutiae of the metaphor. We present an opportunity to the client to make some alteration as he discovers more information about the metaphor. We are not telling the client to do that, but that there is the possibility that he may take the opportunity to do that. This is one good reason to go through the procedure.

We may have to take a more active role in doing something with the metaphor. When, for example, we get into an active role in our intervention with symbols, we can take one element and then another and mold them together and transform them. This is usually not desirable with metaphors. If a metaphor is dysfunctional in some way, and it represents a dysfunctional part of the client's life, we make the minimum alteration that will help the metaphor to be functional again. This does not require dissolving the whole metaphor. It usually requires making some small alteration.

We want to make the smallest possible alteration that will have an effect, and just that effect would seem to make all the difference. As we become more actively involved, we want to determine what features of the metaphor we can change minimally and that will have some impact. The next intervention can be direct or indirect.

Direct intervention on metaphors. Direct interventions on simple metaphors can be quite effective. By a simple metaphor, we mean one such as a simple screen or a filing cabinet; something that does not have a lot of complicated features. A tape machine that goes to a screen, that goes down a conduit, that speaks out of a person's mouth, is more complicated. In the direct approach we treat the metaphor as we would a memory or a symbol. We do not know whether the procedure is going to work. All we will know is when it works and when it does not. If it does not succeed, we move on to something else.

Thinking about the metaphor as though it had the properties of a memory we can go through the triangle protocol.* The first move is to change a point. The client picks something he does not like and changes it, finding an item to go in to take its place. Next, we introduce items or people from the knowledge we have of the client which could go into that metaphor and help alter aspects of it. We can also use symbols to do the operation independently of the client's conscious will. This is

---

* p. 107 seg.

also a direct intervention. Using symbols on metaphors is a preferred way because it removes much of the complexity of making the alterations. We can make powerful interventions when we get the symbol right. Symbols will make alterations in the structure and function of the metaphor, resulting in congruent changes.

Indirect intervention on metaphors. The indirect ways of intervening within a metaphor involve events that have occurred in the client's experience and that are represented by the metaphor. Client: "I have a wall around me and it is black and it completely surrounds the front of me. I cannot see either end." Rather than intervening directly, we find out some of the history of this wall, as distinct from its structure and function. What we could discover is that the bricks in this wall are made up of memories: "There was a time when I never had this wall, when I was eight my father left the family, and that was the first time." 'And have there been other times in which you have had *wall?* ' "When we moved to another town."

We get some of the components in the client's experience which let him know how it was possible that he has *wall;* the first time he had *wall* and the subsequent times. And now we list the times. We treat this in a similar way to that of physiology and symbols picking up memories (see p. 116). We take the wall back through the client's past. We have him list his experiences of wall. Now we have the history of wall formatted into memories, and the experiences in which the client had wall. We have the client take the memories one at a time and restructure each. As he works on each memory, we keep checking: 'Has anything happened to the wall?' By altering memories we expect to impact directly on wall. As we do the first memory, the wall may turn to gray and it seems to have got a bit smaller. When we work on the second memory, some holes have appeared and it is now thinner. By the time we have done all the memories, we may find that the wall has collapsed into rubble.

The client has made the wall crumble. That is the first phase of the intervention. We have used memories to break up the wall. We did not know the wall was going to break up, but that is what happened. We need to be active to restructure that wall. We take the rubble and might use symbols, symbolic intervention or a generic intervention to take that rubble and help the client transform it into something useful.

'As you consider about all those pieces of that wall, and you know about how that wall protected you, and about all the things that that wall did and about what that represents: so you take some time now, to think about what could that rubble be made into that would give you some of the things that wall gave you and yet could also give you some of the things that you need to have now, because some of the things that wall gave you are simply not useful any longer. It is interesting to think about all the possibilities of what could be there instead of *wall*.'

We have surrounded what was left of wall, and the client may take the rubble and construct a house that has doors and windows. The client can go in and out because now he has a way to do so. When he needs protection, he can go back in through the door. This has altered both the structure and function of the metaphor: as from out of the rubble rises this house. The client may need to get to know some of the aspects of being a house owner, as until now he only knew how to be a wall owner. Now we can discover with the client what it is like to be a house owner, about where the house is situated, the paths that lead up to it, the gates, the fences around the house. Who does he invite in the house and who comes uninvited up the path? How does he control the door of the house, so that when the client locks it he is safe from those on the outside? He can know who is on the outside and he can decide whether he wants to let them into the house or not.

That is the procedure of going back and picking up memories, altering them to change the wall and then working directly to rebuild the wall into something useful. With the new metaphor, the house, we leave the client with a useful structure and function.

We also might go into feelings: 'So when you have that wall, how do you know that you have got *wall*? Do you get any sensations or feelings in your body when you have that?' We are mapping out the physiological components of that wall. There may be a particular feeling, a particular quality, in getting wall located in the body. The client gets a physiological symbol for the wall and then we work on the physiology, using our standard symbolic interventions. We have the client alter that feeling by getting other feelings from other, positive memories. We may have to go into the future as the metaphor may not change because of some negative future expectations that the client entertains.

Another indirect way of working with a metaphor is for the therapist to bring in additional information, and there are several ways of doing this. We can talk about our own experience with walls. We can do an Ericksonian metaphor looking at the properties of walls that you have known and walls to live by.

Behavioral intervention on metaphors. We may assign behavioral tasks. What behavioral things can this client do? He may need to go to a museum and learn about walls. He may need to go to a bricklayer and find out about how bricks are laid. He may look at the fortifications of a city. We can have the client do the behaviors that will teach him and give him knowledge about his metaphors. Even though walls may sound quite terrifying, that is not for us to judge. One of the things we can do is to introduce the client to walls and help him learn, because he does not know much about walls and he can learn to appreciate all the things that walls do. The wall becomes more real. This is not just any old wall. This is the client's wall and it has nooks and crannies and very special properties.

The semantic intervention. The semantic intervention is perhaps more complex. It can be hard to capture the it-ness of a semantic language because the very medium in which a client is delivering the information also has, in fact, a close similarity to the message. We have to listen attentively to the meaning of the words the client uses to refer to his experience.

It is more than just the meaning of the words, it is the construct that is important. Put together, the words form a particular construct, a particular idea, a particular sense, and it is that sense that would be similar to the metaphor.

If we consider a continuum of semantic constructs, the words at one end of the continuum form together to make ideas and as we extend that a little further, we get the semantic form in which is contained a parable or a particular story. Meaning is inherent at a number of levels in the story itself, and in that semantic way we are looking to discover the essence of this particular language. When we put a feeling into a form, in the body, it has a *there-ness;* but, in a semantic form, it all exists in a construct which hangs in the air, or exists in an idea that cannot be circumscribed. Memories and feelings can be contained in a symbol or a visual representation, while semantic forms cannot. Yet a number of clients that present semantically couch their language in visual, auditory or kinesthetic terms.

Those sensory terms refer to the idea, the story, the parable or the mythology. They are terms that relate to the concept in an external way: "I would like to *have a view* of the situation," "I would like to really *hear the music* of this drama," "I would really like to *get a handle* on the situation."

We cannot take those words, like 'get a handle', and make them into some sort of bodily affect. They will not translate and so we examine the meaning of the word 'handle' or the meaning of the word 'view': 'From where do you want to view, from what perspective; and what ideas are contained in the word view? What is your definition of view?'

What we are observing here is changing at two different levels. We challenge the idea of the meaning of the word 'view' or 'handle'. What does that mean? Not, what does that feel like? We seek the meaning of that word at a micro level and then a macro level, which is the wider global view. What is the meaning inherent in the whole construct?

We want to identify the phrases that represent what the client is referring to, but it can seem such a chaos. We have to take a wider view, scale up to a different view, because the client is delivering it in a linear manner: one word after another, and it takes a while for him to create this construct that exists in his language of words. It is easy to get caught up, do one little point, and get information out of that alone.

"But the situation just is not right, and I have to get some order into it, and until I get some order into it I cannot catch the music of the words." That is a complex total. The client needs time to review the information. If we can stop it, we stop it, and strive to extend its significance downwards. Apart from that, it is a matter of staying on the surface and intervening in terms of time: 'How long has it been like that?' When we ask that question, we are asking it at a surface semantic level. We are asking: 'How long have you had that concept?' rather than, 'Tell me what happened at that time.' And we are staying at that concept level: 'So you have had it this long, this concept, and you do not want this concept any longer. What other concepts did you have before that?'

We are talking about concepts and constructs in a similar way to philosophers arguing about meanings. This is what is inherent in this language. When we are preparing to make our intervention, we have to decide: are we going to make interventions on meaning, or can we extract one word first and then get the meaning of that word, and challenge that word in a variety of ways?

We take a word and we want the client to explain what that word means. As he explains what the word means, we can ask: 'Are there any other meanings to that word?' As the client defines that particular word, he looks at the relationship between that definition and how it fits in with the phrase he has spoken.

"Things are just *wrong*, and they have been *wrong* for a long time, and the way she behaves is *wrong*, and everything is *wrong* in my job. It seems to me that everything I do is *wrong*."

Here we have the word *wrong* and a number of events which are related to *wrong*. We know about times when these things have been wrong and we are going to search to find out how the client knows it is wrong: 'So when it is wrong, how does it let you know?' We are not likely to get at: "I *feel*— I just know it is wrong." Most often we get: "It is wrong because of this and that... it is wrong because it is wrong!"

'Now is it the same wrong when it is wrong at work, or is it a different wrong from that wrong? In other words, do you have a variety of wrongs?' It is getting the word, examining it and challenging it for the meaning of the word. We also get it descriptively based. We are enhancing and imparting other characteristics to that word. Assuming that we cannot take it down to a feeling, or relate it to memories, we relate the word to external events.

That is a factual descriptive process. We are working in the client's language. We are working in the language of words. We are not going down inside a client's experiences. How is the client able to say these words? That is looking at the minutiae of it and pulling it apart and trying to get at either meaningfully based or behaviorally based information. "The cat is fed," says the client. The therapist asks: 'Who gave what to which cat?'

'Who said what precisely to which lady?' That comes first, taking specific words and getting meaning to the words in semantic and behavioral forms, getting it descriptively based; getting 'video tape' descriptions.

The next step is to take a global view. What are all these things doing together? We can listen at a higher level that does not get us caught up in the minutiae. Now we ask ourselves: is there a story here, is there a moral to it, and is there a parable? How can we distill the meaning of all this into one form? In the same way as we distill into a metaphor or a symbol, how can we distill it into the actual essence of this particular moral, this particular unique statement, this parable? How does this client see the world?

We want to reduce that to the simplest possible expression. A parable gathers data or information, focuses it, distills it to this one focal point. We distill all this verbiage to one point, or to several points; down to the simplest possible statements. Most likely we have to deal with some sort of belief about how the world is, or even how the world ought to be. We want to get it, reduce it into those parts of statements that will have a great deal of meaning.

Some of the ways of assisting the client to evolve his ideas, his non-functional belief or pattern, are:

1. Telling a counter example: a different story, a parable that puts a different slant or shade on it.

2. Gradually casting aspersions: by casting a little doubt; by asking questions, so the client describes more and more how he has that belief.

3. Using the techniques of history-taking. That is looking at the development: 'How long have you had it? What did you have before that?' Putting the idea in juxtaposition to its relationship with beliefs that the client had before. Beliefs have a time period and we question: 'How long have you had this one? Was it as strong two years ago as it is now? Or three years ago?' We can move blocks of the client's experience over time: 'And do you expect always to have this belief? Will it be as strong as now? Is it going to get stronger in two years time?' A useful operation is moving data. We are not altering the belief directly. We are examining the interrelationships.

We think this is important because it keeps all the ideas intact without chipping away at them. That is what is important in this approach. We are taking a global view. This is a global intervention where we keep the client's ideas in context and set them in relationship to the origins of the symptom. This approach will also cast aspersions globally without going into the minutiae and pulling out parts semantically.

Often we have to deal with the tyrannies of the shoulds, the ought-tos, the I-needs, the I-rather-hads, the must-haves, and the I-can't-live-withouts. If we can get the client to formulate our language forms, we circumvent all that anyway. When we cannot, the client's problem procedure stays in there and we have to challenge it with established skills. We think it is helpful to think of the client both in a global view and in a specific view. We want to respect the client's ideas of his uniqueness and his identity as a human being.

In designing and agreeing the intervention, we want to be very respectful of the client's integrity. We think about doing therapy the same way that an architect might approach a building with his client: by mutual agreement. The client learns that our job is to help give form to what he wants and then to plan an intervention which will take into account what the original commission was: "I want you to take away this phobia from me." When we have planned the intervention, it is like an architect's plan. We present a model, blueprint, plan, sketch or outline to the client. The client is not interested in the beam that goes in or the whole infrastructure of the building: that is for the architect to work out. The client is interested in the overview, in the appearance of the building, where it is going to be situated, how it will function, what shape it is going to be, maybe the colors; what rooms there are, what size the rooms are, and how one gets from one room to another.

Have we, in fact, designed the building that the client wanted, or have we designed one that we thought was a good idea? Have the client's wants of the building evolved during the planning process? That is part of our intervention, as we formulate the ideas and the plans together.

The emphasis here is that the client agrees. How does the client agree? In the design phase it is important to introduce our intervention to the client in a language that makes sense to him. What we are striving to achieve must make sense to him. In order to enable the client to meaningfully agree, we have to prepare the information in a form that the client can understand.

When the client presents in strongly semantic language (see Table 5, semantic intervention), he might say: "My marriage is unhappy. It is because my wife is immature. We are incompatible." 'And when your wife is immature, what happens?' "She does no housework." 'And when she does no housework, what is it she does not do?' "Well, one would expect one's wife to dust one's books and keep one's clothes in order, sew one's buttons, order one's papers, not throw out one's property, turn the lights off, keep the heat down, and just do all those normal things that right thinking wives are normally expected to do."

'And when you are incompatible, what happens?' "My wife always disagrees with me." 'And tell me when she disagrees.' "She disagrees about the television, the bowling, the pool, the

TABLE 5. — Table of Major Interventions

Intervention	Presenting complaint	Description	Operations / Procedures
Restructure Single memory	cot death (A)	format → (−) memory deformed face	restruct. → (+) memory healthy face ⟶ healthy face **A'**
Feeling from memory	cot death (B)	format → (−) memory deformed face	access feeling → (−) symbol knife in back — evolve → (+) symbol ⟶ flowers **B'**
Multiple memories	cot death (C)	format → (−) memory deformed face ↓ access ↓ (−) feeling	restruct. ⟶ (+) healthy face **C'**
		(−) feeling → (−) symbol knife in back	access → (−) memory own face scarred — restruct. → (+) puppy face **C''**
			access → (−) memory teased as child — restruct. → (+) kind words **C'''**
Symbolic Synthesis	anxious (D)	format → fist	name qualities → tight — go for opposite → relaxed
			format → lake
			fist (+) lake — integrate synthesis ⟶ happy island **D'**
Evolution	anxious (E)	format → fist	evolve → open hand — evolve ⟶ happy island **E'**
Import	anxious (F)	format → fist	evolve → task assign — epiphanic moment → open hand
			evolve ⟶ happy island **F'**
Combined mem. & symb.	anxious (G)	format → fist	access past → (−) memories — restruct. → (+) memories
			forgive ⟶ happy island **G'**
Internal	(−) memory (H)	access → (−) feeling	specific feeling named → idiosyncratic opposite (+) named
		→ (+) memories	→ (+) symbol — integrate with memories (−) → transformed memory **H'**

TABLE 5. — CONT.

Intervention	Presenting complaint	Description	Operations / Procedures

Complex comb. mem. & symb.
(−) memory (I) ⟶ feeling ⟶ symbol — collect ⟶ list of (−) memories

restruct. mem. (−) — (+) mem. resources ⟶ altered symbol ⟶ (−) scenarios future ⟶ (+) scenarios future I'

⟶ behavioral check

Metaphor Evolution — confusion — format ⟶ disfunct. symb. blank mind — evolve ⟶ funct. metaphor computer screen ⟶ 3rd metaphor control panel skill

Importation — confusion — format ⟶ ditto — import Pa's voice ⟶ ditto — task assign. ⟶ ditto skill

Combined — confusion — format ⟶ ditto — access ⟶ (−) memories — restruct. ⟶ (+) memories skill

---

Semantic — unhappy marriage — format ⟶ "immature wife" — format ⟶ "incompatible"

specify ↓ criteria   specify ↓ criteria
"no housework"   "always disagrees"
↓ list   (+) history (−)
↓   ↓
future wishes in excruciating detail ⟶ double bind crisis / epiphanic moment

---

Symbolic alternate
(−) memory metaphor symbol ⟶ transformed memories metaphors symbols ⟵ integrate symbols — (+) symbols blanket lake sleeping baby ⟵

↓
idiosyncratic description qualities (semantic)
↓
cold fear
hot anger
burning sad

isomorphic opposites ⟹ warm comfort cool calm soothed contentment ⟶

(+) memories ↑

beer, the boys, the evenings out with my friends, politics, basketball. She does not agree with me about anything. She always disagrees." 'And tell me about all the times she disagreed with you.' "Bowling...football...boys...TV...President Reagan...the furniture...where to go...etc." 'And does she ever agree with you?' "Well, hardly ever. She does agree about saving money, the boys' school work, holidays at the beach, and the new car." 'So she agrees with you some of the time?' "Yeah, but it's not often enough." 'So what you want is for your wife to agree about the TV, the bowling, the pool, the bars, the evenings with the boys, the politics, the gun club, the football, the president, the basketball players' uniforms?' "Yeah, all those things, and of course the housework." 'And the housework. She should dust your books, and keep your clothes, and sew your buttons, and order your papers, and keep your property, and watch the utilities, and save water, and scrub the floor, and vacuum your car, and not use too much soap?' "Well...." 'And I wonder what else she could do to serve you better, to agree with you more completely? What more housework and agreeing could she do that would make her less immature and less incompatible?' "Well...." 'And so take some time and know about what it will be like to have her do one hundred percent housework and one hundred percent agreeing with you, and really know about that, and when you know about that let me know that you know, and what that's like and what more you would like to have her do for you.' "Well, now wait a minute, let us not take this thing too far...."

What skills do we have as a therapist, what techniques and resources do we have that would seem to be useful in this particular case? We format those skills, like a blueprint or a plan, so that the client can look at it, can feel it, can get a sense of what we are about to do. When it makes sense to the client, and he agrees, he commissions us to go ahead. It is important at this phase— the agreement phase— that the client *proves* to us how useful this intervention is going to be for him.

The client is not only agreeing, but the onus is now on him to convince us that this is the intervention he wants; that this intervention suits his purposes. He already *knows* ahead of time that if he can do this, he will get what he wants.

'So now you have these memories, and you know that in some way these memories have limited your life, and what you also know is if these events had not happened, you would not have what you have now. The fact is that it did happen, and the way that it limits you now is because of how you stored that information, how you have that information in those memories, and that this limits you in some way. Does that make sense?' "Yes." 'So, if it were possible that in some way you could remember those memories differently so that you did not have *jelly*, would that be useful to you?' "Yes."

We have put the intervention in terms that the client can understand experientially. The client has these memories, he knows it happened, he is not denying that, and we are relating the client's experience to something that could be achievable.

'If you could remember these memories, and in remembering them you did not get the feeling of *jelly*, would that be useful?' At this point, we are asking the client to convince us how the intervention would be useful. We do all this before we perform the procedure. If at this stage our plan makes sense to us, and to the client, and we both think this is what we want to do, we can go ahead and perform the intervention, restructure the memories and see if that takes care of the *jelly*.

Another example: 'Now you have this *apathy*, and when you have this *apathy* you get very confused and you freeze up in front of people. Now if it were possible in some way that *apathy* could be different, would that be of use to you?' "Yes." 'How would it be of use to you?' "If I did not draw a blank, I would not freeze up and then I would be able to go out with my husband to his business dinners." 'And how do you know that?' "I know that because I know I would be able to do it, because it is when I go blank that I get so confused." 'All right. So if it were possible for us to discover how you could control the ways that *apathy* occurs, then would that be what you want?' "Yes."

Now we plan an intervention to alter *apathy*. We have translated it into the real world of something behavioral. The client believes that the alteration can happen, and now the therapeutic task is to assist the client not to have apathy. Our intervention, once the client has agreed that she does not want *apathy*, is to do this by altering a metaphor of apathy directly, or we may choose to alter memories of apathy experiences.

5

Memories as Intervention

Precis

Restructuring the content of specific memories provides a useful way of changing unwanted feelings. When feelings are overwhelming, or thoughts intrude, working with memories loosens the soil from which overwhelming feelings grow. The purpose of restructuring memories is to change the physiological feeling attendant to the traumatic memory.

Treating Traumatic Memories

An important consideration in selecting the different interventions is where the client is oriented in time. Memories usually play some part in presenting complaints. If we think that memories are going to be an important part, then our rationale for working with them first is:

a) There is the possibility of an intervention on memories being all we need to do. Altering the memories and restructuring them will be the intervention.

b) It may be that in working with the past we can prevent it from sabotaging the therapy. What we want to do therapeutically is in the present or the future. We use memories to loosen the fabric of experience, to make the infrastructure malleable so that we can work with a more present- or future-oriented therapy.

c) We work with memories to restructure the past experience so that we will have resources in memories that are not there currently. By restructuring the memories of a negative experience, we obtain positive ways of the client being in the old situation. The client thereby generates positive experiences to take the place of the negative ones.

d) Restructuring memories is a healing alteration. We can heal past wounds and that may be all a client wants. He can then go on and start off with a clean slate.

e) Working with memories can be part of loosening the infrastructure in a metaphorical or symbolic intervention. When the client has a metaphor of a wall, or a symbol such as a knife in the back, we may format the memories around that. The client alters the memories so that the wall crumbles, the knife loosens, or the knot in the stomach unties.

Memories are an effective first intervention. Working with them in our way loosens and makes the pathology more malleable. Client: "Well, yes if I did not have those memories, then I would not have jelly and then I would be able to do this." We are also striving to make— and here we construct a fiction— memories represent the pathology by way of a syllogism.

"I am scared in front of groups and, when I am scared I have jelly, and when I have jelly I remember all the times I had jelly before." And we are taking these times of jelly, these memories, and we are saying: 'So if you do not have these memories, then you will not have jelly and you will be able to stand up in front of groups.' We are making an assumption that may or may not be true.

We go on to find out if it could, in fact, be true. If it is not, we develop a different plan. We do not know in the design phase if the intervention will succeed. We will discover this during the operation. If we take a metaphor, we may choose to work directly on the metaphor, or we may go to a feeling part and/ or a memory part of that matrix. We see which one of these seems to be the one that, when altered, will cause a change. We strive to make a minimum intervention which will have the most widespread effect.

The language of memories is what the client uses when he presents his complaint in terms of an unwanted, painful past event (or events), and he couches his presentation in verbal terms, in memory terms. The expression is direct with words, not with symbols or metaphors. The density of the presenting complaint is expressed in words and associated with specific past events. These factors will be indicators for performing an intervention on memories. Whatever other language the client presents in, be it feelings, metaphors or semantics, the development of that pathology is likely to be linked to particular events that occurred in the past. Hence the therapist often uses memories, as many presenting complaints can be molded into a form that will produce memories representative of the pathology.

The client presents and says he is scared of a phobic object. The therapist asks the client to examine the times in the past when he had the same feeling, and to gather together the memories of a number of instances when he had that particular feeling, fear or phobia. A list of memories is obtained and the client equates these memories with the fear. Thus, the memories become symbolic of the presenting pathology.

That is the syllogism, and the therapist asks the client: 'Is it possible that these memories could alter, so that they could be remembered differently in some way? Is it possible that that might be useful to you in some way, that it could change how it is that you feel?' If the client says "Yes," the therapist has a good case for using memories solely as an intervention. Altering these memories that stand for the pathology will possibly change the pathology.

'It appears your complaint stems from all these things that you told me that happened, all these memories that you have of these things that you say happened; and so would you be different today, would your situation be different today, if your memories were different?' That is the presuppostion. A normal person asked that direct is unlikely to give a congruent response. The question will not be asked until just before the intervention. At that point the client will be in the matrix and in answering that question he will do so experientially *in matrix.* When asked cognitively, the client may answer: "I had those experiences; there is nothing I can do about it." It is a different perspective for the client inside the matrix. We help the client to alter the structure of the matrix, of that memory, of the perceived reality of that memory. Together we then discover what benefits this can bring to the client. The therapist may choose to work with memories first, because although it might not be the complete intervention, it has the ability to loosen the fabric of even a very ingrained pathology.

The client presents with a pervasive piece of physiology. He has this black mass on the heart. In talking about it, the client has strong affect. We ask the client when the last time was that he had the black mass, then the time before that, and before that. The client regresses to get a list of memories. Then all those memories are altered. The object is to evolve that black mass. There may be six or more memories to go through. Once those memories are restructured, the therapist asks the client how much the mass has changed.

In restructuring these memories the mass is no longer black. It is now a grayish pink, lighter, but still fairly big. What is accomplished by altering the memories is that the structure of the past is loosened, allowing the therapist to intervene directly on the heart. It is much easier to intervene directly on a heart that is pink and gray and light than it is on one that is black and thick. The work with the past has loosened the fabric of experience. Without this loosening preparation the symbols cannot move the mass.

Another operation is to use the memories as a way of preventing the client from sabotaging with memories. With some clients who are historically oriented, every time they are asked to do something, it is always the same refrain: "Yes, but I would do it if this awful thing had not happened to me." The client is using the past as the excuse for not doing something. The therapist may want to change the structure of the past experience so that the client can no longer have access to that precise experience. The client says: "I am unhappy, I am depressed, I am lonely, I am afraid, I cannot maintain relationships, I destroy relationships, I make myself unhappy,

I had a very bad childhood. My mother died when I was twelve, my father died when I was fourteen, and then I continued with my grandmother. I had a very unhappy childhood and basically I have been making a mess of everything ever since. How do I make a mess? I make a mess because I keep saying the wrong things to people, doing the wrong things to people. I have a man I love that I want to be with, that I want to marry, and I tell him how stupid he is. He does not want to see me any more. I mess it up with everybody, and that is because I had such a bad childhood." The pattern is: *"Because I had a bad childhood I do bad things."* (Also: *"I am all messed up now because I had a bad childhood."*) Although the density of the presenting pathology is certainly oriented in the present in terms of the behaviors, the etiology is in the disordered childhood. That is what the client says, and it may very well be true.

We may want to relieve the tension, or the tendency to keep getting stuck in childhood memories, before moving on to do things in the present: it is lot easier to proceed without having to fight the ghosts of the past. To do that the therapist obtains a physiological response, internal symbol or metaphor, using it to go back and select memories: 'When was the last time that happened, that you got that particular feeling, and when you were ill-treated in childhood, what was that like?'

With a client who was abused in her childhood, the therapist may find that she has a feeling, a sensation of fear which can be like concrete. The therapist obtains half a dozen memories about it. The client may get a feeling of being angry: like a hot flame in her chest. She may get three or four memories about that, and another feeling of being hurt, for which she gets half a dozen memories. Each list of memories of each physiological set has to be established. The therapist activates these memories in order to loosen the past to enable her to work in the here and now. It is easier to work with a client when she does not refer to the past all the time. Many issues can be dealt with in the here and now and in the future. This loosens the whole fabric of the client's experience. We have the client gather memories into classes determined by the same physiological feelings.

Every intervention deals at least in part with either internal symbols or external metaphors. When dealing with memories, they are presented verbally at first. With clean questioning, many clients will present metaphors or symbols related to those memories. We sometimes work with memories in order to make the client more accessible to intervention in the present. They are used in this way to loosen the structure. The therapist does not have to make distinctions between memories, be they actual events or things the client thinks have happened. There is no distinction of any reality inside the matrix.

Memories can be real, imagined or constructed in the future. They have as much power being memories in the future as in the past. Indeed, depending on how clients construct their reality, memories in the future can be even more powerful than anything that happened in the past. It is useful to determine where the client is focused: where does he spend his time, where does he actually live in time? Does he live more in the past, the present or the future? An agoraphobic client is going to know about the future. He knows about the past and translates this knowledge into his life in the future, where he imagines catastrophe. He knows little about the here and now.

The client who lives primarily in the present does not learn much from the past. He does not plan for the future because he is absorbed by the present. A client who lives in the past is not likely to know much about the present or future because his thinking is primarily about the past. He is unlikely to have anticipatory anxiety simply because he lives in his memories and he thinks only about them.

A client lives in the present. She accounts for the miseries of the present due to events in the past, and looks towards a bleak future where she will continue unmarried, without a child, lonely, and sad. She is a businesswoman. She goes to work every day. She does this, she does that. This is a tri-modal presentation: let us say seventy percent in the present, fifteen percent in the past, and fifteen percent in the future. We use a different language to make our intervention in each place. It is good to do something in the past and she keeps referring to this, although she is seventy percent in the present. We therefore start off with the past and, as a result, pre-empt a lot of problems. We want some change in the past to make the client more accessible in the present. To do this we may decide on an intervention in memories.

We have to discover whether this makes sense to the client, because it may be that she is so focused in the present, even though she refers to the past, that she does not see any direct connection. After the client has set up the memories, and has them listed, and is inside a matrix and connected to these memories, we have to ask the question.

Were we to ask with the client out of the matrix, we would get a verbal external indication; an external reference. It is not the same in the matrix now, with all those memories lining up as she experiences them. It is as if a whole panorama of her history is beside her, and then we ask the question: 'Is this going to be useful? And if it is going to be useful to activate these memories, how will it be useful?'

We put the memory into a form that fits the client's experience. If he cannot recall a memory, we do not force the client or trick him or use hypnotic techniques to relive or vivify the memory. We treat the memory gently, as we would any traumatic memory. We do not open it up for explanation or to make sense of it. The memory is stored internally in the matrix and we strive to heal it in the past. Any number of therapeutic techniques would involve going into the past, getting the memory, vivifying it, reliving it, bringing it into the present and understanding it here and now. That would be a good way of retraumatizing the client. We want to make the now, the present, not to be here any longer. After this we want to transport, to orient the client back into the then, the then of the memory. This is a form of age regression. To do this we have to watch our verb tenses and we have to keep the client in a matrix. Interaction as a therapist is kept external to the client. To keep the client inside the matrix and to orient him in time back in the memory, the I-ness of the therapist as a person should appear to cease to exist. Making statements such as: 'I want you to do this,' or 'How do you feel?' would orient the client out of the memory and retraumatize him. The client would be split between two realities: the feelings that he has back in the memory and now. That is most often where therapists cause a client to weep. There is not much that can be accomplished while the client is sobbing and traumatized. It is not necessarily cathartic to cry. Sometimes it can have a beneficial effect, while on other occasions all it does is embed afresh the negative internal physiology. When a client is crying his system is overwhelmed. While he is crying the therapist cannot trigger any change in the system. The primary focus of an intervention on a memory is to change the way this memory is stored, so that it will not evoke an unwanted emotional response. If the client is crying, he already has an emotional response and our words are not going to be effective.

We want to start out by doing minimal interventions because we want the client to use his own internal resources to discover his resources in the matrix. In this way the therapist enables the client to make alterations that are within his experience and are going to help. If the therapist delivers information into the client's matrix, it may be rejected later on. The process we use with a memory is to first put the memory in a form and then evolve that form into another form.

This is very different from guided fantasy or the introduction of suggestions which are then added to a memory. We have the client take the original memory and make small perturbations, small alterations, that will evolve out of its original form. The memory will differentiate out of itself. Finally, the memory cannot return to its original form. We do not seek to replace the memory with another because in doing so the client can get the old memory back. We prefer to differentiate, evolving the memory out of the original form so that it creates another *there.*

The first step in approaching a traumatic memory, once it is decided that this memory is to be altered, is to prepare the memory by making it more malleable and amenable to alteration. Memories can be quite rigid and we sometimes have to approach them indirectly. Were we to take a client's unprepared memory and to instruct him to alter something in it, it is fairly unlikely that he could do so. Instead, we gently create an environment around that memory. This is distinct from going straight in and making suggestions to the client. That procedure would introduce new factors into the memory. We do not want to do that to begin with. Our objective is to surround the memory in an environment and choose our words to use that environment. The client can then discover that he can have his memory in another way.

Developing the memory. The memory is developed and made present in the past in its modalities: visual, feeling, and cognition. At this stage the client does not know whether the intervention is going to be visual, or feeling, or whether it is going to have a big cognitive component. The therapist puts the questions in a generic form to manifest the memory so that the client can experience that memory. The verb tenses are kept historically oriented so that it is about that memory *there then*: 'Take some time to think about that memory and all that happened *there then*. And as you do that, put in all the detail so that you can know what happened and know what that felt like *there then*. And let me know when you have it fully developed.' When the memory is accessed with words like: 'Take some time to think about that memory and all that happened and put in all the detail,' interjections like 'see it' and 'feel it' are avoided. That allows the client to develop the memory generically, in his own way. That is the first part of making the memory present.

Freeze-frame. The second step is to focus on the very worst moment of that memory; where it is most strongly physiological. To do that, it is often easiest to freeze-frame the memory at its most intense moment: 'See if you can freeze-frame. So make a picture of the memory at the very worst moment, and make sure you can see yourself in it. Now put a frame around it that would seem to be just the right frame for that memory and develop all the detail fully.' If the client can freeze-frame the memory, a simple technique is to make some of the facets of that memory less real. One way to do that is just to put a picture frame around it: that gives the memory a boundary and an unreal quality.

Dissociate. The third step is to dissociate the memory. This is especially important in treating a traumatic memory. Often the client is associated, looking out into the memory through his own eyes. The therapist may want to get the client dissociated. Sometimes the client is already dissociated and that may be part of the problem.

The therapist asks the client to change the perspective in which the latter holds the memory: 'As you have that memory *there then*, just see how you can change your perspective or point of view so that you can look at it from a different angle.' This pattern will facilitate a change in the client: if the client is dissociated, he will dissociate to another angle; if he is associated, he may dissociate. At this point the memory is prepared for an intervention. This prepares the memory for a freeze-frame, and we can go on to a restructuring protocol.

Moving backwards. If the client does not freeze-frame the memory and it runs on like a movie, we want to make the sequence of events more malleable. If it runs like a movie, it may be difficult to alter. We want to loosen the memory, make it more supple, and add a new ending. By running it backwards, we may have the client find a new beginning. In extending the memory, we are not asking clients to invent anything, to alter anything, to fantasize or to imagine. We want the client to add in all the extra detail. Running it backwards helps to build up the memory to retain more: 'Now run the memory from beginning to end, and when you reach the end, make it end at a later time than the end you remember. And then run the memory backwards to the beginning and begin at a new beginning, before the beginning you remember. And do this three times very thoroughly, and notice all the extra detail that you did not notice before.'

Making malleable. By having the client repeat the memory three, four, five times, we make the memory less rigid and allow it to become somewhat unreal as the client runs it backwards. Once the memory is prepared, we can proceed with the interventions.

Restructuring protocol

Each of the therapist's steps becomes increasingly invasive. The objective is to do as little intervening as possible in order to allow the client control over completing his own Gestalt. When the memory is in a movie or a freeze-frame, it is in a form in which we can do the procedure.

1. *Change about a point.* This, the first step in the restructuring protocol, is the minimum alteration that we can perform. We make sure the client is dissociated, that he has another perspective. We simply invite him, as he looks at the memory from this different perspective, to pick a point in that memory that he would like to alter. That is the end of the instruction and then we wait. Only three things can happen. The client will signal that he has altered the memory, or will say: "I cannot." Or it does not make sense. (If he cannot, or it does not make sense, then we go to step two.) If he can do step one, we say: 'Pick another point and alter that.' If he can change one point, then he can change another. We give the instruction to alter a second point and perhaps a third. The method is to have the client go through and alter a number of items, until he is satisfied that he can remember what happened differently and feel differently about that memory, while still 'knowing' what really happened.

Outside of his matrix it would be unusual for a client to 'remember' how it was and yet have the memory altered. After going through matrix there is a split in reality. We want to connote the reality of that split so that the client can 'remember' the scene and feel differently in this new way. He can still 'know' what originally happened, what really happened; yet that knowing now no longer has the strong physiological valence that it used to have. The object is to alter the memory so that the client feels quite differently about it.

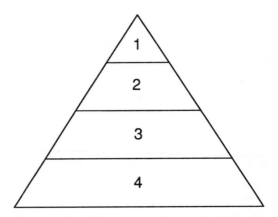

Fig. 2. — **The restructuring diagram**. 1. change about a point 2. people and knowledge
3. detail 4. external implications. See text.

2. *People and knowledge.* As we go down this triangle [Fig.
2] we become more and more directive. If the client cannot alter
the memory in step one, we have to give him some assistance
to discover another resource. We now want to introduce
elements into the memory, and we can do that either by directly
suggesting some things that we already know from the client's
history or by using the generic form of people and knowledge.
When we introduce these elements, we have to remember that
people and knowledge can come from different times. There are
resources of 'now' and 'then', from the time when the memory
was formed. When using people and knowledge, that
introduces matters from outside the matrix, and that is more
invasive of the matrix.

Sometimes a memory needs resources added to it from a different moment, time or place. This step introduces these resources to assist the client in changing the memory that he could not change in step one: "If only I knew then what I know now." This wish can possibly be granted by introducing the concept into the memory at this stage. This step requires a light naturalistic trance.

'Now take some time to think about that memory and to think about what you knew *then* and how different that was from what you know now, and how what you know now can go back to then to change *then* so that it can be different, and the people that you knew then could change *then* in some way so that it could be different, and the people that you know now could go back to *then* and do what they need to do so that *then* could be different. And take some time to discover how that could happen and make any adjustments that you need to make so that you can remember what happened differently, and feel differently about it and you can still know what happened.'

If step two does not work, we go to step three.

3. *Detail.* We may have to be even more invasive. If 'people and knowledge' has not worked well, we want to find what stopped it. We want to discover some of the details about the memory. Up to now we have not needed to know much detail about the memory. At this stage the therapist is getting ready to make suggestions to alter the memory. First the therapist finds out what stops the memory from changing; what the client would need to have. Then, if necessary, the therapist generates ideas and suggestions that the client can take into the matrix. The therapist makes suggestions in such a way that the client can take them inside and alter the memory. We give him two or three suggestions and tell him to come up with ideas of his own. The purpose is to confuse the memory, to make it evolve from the way it presented and generate an alteration.

4. *External implications.* This step requires the therapist to get the detail about the memory and then to generate a series

of suggestions about how the memory might change, giving at least two or three alternatives. The therapist becomes actively involved in loosening the structure. At each suggestion the client is instructed to go inside to test the solutions suggested by the therapist. The therapist works with the client in a participatory process to make the memory evolve: 'What stops it from changing?' 'What would have to happen in order for that part to change?' 'What would you need to help you so that it could change?' 'Who would be able to give you advice on what you might be able to do?'

The therapist now relates the reasons why the memory will not change to external factors that may have a bearing on the situation. These factors may require a behavioral task and may give a direction for intervening with another therapeutic approach.

When something in the memory will not alter, we may go outside of that memory, outside of the matrix of experience, and find what it is that stops that memory from changing. What behavior would the client need for the memory to change? As we focus on the internal process, we want to find out what external factors prevent this memory from evolving: 'So as you think about that memory and the things that stop it from changing, what do you think is occurring in your life now, or that has occurred, that stops the change in the memory? Maybe there are some things that you have to do externally, or behaviorally, in order that whatever stops that memory from changing, could change.' The client might have to confront someone, or say that he is sorry, or make some recompense. If there is to be a corresponding change in reality, and sometimes there is a secondary gain or hidden agenda which can prevent the memory from changing, then we want to explore the external factors that interfere with evolving the memory.

5. *Derived symbols.* A symbolic intervention is a sophisticated approach that requires no effort to restructure the memory on the part of the client. The memory is formatted and then an array of positively valenced symbols is derived. These symbols are introduced into the memory and do their

restructuring independent of the client's conscious will. This intervention is called for in dealing with major traumatic events which have a pervasive quality, such as incest and other memories that prove intractable.

This fifth restructuring technique is called derived symbols. Instead of having a symbol at the center, we are going to use the memory. We make the memory present in all its detail. We ask the client to translate the memories onto a linguistic level and get the words, sensations, and feelings that come with that memory. We get the opposite words, and from those opposite words we get positive memories. From the positive memories, in turn, we develop positive symbols. These positive symbols are introduced into the memory; the symbols do the restructuring. The advantage of this pattern is that the client does not have to be actively involved in searching his experience to make changes. Particularly in cases involving trauma, the client need make no effort while these positive and powerful symbols do the memory restructuring at a non-verbal, non-cognitive level. This is in contrast to the previous processes that involve quite substantial effort and cognition on the client's part.

Derived symbols take care of the whole memory, all in one moment, when the intervention occurs. The methods of 'change about a point,' 'people and knowledge,' 'detail,' and 'external implications' are slower. They are processings and restructurings that occur in a methodical and orderly way. 'Derived symbols' is a highly symbolic intervention; a change that occurs in one moment, when the client integrates the symbols into the memory.

Treatment of Single Traumatic Memory: Summary

1. Client presents in therapy with some limitation on his behavior or feelings.
2. Specific events from the past are believed to cause these problems.
3. The client agrees that if he could remember these events

differently, and not get the same feelings, he would not have that limitation.
4. The memories are restructured by altering some of their components, until the client's feelings are changed.
5. Because he feels differently about the memories, the client can now demonstrate behaviorally that he has overcome his limitation.

Multiple memories: An Overview of Treatment

How do we formulate and design a therapeutic intervention around the changing of memories that makes sense to the client and holds some promise of achieving the desired therapeutic outcome? Traumatic experiences often occur as multiple events and there is a great variety of significant events that may have occurred over time. Hence we need to organize the memories into classes of memories, each class around a common physiological feeling. Now we are treating sets, groups of memories, and this has several advantages:

1. It organizes the client's memories and orders them into a structure that gradually begins to make sense. When memories come intermittently and clients get memory flashes, it can be particularly disconcerting to those whose memories are stored in a confused manner. Organizing memories into groups with common characteristics can be important for the client, and also helps us to decide what intervention to employ.

2. The client gathers these memories in an order that is predicated upon internal reality. The internal reality may have nothing to do with the sequence of events or a common factor, such as memories to do solely with the father or the mother. These are external criteria, while memories have to be organized internally within a matrix in terms of their primary presenting pathology and that often is the physiological affective valence that a memory carries.

Our primary organizing factor must not be time or similarity of events. Our organizing must be particularly around the physiological feeling that the client has at the times he has that memory. We use that physiological feeling to aggregate other memories that have the same physiological feature. When the client makes up lists of memories, she puts a name to each list and that name will be symbolic for all the memories on that list. When we refer to that name, the client will know internally that we mean those four, five or six memories in the group from which that same particular feeling is elicited. This may or may not have anything to do with chronology. Some typical names of lists that clients use are: rage, fear, and fright. There are different physiologies involved, although the client may have had the fear in one part of the memory, and then the rage one minute later. The two separate memory components are treated as different, distinct memories because the physiology is different.

The purpose of this operation is to organize memories into a structure that is going to make sense to the client and is going to be therapeutically serviceable in an intervention to alter the memories. In changing these memories, we expect to alter the feeling, the affective component, caused by these memories. Having changed the affective component, we ask the client to translate that from the matrix into a behavior that the client wants to achieve.

In the following case example, we use memories to alter the internal experience and validate that change by an external behavioral indicator. This is one way of translating to the outside. Once the client has got the memories gathered, we set up a syllogism which makes the memories stand for the pathology: 'Now take some time to think about these memories, and if it were possible that those could be altered in some way, would that be useful to you?' We want the client to tell us the possible benefits. We examine the client's ability to feel differently inside. Having altered the ball in the chest, the client might be able to go to her father and talk to him more comfortably. Altering the memories that are associated with ball, the client makes a guess— it is only a guess at this stage—

that altering these memories may change the ball: "Without this exact ball I may be better able to talk with my father."

This is an internal check. At this point we do not ask the client to go to the next level to do something in the real world. We ask her to check it experientially *in matrix*: 'Is it now comfortable to talk to your father? Would this result in some desired benefit?' Now the intervention is in place. We have the memories gathered together in a group, have found out if we can alter these memories, and what benefits are likely to be derived. If the benefits are not likely to be sufficient, we leave these memories and perform another intervention.

Before we begin the intervention, we ask that the intervention should make sense: 'Take some time to think about all those memories.' We re-orient the client into the memories: 'And as you do that, if it were possible in some way, and it does not matter how it could happen at the moment, but if it were possible in some way that those memories could change so that in changing you did not have that round ball, how would that be of use to you?' At this stage we are skipping over the question of whether these memories can or cannot change. This is the 'as if' pattern. We ask the client to behave as if these memories could alter in some way, and, if this were possible, we ask what benefit could be derived. We do not ask for a change at this point, nor do we ask the client to pretend that it is possible to change: we only ask that *if* the memory could alter, what benefit might it bring? Then we ask the client to consider what behavioral benefits she would obtain.

There is little likelihood of resistance because we ask the client to tell us whether or not this is a valid intervention. This is part of the participatory process. It is not participatory if we decide what is best for the client. We have provided a context; we have organized the client's memories into a form, associated the memories with the physiological feeling. We then say: 'Now, check this out and see if it makes sense to you.' We are asking the client for her input into the design of the intervention. If she comes back and says: "This does not make sense," we are not going to do it. We would make another intervention. If the client says: "Yes, it does make sense," we will ask her to prove it to us.

Otherwise the onus would be on us to prove that this is going to work. We do not want to do that, as it puts us in the invidious position of having to 'heal' the client.

We have given the client a different internally experiential way of organizing these memories, and we have suggested the possibility that the memories can alter. At this moment the client decides that, "This makes sense and will get something I want". She has to prove to us what benefit she will derive: 'So as you think about these memories, and the possibility that if these could change in some way (we are changing the memories and so we can change the internal symbol), and if that could be different, would that be useful to you?' If she says: "Yes," we reply: 'How could it be useful to you?' "Well, I would feel better inside. I would not be so nervous when I was around my father. I would be able to go for Thanksgiving or Christmas, whereas I always make excuses and he is getting old now and I really want to be able to sit down and talk to him." We say: 'And if you did those things, if those things happen, would that give you what you want? Would that give you what you are here for? Would this be a successful intervention? Could you be satisfied if this ball were to change and you could do these things?' We use these aims as criteria to check later. The client has convinced us and now we can ask her if she would like to do the intervention.

Before any intervention is selected from the four in the triangle [Fig. 2] we mobilize the energy. We have set up an environment in which the client can learn for herself and discover for herself that this makes sense. This way we pre-empt a lot of resistance. When clients have held onto traumatic memories it may not seem possible that anything could change. We are not saying it is possible: we are only discovering if it is possible. This is a useful attitude to take. When we alter a memory, we are quite surprised when the memory changes. We seek to find out what might or might not change. That is different from starting out with the presupposition: 'I can change this memory.'

Let us consider the first sequence of events when we work with a traumatic memory. We take a case of a single traumatic memory that has presented and how we go through and organize an intervention around one traumatic memory. (Then we will look at multiple traumatic memories which are sequence based on this particular process.)

The client knows the incident and we ask him when the incident was, and to go through it in detail from beginning to end. As he does that we want to ask the client about what happened. Generally the client will give surface information and external details. As he does that, he helps to create that memory. Now we extend the significance down, inwards, by asking: 'And when that happened, what happened inside?' A large proportion of automatic memories are linked to a physiological feeling component. There are few clients for whom the memory related appears to have no physiology at all. We treat those clients differently. Most clients have the physiological feeling components and we establish this physiology as an indication, as a control of the intervention. We ask: 'When that happened, what happened inside?' "Well, yeah, I got upset."

For control we establish a physiological attribute to memory, so that we can test the efficacy of a memory intervention and use this physiological internal symbol to sweep up other memories which have, or elicit, the same basic feeling. The design of the therapeutic intervention assumes that if we alter the memories in which this feeling has its origin, this will ameliorate the feeling. After the intervention, when the client recalls any of these memories, this particular feeling will not be present.

We find the first memory associated with the knot in the stomach. The client gets this knotted feeling when he thinks back. We develop that knot; it is a knot like a *ball of string*. We take that *ball of string* and regress the client through its history. In passing this *ball of string* through the client's history, that physiology attracts memories in which the same feeling of *ball of string* was present. This is a more potent procedure than just asking a client to think of the times he had that feeling, or think of the times that were similar to this bad memory. We get different sets of memories when we ask for memories in different ways.

This is why deriving a feeling from the memory and using that feeling to collect the other attendant memories is important. The object is that by altering the memories we change that feeling. The feeling is our indicator: with it we can check our work and know how effective the procedure has been. That is the primary purpose of working with a feeling first, of deriving the feeling from a memory. Once we have got the memory established, we can go on to multiple memories.

In multiple memories we use the same pattern. First we get a significant memory of the event, or the last event that occurred. When we have one of these, we take one memory that is fairly intense and as the client talks about it in terms of external criteria, we focus at a point at which we can extend the significance down to the feeling. An example of our wording would be: 'As you think about that moment when that happened, what happened inside? Did you have anything inside?' We are striving to then get at: "Yes, I started shaking." 'Where did you shake?' "Well, I started shaking in my knees and in my stomach." 'And did you shake more in your knees than in your stomach? What was the shaking like?' We get to a symbol of jelly in the knees, or gray jelly in the stomach. When we have established this, we go through and collect memories through the client's history. That is our age regression. In traditional hypnosis, it would be called an 'affect bridge'. With traumatic memories, if we were to get a client to give details about the memory, we would retraumatize him. Should the client delve into the details of the memory, it would start to vivify. As he works to tell about it, he would also have to struggle to control his feelings. This would cause unnecessary distress.

By using the feeling and having the client go back and think of the times, right back to the first time that he had this jelly in the stomach, we assist the client to float over his whole history and pick out the significant events at which the jelly feeling occurred. Our instruction enables the client to come up with a number. If we were to tell the client to remember the memories, he would go on to the details about his one and that one. That would pull him out of the matrix and also increase the chances of his being traumatized. When we tell the client: 'And as you think back on your history, and take that jelly, and let that jelly just pick up the memories when you had that same jelly feeling, and when you have done that just tell me how many memories you have picked up.' This is a helpful instruction because it teaches the client to stay inside and survey his history; not to come out and tell us about it. He is not looking for all the bad things. He is instructed to count incidents: a very natural way of dissociating the client from the trauma.

We do not want to treat the memory until we have the client adequately prepared. By asking the client for the number, we have a way of obtaining analgesia. When the client comes back out, we want a number like five or six. Saying a number like five or six is not going to hurt. Relating the dreadful things which happened when he had jelly would, on the other hand, be very stressful. Now the client makes a list of memories to organize. This may be the first time that the client can organize his traumatic memories. Putting something that is horrible into an order does something to it. It gives it a form that is less chaotic. Even though the events are exactly the same, the fact that the client has got one memory located in relation to another (not necessarily by chronology) imbues certain characteristics in the way these memories are stored. This has to do with the architecture of memories. When the client retrieves memories from a chaotic mass, the problem seems much bigger than when the same memories are retrieved from an ordered source: "My mind is all confused. I used to have many memories all together and then this tragic event happened, and now it is like everything has just spilled out over my mind."

This client is referring to the structure of his memories. This is where the density of his pathology is. It is not in the memories themselves, but in the way he remembers them, and that they constantly recur. The simple intervention is to alter the architecture. We return the shelf to where those memories were, and we place each memory on the shelf. The client puts the memories into bins. Some bins have locks, some are transparent, and some are open. Each memory is sorted out and stored in the client's mind in an orderly fashion. When this client has got his memories ordered and stored, he has his whole experience and he has ways of controlling access to it.

For memories that are best locked away, the client may leave the key with someone else. Now that memory can come out at certain times, that may be all an intervention has to accomplish at this stage. With this intervention we are almost beyond the memories; we are changing no data at all. No memory has been restructured. The memories are exactly the same as they were before we started. What we have altered is how they are stored, the order, the architecture: this is all that this particular client may want.

One of the important facets of the syntax of the language of memories is positioning. Putting items into position is like changing the punctuation in a sentence. It changes the reference, the relationship between one memory and another. An important aspect of symbolic forms is to do with similarities, differences, and relationships.

The ordering of memories, and its preparation, may be vital to the success of an intervention. This part may take up three-quarters of the time involved in the procedures. The actual alteration of memories may take just a few minutes at the end. We may want to devote a lot of time and care to the preparation, as this is part of building a domino effect. We set up memories to create a maximum effect. We focus the intervention to arrive at the point where the client can get exactly what he wants. Clarifying relationships and ordering memories at the beginning helps to enhance this focusing effect.

Picking out just one memory and acting on it may change the jelly from gray to pink and reduce it to half its former size. That may be only part of the intervention. In getting a string of memories, putting in a structure, and going through and altering the memories, we may find that not only is there no jelly left in those memories, but in its place the client may now have a positive resource. He now has a rubber ball that gives a warm, solid feeling in the stomach. What we want from the intervention is not only to neutralize the negative physiology, but to replace it with something that can be positive.

This is part of reweaving the structure. The fabric of negative experience is used to create a usable past that is manifested in a positive physiology and replaces the unwanted symbol. That new, warm, positive symbol may be manifested in the exterior world in a new and positive mood; in new and positive behavior.

We take care of the internal reality first and then facilitate this to translate externally. This is the rationale for listing memories and giving them order. Developments happen inside the client that are like an intervention. This prepares the fluidity and makes for an easier intervention when we get things ordered. Before we perform an intervention, we want the client to represent his memories in a different order and a different sequence. That makes the pathology more amenable to change. These alterations increase the mutability of symptoms and the client's ability to further alter his internal experience.

If the client presents memories in terms of chronology, we ask him to organize them in terms of intensity and vice versa. It suffices that the memories are presented in a different order. The changed relationship eases the bonds between the memories so that they are not nearly so fixed. There may be a great deal of energy invested in maintaining that memory, but there is not usually much energy invested in thinking about one memory before another. In altering the sequence we are loosening the weave.

For multiple memories we have the client list the memories and put the name which identifies the feeling (jelly) at the top of that list. Naming internal states is of the utmost importance. There is power in naming something and we take great care in giving the client the opportunity to name his feeling precisely. To name that list, the client may have two names that can be symbolic of it. The first will be some reference to a feeling such as anger, pain, hurt, sadness, and depression. The content of these names shows that they are not powerful. Translating into another, idiosyncratic, name is much better. The idiosyncratic name comes to stand for the incidents when the client had jelly, knife, heat, compacted tennis ball, whatever. That is unique and we no longer have to deal with ideas about depression or sadness. We are now dealing with *jelly* and what this client would like is not to have *jelly* there. The client may not be sure what he would like, but he knows he would like something other than this jelly.

For the moment we restrict the issue to one particular thing inside experience, which is *jelly*. Under the heading of jelly the client lists up to six memories. We rank the memories according to affect because that helps break up the chronology patterns: "Really, the worst memory was not the first time, it was actually the second time. I did not realize that before." While the client is steeped in those memories, he has new insights and cognitions. New associations are now in sight. This is the essence of changing multiple memories. Using these techniques we have the client alter all those memories. Often, if it is a major core, we may start with the least valenced memory.

We are teaching the client a skill and our object at this stage is to do the absolute minimum in order to effect a change in a memory. The work is done by the client. It is easier to teach him in great detail about only the first memory. We spend a lot of time on that. We spend less time with the second one. By the third and fourth memory we may be able to give a simple injunction such as: 'Now go ahead and change numbers three and four in a similar way as you did with the others.' Our instructions are brief; the implication being that the client goes inside himself without our even asking for it. When he exits, he tells us whether or not he has done it. It becomes a very simple procedure. This is how the algorithm works: 'Now that you know how to do it, do it again and let me know when you have done it.' We need not say anything else. The client goes ahead and runs his problem-solving routine, as if solving a mathematical equation, and comes back out and says he has done it.

Assembling different memories. Depending on the nature of the events, the first one we examine may be the precipitating event. We are now going to build on this pattern of lists of memories to determine how to put groups of memories into a form which fits closely to the client's reality.

In a precipitating event we are seeking a particular memory, event or turning point that occurred in the client's experience and changed his life. Typically this is an original, full experience or trauma that seemed to change the course of life, caused by, for example, a death, losing someone, somebody leaving, a divorce, changing school, changing neighborhood, a kiddie group breaking up, etc. Instead of organizing memories from the last instant, we are going to organize the memories around this precipitating event, which will be the focus around which we perform our intervention.

The precipitating event becomes our point of reference. From this event we are going to construct a sequence of events or memories that go forward in time, and a sequence of memories that go back in time. The sequence of memories that goes forward is composed of consequences stemming from the precipitating event. The subsequent memories may have nothing to do with the nature of the precipitating event. Because that thing happened, the client *says* his life has been limited in some way and these one, two, three, four, five major things that occurred later are the alleged results of that original precipitating event: "Originally I lost my confidence, and then I could not keep up with my school work, and then they put me into the lower stream, and then the wrong stream, and now I am digging ditches instead of being a microbe hunter."

A woman's father died. She had been very close to him. Since that time no man can measure up to her father and she has had difficulty with relationships. That is a precipitating event, as a consequence of which she has a number of incidents where she has found it difficult to relate to men. She has problems at her office. She has fights with her mother because her mother is going to remarry, and how could she do this after such a short time, etc. We call this the Expulsion from the Garden of Eden, or the Fall from Paradise. Everything was wonderful until...but...ever since...everything has gone wrong.

We gather these subsequent events and we have the client make either a single list, because it will have one form of common feeling that runs throughout. Or we may have several lists with different feelings attached to it: one of the significant memories of events that occurred, and one of the events that happened after the precipitating event. We have a single precipitating event and there may be five or six incidents that occurred by which the client's life has been affected.

Sometimes it is quite difficult to do anything to alter these memories because the precipitating event was so traumatic. We assemble the panorama of this client's experience into an order and examine ways in which we can use resources from another time to ameliorate things that happened after the precipitating event. The memories of events before the precipitating event are what we call sensitizing memories or sensitizing events. These are events that made the client susceptible, so that when the precipitating event occurred her life changed.

The sensitizing memories could be negative, but very often they will be very positive. We ask a question regarding the precipitating event. How was it possible that this woman was so dramatically affected when her father died? That may have been because she had such a strong relationship with her father and loved him very much. If she did not love her father, she might not have been so affected at that time. What if there was a sister in the family? The father dies, so the sister is subject to the 'same' precipitating event and she gets over it. She is much less affected. She does not have the consequences that occurred in our client. The difference is that she did not have the same relationship with her father. Her sensitizing events, her memories would likely be very different.

We may get a sense of the nature of the memories that we are to obtain: 'What are the things, the memories, you have of your father that made his death such a momentous event in your life? And can you remember the last memory before he died?' "Well, I remember going to the theatre with him." 'And what about a time before that?' "Well, I remember when we would go to the beach." Then as we regress the client, we have her pick up the memories that have a common physiology of, say, love and enjoyment; all the way to when he used to read

Bambi to her and take her to the movies when she was a little girl. These are the sensitizing memories. The physiology here is love. The physiology or memories after the precipitating event—the death—have to do with qualities of loss of confidence and depression.

'And consider the course of your life prior to your father's death, and think about all the things that happened, and know those things that may have affected you when he died, and then think back to the first and the last thing that you really remember that has that quality.' That statement is fairly general. We want to narrow it down after we find that there are two or three qualities of feelings. There are parts of her father that she loved and parts that she did not. She did not like the way he treated her mother, or that she always had to be the golden haired girl. We might have to have her split that. We obtain a list of surface memories and we order them as well. Related memories can be put under the heading: 'I love my father.'

This is the panorama. We have the events leading to the death. We have the sensitizing events, the precipitating event and the consequences and two types of memory. The general principle is if these sensitizing events had not happened: 'And if you had not loved your father in this way, would you have been affected in the same way when he died?' We might get the answer: "No, I would not have been so affected." This is a way of discerning which memories should have been on that list. We want to make sure which memories really affect this pivotal point, by repeatedly checking the sensitizing memories: "Yes, you know, it was so vivid, the time we were at the beach, and that is when I really knew that he cared for me, that he really loved me because he gave me this special attention."

These sensitizing memories influence the precipitating event and all the consequences. The client has assembled this data. How can we change the client's experience about the precipitating event and the subsequent events that occurred? We have the sensitizing events, all of which may be positive, and we want to determine what resources we can use from those positive memories. These are resources that we can transfer over time into the memories of the precipitating event, and past the precipitating event into the subsequent memories. We are going to have the client look for symbols or resources in these positive memories that we can introduce into the other memories. We want the client to restructure memories; her perceived experience of those events.

In letting the client re-experience each of these memories, she would: 'Take a symbol such as a ball, such as the book of Bambi, and from each of these memories pick something very special that represents your father's love and just store those in some place, so that you can use them later.' What we have now, in a mobile form, is a group of positive sensitizing memories. We have images that have a special meaning, such as the beach ball or Bambi. With these we induce a restructuring of the precipitating event.

We have the client take the positive elements (ball, Bambi) and the precipitating event to make it present and develop its properties. The injunction is: 'Now, take those symbols and introduce those into that time, when you first heard your father had died, and just allow those symbols to go in there and do what they need to do to give you what you need *there then*.' We are transferring those symbols, bringing them forward in time. At that time the beach ball can come, Bambi can come, so when the client hears of the death on the phone and screams, Bambi comes in and leaps into her arms. She can cuddle Bambi and at the same time, as she screams, the beach ball is inflated by her scream. She no longer hears the sound of her scream: the beach ball captures it. The colors and warmth of the beach ball change the scream into a musical note. The trauma was partly in that scream, and her hearing herself scream, and partly in that hollow sound. Now the beach ball has changed that and Bambi is in her arms. She now knows that the good *qualities* of her father can go on living with her.

We might go on to the next event and carry out the triangle protocol, or we could use other symbols. We are teaching the client to use things from her distant past, to bring them forward and heal her near past. The distant past comes forward into the near past, beyond the precipitating event, and can change the qualities of those memories and the resultant internal response.

A beach ball or Bambi can occupy the place of jelly or a knife and that is what we want to replace. She heals herself in the very ways in which she was wounded. The intervention has to make sense to the client. This represents the panorama of her life, and it fits. We discover together what we can do about it to make it change. With her, we discover the way of using memories.

It may be that the sensitizing memories are in fact negative. A woman has an obsession about her hair. She is obsessed with losing it. Something happened five years ago and ever since, every day, she counts the hairs. When she has a shampoo, she takes all the hairs out of the bath and counts them to see how many she is losing. She keeps plucking out hairs and counting them as well. Her scalp is red and this has grown progressively worse over the last eighteen months: "I went to visit my grandmother. She had been treated for cancer and her hair was falling out, and when I saw her red scalp, something just happened, and now I am counting my hairs, and I am so scared that I am going to be bald."

That identifies the precipitating event. The consequence is that she says she cannot go to work as she is so embarrassed because she is starting to go bald. We have noted the precipitating event and some of the subsequent events. Now we look at sensitizing events. We ask this question: 'How was it possible that when you saw your grandmother you were influenced in such a way that from then on you became worried about losing your hair?'

We get the feeling physiology established at the precipitating event: 'What is the feeling you have?' "Well, I feel fear and the fear is like a lump in my throat." 'Now, before you saw your grandmother, was there any time before that in which you got a similar feeling; it might not have been seeing your grandmother or anything like that, but did you get that similar feeling, like that lump in your throat?'

We give the client time to go back and we hear: "Yes, there is a time, two years before, that my girlfriend had lost her hair and when I look through fashion magazines and see ads for shampoo, I get the same feeling." As she goes back we find that when she was a little girl she saw the picture of an Irish woman who had her head shaven by the IRA. This picture prevails in her thoughts and that is the first time she remembers the lump in her throat.

The client now has a list of negative sensitizing events and we restructure the picture, the times of reading shampoo ads, the time with her girlfriend. Having restructured those negative sensitizing events, we come to the precipitating event. Now it is easier to restructure the memories of seeing her grandmother there, because it has been loosened by restructuring the childhood picture of the Irish woman. That picture is easier to restructure than the one of her grandmother, which is so vivid to her. The client now alters the precipitating event and the subsequent events as well. Every time she has a lump in her throat she knows that she gets that fear which, "...makes me count my hairs," and she also gets the lump that is always present when she keeps pulling at her hair. We want to alter the lump, first by restructuring memories and then by getting qualities of the lump and inducing symbols to help de-potentiate the lump.

We search for a powerful symbol from granny when she was still healthy. We look for some memory that could be applied: "There is something about a 'special tortoise-shell comb' that my grandmother had, and if I can use that as a symbol, then I can put it right on my throat where that lump was and use that tortoise-shell comb to drive out this lump of fear."

We have seen how to format and put a structure to a single precipitating event. What come before are sensitizing memories and these are followed by the resultant subsequent memories. We cause those sensitizing memories to alter first and loosen the structure of the memories around the precipitating event. We alter the client's internal experience of the past before we deal with the present or the future.

Organize memories over time. A ruler can show a way of organizing the sequencing of events or memories into a form over time. This form can enable us to manipulate groups of memories, or to give a logical sequence to a complex problem. When clients present with many things that have gone wrong in their lives, it may be hard to make some order. The use of the ruler may introduce the order that enables us to formulate an intervention using memories.

We think of a twelve foot ruler. On it we have the mid-point we call six, and the ends we call zero and twelve. Six represents the present and twelve represents the future. The client comes in at six and presents with something being wrong. We have to use unspecified references to move data around. When the client comes in, particularly if he is incoherent, and he does not know what he wants, all we can say is: 'What you have now is not what you want.'

'You want something else, and how long has it been since you have had what you have got?' We establish that as zero on the ruler. "I've been like this now for three years." 'And what happened three years ago?' "This event occurred at zero and when this occurred, then life has been different." We fill in other significant subsequent events at the other numbers: one, two, three, four, and five. These gradually lead up to the client at number six, and right here, today, in our office.

Zero stands for the first time the client has what he has got now. We examine what happens before zero. We extend the ruler: 'So what happens at minus one?' Minus one is in the area of sensitizing events. These events happened: just before zero this happened, just before that minus two happened, minus three, etc. These are significant sensitizing events that occurred. We are going to build a panorama of the client's history and it is all focused at his presenting at number six. These are events that happened to the client to make him susceptible at zero, leading to other, later things happening after zero. We trace back and disentangle the history. Minus six represents the client's birth, and we go back from minus six to minus twelve. This represents ante-natal events, the parental history. It can represent the family rules, in the mists of time. Those events have come forward in time to have an effect here.

Grandmother one day told the client what his mother was like as a little girl. An auntie tells some of the family stories. These tales function as if they were memories, although they are not. Because the client has constructed it, it becomes part of his mythology, whether he was there or not, whether it happened or not, whether it was true or not. That is in the nature of myths.

Sensitizing events. The client may not know what he wants at this time. All he knows is that he does not want what he has got, and what he has got is at number six. The desired objective is to get to twelve in order to make some progress. Because the client does not know how to define what he wants as yet, we bring him to seven. This is a way of organizing the panorama of the client's experience when it is a complex story, and of making some sense out of the sequence. What we might do is to go back to minus twelve, look at the mythologies and restructure them as if they were memories. This challenges those presuppositions. We go back to undermine the history, restructure the mythologies; renewing them into more operational ones and then moving forward in time. We use the momentum of change developed in the distant past to favor a change in the near past. Then we examine the memories from minus six to zero. These are the memories that sensitized the client, causing him to be affected at zero. When we have done that, we restructure the memories from minus six all the way up through the consequences to the last one at five.

We have strung out the history of the client: putting it into a form and altering the history to change the mythology. Having altered that history, each of these memories will now have a different feeling, a different physiology, attached to it. In doing so we want to assist the client to discover what could be accomplished at seven or eight. In altering the history we search for some resource that will create a shift: the client does not have to be stuck where he is with all his history; he can move to seven or eight. The client's perspective has changed.

Once a bit of that history has changed, it is as if one layer of the onion has been peeled off. Now something else comes up, and whatever that is, it comes up here and now, at six. The old number six, that came when he first presented ("I cannot get up and go to work in the morning."), has been resolved. Now when the client comes in, number six becomes: "I need to get in a good relationship and I do not know how to do that." What the client wants in the future has to do with relationships. We might do something with how he knows he loves. The experience back there of when he lost his love, and other lost loves, would be before zero. "Our family knows about love," would be at minus twelve. What he has now is a life in which he does not know about love.

We go back yet again to construct the history. This time it has to do with love. It no longer has to do with not getting up in the morning and depression. He wants to get married. We move from this, restructuring the mythologies having to do with love. The ruler helps the client to understand his history. We put the history in order. Then we help the client alter the different sets of memories. He may no longer sabotage this by referring to the past because we know about the past and it is ordered and sequenced. If the memories have been restructured, they no longer present an issue on which the client gets stuck.

The ruler gives the therapist a way of asking questions that helps keep him specifically oriented in the right time frame. One of the problems in dealing with the past is that it is too easy to leap over many years. This confuses the intervention. Where we orient our questions in time is vitally important. If we are at six and we ask the client for information between zero and six, we have got to be consistent in asking for this information.

The client makes a statement that life is suffering: "I do not know anybody who has not suffered." When the client makes that statement at six, it is only possible to have done so because he knows about experiences from zero to six. If we were to reply: 'I do not think that is exactly true, I know people who have not been like that,' we are making a reply at six. We would be challenging the statement at six itself. If we were to do that, the client would have all his experiences that help him to maintain the 'truth' of his statement. The client would use his history in arguing that it is in fact true, and he can give examples. By asking the question *in the present* we would set up a resistance because it implies that we want the client to go against his own experience.

A very different question that we can ask is: 'How long have you had this concept about suffering?' When we ask the question like that, it puts the client back to zero and it also implies: 'How long have you had this feeling or idea?' We are not detracting from the feeling, we are asking for: 'How long?' When the client answers that question, he may realize that before zero he had some other construct. This, without any challenge, starts to create some doubt about the validity of the client's concept: "I have had it ten years, ever since my mother died of cancer." 'Was that the first time? Was it as strong then, or did some other things happen from ten years ago to today which will support that?' "These are the events that occurred in order for me to be able to make this statement." Therapists often ask a lot of questions at six, challenging concepts and beliefs in the here and now. We prefer to ask the question at seven or eight, and this could be a question such as this:

'You have had this concept of suffering for ten years, and we know before ten years you didn't have it, and now you have it. Do you think that ten years from now you will still have the same concept or will it alter in some way? Do you still want to have that same idea or would it be useful to you to have modified this idea?'

That is asking at eight or nine. We are asking about a possibility in the future: will that same idea still be held or will it be different? We are orienting our questions in time. The ruler helps to keep it straight. When we ask at zero and at one and two and three and four, we begin to get a series of events that occurred, enabling the client to make his statement at six, at this moment, here and now. Then we can go back to: 'All right, what things made you susceptible, sensitized you?' "My parents were in a prison camp. I keep hearing the stories that they told." That goes back from minus six to minus twelve. We can get a profile of how it was possible for this client to be able to make this statement at six without ever challenging it. If we want to alter the belief in some way, we do not alter it at six, we go right back to the development of that belief. We question 'memories' back there first and that undermines the support. We orient our intervention in time to alter that history of experience. Then the client can alter that unwanted belief.

This is a way to change beliefs without having to challenge them, without creating a conflict or a confusion or chaos within the client's mind. If we introduce into the client's experience, right now at six, the idea that in an hour's time—which is number seven—we are going to alter this belief, a great deal of energy and effort are required and we may very well not succeed. If we go back to the history and alter it very gently, undermining the beliefs, the mythology, the 'events' that helped to create that unwanted thought, then by the time we get to six that belief will possibly already have changed. Now the client has a healthier belief, a healthier rule to live by without us ever having to challenge him.

If we challenge and bring proof, we are going to bring it in a future time from, say, seven or eight: 'You do no have to live your life like this.' This is to suggest that the future does not have to be like this. If we go back and alter his history, we have a better opportunity of altering his beliefs by changing the structure of the experiences that enabled him to hold those beliefs.

The ruler helps the therapist to ask questions that are focused in time; that make sense to the client without our asking questions that will challenge the validity of his belief. We tend to leave six, the here and now, alone and find out how is it possible that this client could make this statement at six. The therapeutic result is achieved at seven, eight, nine, ten, eleven or twelve. We move the client into that area by evolving the etiology, the development, and the events that led up to the status quo, and then asking about the future.

The ruler helps us to map out the development of a belief. The belief itself will change if we have undermined the experience the client has that maintains that belief. Beliefs are often difficult to change in the realm of ideas. We take the foundation, the very development, and subtly evolve it. This does not deny the reality of that belief. Rather, it lets that belief evolve in a way that could be more useful to the client.

We chip away at the pillars of dubious wisdom that sustain that belief. Out of the dubious wisdom the client evolves another belief which is more useful and functional. The original belief was carved out at a point years ago, and although it was a functional belief then, this is no longer the case. We do this gently and always connote the client's reality. We do not want fragmentary ruins strewn along the path. By going through the client's history in this way, we evolve the existing material of the belief and help the client reshape it.

The Child Within

In working with memories, we often find with early childhood memories that there is a child trapped within the context of a particular moment. The child is frozen in time, and it becomes necessary to free it.

There are at least two ways in which the child within is found. It can be found in a psychosomatic pain. There will be a particular feeling in the chest or heart: a hollowness for example. Hidden in that hollowness, under a rock, behind something, there will be a child. The client describes a rock. Suddenly there is a phrasing which is slightly unusual. In response to: 'Is there anything else about that rock?' comes: "I'm scared." A tonality, a change in the voice and a personal reference which was not there before are the first clues that somewhere in there is hidden the child. That is the child talking and we ask clean questions to provide a form and context to enable him to come out.

Often, as the rock is described, we will be spontaneously taken into a memory. The client will be describing the particular pain, and the affect, and then at the next moment there is the child within. It will be in a memory, which itself can be hidden within the metaphor.

The task is to define the child and the various characteristics of the child rather than the memory. We can do this by dressing the child, finding out what clothes he had and then finding out what the child wants. That way we may find the personality and the characteristics of the child.

Another way is to find the child in a memory. We search the unresolved memory. As we work with it we find that the child is frozen. It cannot escape. It is locked in that time. Again, our object is to help that child out of that warp. As traumatic events accrue, some aspect of the child is frozen at that moment. The rest of the persona grows up and some aspects of that child remain behind. The adult now lacks some facets because their development has been arrested. When the child within is freed, that child grows up very rapidly and the adult can now have access to the missing facets. The child will often ask for particular things it wants and these things usually have a unique character. When we find the child within, it has the primordial facets that the adult is lacking.

Child the father. A forty year old man comes in and says: "I want to be happy." 'And how do you know you are not happy?' "Because I don't feel happy." 'And when you don't feel happy, where don't you feel happy?' "Just all over." 'And where all over?' "Well, all over inside." 'And when you don't feel happy all over inside, where inside?' "In the middle of my chest." 'And when it is in the middle of your chest, what is that like?' "Well, it's like a hollow". 'What kind of hollow?' "I don't know." 'And is there anything else about that hollow?' "I don't know, I'm scared."

The client has just been describing the hollow. Suddenly there is a change and he does not know how to continue, saying instead: "I'm scared." We determine how he knows he is not happy. He gets pains in the chest and has hollow. Now the tone changes from hollow to: "I'm scared." To which we reply: 'And when you are scared, how do you know you are scared?' or 'When you are scared, where are you scared?' or 'And about how old would you be when you are scared.' "I'm little." 'And when you are little, and you are scared, just how old do you think that little boy could be?' "He is three." 'And when he is three and he's scared, what's he wearing?' "He is in his pyjamas."

At this stage, the personal pronoun changes from I to he. This is important in facilitating the child within: 'So *he* is three. And he is in his pyjamas. And when he is three and in his pyjamas, is there anything else about him?' "Yes, he is standing." 'And when he is standing, where is he standing?' "He is standing in a doorway." 'And what else is there about that doorway?' "He is frightened and he is frozen." 'And when he is frightened and frozen, what else is there?' "His parents are arguing in the kitchen and he doesn't know what to do or where to go. He is just frozen, and he is frightened."

In this memory the child has been locked in the same context for the last thirty seven years. This little boy is frozen in that moment standing in the doorway. The intervention is to free him from that doorway and it must be in terms of a solution that a three year old can understand. We cannot use adult solutions for a three year old's dilemma. The intervention must be something that a three year old is able to do when he is frightened and frozen in a doorway: 'And what is it that he would like to have happen? What is it that he wants?' "He wants his mummy." 'And can he have his mummy?' "No, she can't come." 'And is there anybody else he could want?' "He wants his daddy." 'And can he have his daddy?' "No, his daddy won't come". 'And so is there anybody else?' "No, there's nobody else." "And just who could there be so that he wouldn't have to be frightened standing in the doorway?' "His sister. His sister could come." 'And can sister come? And what could sister do when sister comes?' "Sister could come and she would pick *me* up." 'And could a sister come and pick *you* up?'

As the little boy arrives at the idea of a solution, we have him take on a very physical movement because we have to move the child out of the doorway. It is not just the idea that a sister could come. We make sure that scene has a real, physical aspect: 'And so the sister comes and picks him up, and then what would the little boy want when his sister comes and picks him up?' "He wants his Teddy." 'And so could he have his Teddy?

And so sister gives him his Teddy, and then what would little boy want?' "Well, he would want to go to bed." 'And could his sister take him to bed with his Teddy?' "Yes." 'And when would his sister take him to bed with his Teddy, and where?' "She would take him upstairs." 'And so could sister take him upstairs to bed with his Teddy?' "Yes." Sister takes him upstairs, puts him to bed and the little boy sleeps. At this juncture the parents were discussing their divorce. They never reunited. That was the trauma.

Now the sister comes, picks him up and puts him to bed. We let him sleep there for quite a while. That is how that child grew up: he just slept through it. When he wakes, the child wants to go out and play. And so he goes out to play. For the first time the child is growing up without being stuck in the doorway. And he wants to find some friends. It is difficult to find friends to play with because he is a lonely child. As he cannot find any friends, he has to play by himself. Then he wants to go to school. He finds out he can go to school. As he goes to school we facilitate the discovery that school is where he could find a friend. We bring the adult into the school and we have *the child teach the adult* what the child knows about being happy. This child has much of the knowledge that the man needs in order to learn how to be happy: "In that classroom this child taught me that the way to be happy is to go out and play with friends." This was the first time that the client *knew* that one of the ways in which he could be happy was to go and play with friends. He may have known that cognitively, but here was the shock and the pure thrill of realization that that was one of the ways *he* could be happy. It is a skill the grown man did not have and it took the child and the switching of their roles to achieve it. The child becomes father to the man. For a dialogue with this child to work, it is essential that the dialogue flow from child to adult. Information does not pass from adult to child. The adult always construes information in an adult manner, and will therefore fail to appreciate the fragile knowledge of the child. When there is internal communication between the child and an adult, it should be in terms of the child speaking to the adult. The adult is sitting in the class and he is being taught about happiness by the child. That frees the child, and the child can then go off and play, and do the things that a child does. That is very different from standing frozen in a doorway.

This adult does not have the skills to play. What the intervention has done is to provide the focus and direction for therapy: the adult needs to learn to play. The child probably had some of those abilities before he was three years old. At this juncture therapy needs to be focused away from the internal to more pragmatic skill-building and practical behavioral programs about the friends he has, and how he is to involve himself in activities with them.

Mathematical rape. This is the case of a fourteen year old who was raped by her mathematics teacher. She is now thirty eight years old, and has been in therapy for twenty two years. She is a therapist and deals with rape and incest. However, she has not achieved a resolution of her own rape. She has been in four major therapies and the memories are still unresolved. Because she has a fourteen year old daughter she is reliving the rape experience. She wants to do something about it.

This case illustrates how important it is to keep the therapy age consistent with the child within. We need solutions which will make sense to a fourteen year old who is being raped. We need solutions she can hear and understand. Solutions that only an adult understands will not do. Information does not travel well from an adult to a fourteen year old who is trapped in this way.

The client is agitated and scared. She says: "I don't know what's going on, but I'm ready for something to happen." 'And what do you want?' "I think I'm going to throw up. It's coming up." 'And as it comes up, what happens then?' "I think I'm going to die."

Here is the first clue that the information is coming from a different age and context to that of the adult in therapy. Cognitively the adult knows she is not going to die, but inside there is the fourteen year old who is chained to this memory at a moment during the rape when she thinks she is going to die: 'And as it's coming up, and you think you are going to die, then you can know whether you are going to die. And how you can know whether you are going to die is to wait; and if you wait then you can know if you are gong to die. And you can wait and know for sure whether you are going to die or not.' These sentences provide information that a fourteen year old can understand. We are using words that will have an impact because the client is trapped in this context, and we want to say words that the fourteen year old might understand. After thirty seconds she exclaims: "I didn't die, I didn't die! I can breathe, I can breathe!"

That was the initial phase of the intervention. The client explained later that she was a healthy fourteen year old girl being raped by her math teacher. Other therapists had her understand, go back and get angry at the teacher, try— in the memory— to hit him or stop him from doing it. She said: "To hit him or harm him offends my morals and ethics. I cannot do it. I am a mousy fourteen year old girl." All previous interventions that were adult interventions did not work.

Our words made a suggestion which a fourteen year old could carry out. We provided the time for her to grow the eight minutes beyond the rape. Here she was a fourteen and a half year old bouncy little girl: fourteen years, six months, three weeks, and two days old, and it is 11.22 a.m. Now we have to free her from that memory; a memory that she keeps going over and over and over again. Throwing up is anathema to many sexually abused women. Throwing up is about the worst thing that can ever happen to them. Part of that frequently is the penis that is inside them. When she says it is coming up, that is what she is referring to. With the words: 'Wait, so you can just wait. Does it continue to come up?' we enabled her not to vomit, but to experience this penis coming out of her mouth and getting out of her body. Previously she would always swallow back and it could never exit from her experience. We simply had her wait, and that is all she had to do. That word *wait* was what a mousy fourteen and a half year, six months, three days, at 11.22 a.m.-old could hear. That word *wait* enabled her to grow up eight minutes to 11.30 a.m.

It was at that moment that she discovered she did not die and that she could breathe. We have just freed her and grown her up. She is eight minutes older and more amenable to other interventions. This is a therapeutic intervention that a fourteen year old can understand. Things are now different for one who has grown up eight minutes to 11.30 a.m. What would she like to do now that she has discovered she did not die and can breathe? What could she do? She says: "I could change something," and: "I can't harm him or hurt him, but I can sass him and give him cheek." She practices saying words to him. Now she has grown up another four minutes. She is learning the skills. She is at 11.34 a.m. Another four minutes of growth and she is learning to scold. Now she is at 11.38 a.m. and she has just learnt how to give him cheek. We find out what else she needs to do, and, as she practices these words, we gradually empower her. Although she cannot harm or hurt him she can set him back, because she is now sixteen minutes older than when we began the intervention. As she develops she remembers that he used to say words about the size of his penis, likening it to a telephone pole. Next she wants these words changed. As she works to change those words, she remembers that there was a power pole outside of her house. She attaches electrical rather than telephone wires to those words, and to the penis. She finds she can 'sprong it'. These words begin to empower her. The frightening effect of his organ has now been diminished: not in an adult way, but in a way that a fourteen and a half year old bouncy little girl can understand. These are not adult solutions; they are solutions that a young girl can do. And then she discovers that what she really wants of this man is not to harm him or hurt him. She wants his respect. She wants his respect for what he did to her. Horses are symbolic in her experience, and she brings in these strong horses, and these horses surround him, encircle him. As he tries to escape they keep him in the circle. Then she gets Aretha Franklin to sing the song *Respect*, and the horses keep him in the circle until she knows that he respects her for what he has done to her. This is her criterion: his respect.

These are solutions that are entirely hers in the context of that time. As an adult she would never have thought of these as solutions. As a therapist, these might not be solutions that she would use for her clients. We are working with a fourteen and a half year old who has grown up sixteen minutes and these are her solutions. They seem relevant to what she wants, to her criterion, and her gender.

These solutions appear to be strange and not of the normal world, but then neither is the experience. We have to use words that she can hear in the midst of that trauma: words that describe something doable, and so the active words are 'just wait'. She waited eight minutes and found she did not die. We teach her to feel, grow, and evolve out of that memory, and through this she becomes empowered. Three months later she stands up in front of an audience and discusses her case without undue affect. She travels to the town where the teacher lives, a town which she has avoided for all those years. She has no more bad dreams or nightmares about her daughter. For the first time she discusses her case without crying. She says: "It's so distant from me now, it's just like telling a story." She has evolved her trauma from being stuck in that one moment into a whole story which has a completeness. Everything is still contained in there, but now it is stored as a story. It is much more acceptable, and it no longer has that awful negative affect.

6

Phobia, Incest, Rape, and Child Abuse

Precis

The client's presenting language reveals to the therapist where in memories, metaphors or symbols the pathology is most heavily represented. The intervention is designed in the client's most prevalent language, using operations relevant to the client's memories, metaphors or symbols.

Phobia. Phobia has a strong physiological component. This implies a language of symbols and that the physiological component *is* the panic attack. When working with a phobia we examine the panic attack and have the symptoms of the panic attack expressed in symbolic form. Generally we find that there are two or three loci at which the onset of the panic attack is manifested: "My *skin* crawls like hairy caterpillars and then I just go frozen with fright and my *heart* thumps like a pounding drum and my *head* starts spinning and I get disoriented and I scream."

Here there are four different physiological symbols: 'crawling skin', 'frozen' ('where in your body?'), 'pounding heart', and 'spinning head'. We put this total manifestation into a form. This becomes our test, our indicator of the client's experience. If we are successful in dealing with the phobia, the client will not experience any of the symptoms of the panic attack. Our tactic is to perform little interventions upon these symptoms so that we can interrupt this pattern and produce a different response.

Small animal phobia. Characteristically these are very specific. For instance, a client will be afraid of a black spider, but not of a brown cockroach. A furry rabbit is fine, but a furry rat is not. We have the client establish the physiology of feeling and determine if this physiology is exactly the same for each variety of these animals. We use the physiology to go back and collect the memories of the worst phobic incidents, regress the client, restructure the memories, and, in restructuring the memories, loosen the sympathetic nervous set. We may have the client actively alter the feeling physiology of the sympathetic nervous set by using para-sympathetically active symbols.

We have the client go back historically and use the panic attack to gather together the memories of the times when the panic attack was most profound. Generally the client finds that perhaps two or three attacks are especially strong and the client makes up a list of between three and six of them. There is always an original, precipitating event in which the first panic attack occurred, in which that physiology first manifested itself. The physiology had never been experienced before that. Some therapists say that phobias do not have an originating event and this may be true in their experience. As yet we have not failed to regress the client to the original phobic event. By using the physiology that we have established, and having the client take that syndrome back through his mind, he can find the last time he had a panic attack (and the time before that), pick up the strongest memories, and make the list.

The task is to restructure each of those memories of attacks. As we restructure the memories thoroughly, we test and check if, in remembering, the client experiences that panic physiology again. We have the client construct phobic events in the future in which he will have the experience of phobic stimuli. As he does that, the client takes the new learning just acquired from the restructuring of memories so that he can rehearse phobic events comfortably, without experiencing the feelings of panic. That is our test for the future.

Sometimes the work with memories will have reduced the physiology very substantially, but there is still some feeling of panic left. In that case we may have to act directly on the remaining feelings by using symbols. Now the mind does not spin as fast, it is merely wobbly. This is a bit uncomfortable. Our intervention is directed to the wobbliness. To give the client some control over the wobbliness, we teach him internal control of the physiology of the panic attack. What remains is to set up an external behavioral task in which the client can enter the phobic situation.

The object is for the client to go into the phobic environment comfortably, naturally, and, without the use of special effort, act quite differently in the presence of the stimuli. If it requires special effort, if the client has to run verbal patterns in his head and struggle to maintain his state of equilibrium, it has not been a wholly successful intervention. A successful intervention is one in which the client knows that he can calm his experience before he enters the phobic situation and goes ahead in reasonable comfort, without effort; as if he had never had the experience of a panic attack. He already knows experientially *in matrix* that he can do it.

In the beginning we establish exactly how the client knows he is going to have a panic attack and what the symptoms are. Our objective is to alter all that, so the client can comfortably go on with just the right degree of comfort he has asked for. This does not mean to say that all trepidation must disappear completely. It might be appropriate to retain a certain tolerable degree of discomfort.

Working with the memories helps to loosen the structure of the physiology of the panic attack and we then work directly on the physiology itself. It is easier to evolve a mind set when it is just wobbling than it is to change a mind that is spinning furiously. Restructuring the memory has slowed down the spinning of the mind so that we can alter the wobble through direct work. This approach appears to be successful with specific phobias. Often this is all that is needed.

Specific phobias are generally easy to dispose of, but there can be a phantom limb effect where the client has the panic without the panic attack. In changing the internal experience the mind acts as if the client should be panicking. It is a hollow experience and this is a very good thing to find because it is a validation of our having derailed the panic. The mind takes some time to adjust to the new response pattern.

The benefits to the client in part come from being understood. The metaphors are understood and, when we name his experience, we tame the devil by giving him a name. We identify each little part of his experience and that gives comfort to the client because he sees that someone knows exactly what that experience is. How can the client understand, when in response to an innocuous stimulus he feels he is going to die? We concentrate on each small aspect of the experience, one element at a time, to make the change rather than trying to confront the whole syndrome. We make one alteration, make sure it persists, and go to the next doable bit.

Complex phobias. With complex phobias, and for phobics who suffer generalized anxiety, the above approach will not suffice. In complex phobias we might apply a similar pattern just to help undermine the structure and also work symbolically with the physiology. Our treatment program monitors the client's internal experience, as well as the external environment, and requires some behavioral task or modelling and external experiences.

The problem with generalized anxiety is that it is hard to pin down to operational specifics and clients tend to display a slipperiness of mind. With agoraphobia we tend to encounter a generalization of the symptoms. In dealing with generalized anxiety and social anxiety, we have the client pin down and sort out the external stimuli, the conditions which invoke the anxiety and list these together. We format the quality of the physiology and then discover whether there is a change in physiological response to the different stimuli. For our intervention to have any significant effect we find that the syndrome must be broken down and resolved bit by bit.

We may also need to work historically in tackling general-ized anxiety: 'When was the first time you had that type of panic attack in that type of situation?' We go back to before that time, to events that made the client susceptible to the situation and respond in this way. We have the client list the different sets of memories that will produce different feeling physiologies. These are the memories, the events that predisposed the client to the first panic attack. We have the client alter or heal those memories and experiences. This helps to loosen the fabric of the physiology. The physiology is going to be the central issue, the criterion we work with: the butterflies in the stomach and the pounding heart ("If my heart did not pound, then I would be a lot better off.") Whatever strategy we employ, we orient the client's response to ways other than a pounding heart or butterflies in the stomach.

Agoraphobia. This condition often requires long-term treatment. We take into account a lot of the external phenom-ena as well as the internal response: the family of origin and the first panic attack. We concentrate on the area *before* the first panic attack. What occurred in this client's life that could have helped make him susceptible to a panic attack which seemed to come out of the blue in the supermarket?

We have the client detail the experiences *before* the panic attack because there is going to be a wealth of information in them. Most of the information we get after the panic attack is simply about the panic. It is about the symptom, and that will be important in terms of the anticipatory anxiety. The primary focus is on what occurred before the first panic attack. We might have to do some normal, straight, therapeutic uncover-ing to clarify the family relationships and the structure.

Often agoraphobics are nice people; too nice for their own good. One way to think about the condition is that these people subjugate their internal experience or subordinate their lives in the social and family structure. Often they subordinate their personal feelings to those of others. There comes a point, like a negative conversion experience, in which the suppressed rebels. At that point the client can no longer control his internal experience.

Usually these clients want to tell us about the panic attacks, the symptoms, and their effects. We must explore the circumstances before that first panic attack and examine the client's view of what went on and what stresses were experienced.

The client really wanted to go to art school, but her mother wanted her to work as a fashion model. The client obeyed her mother. She went on obeying until one day she had the first panic attack. Before the panic attack she was a nice girl who always did as she was told and never put anybody out. We might have to teach her some basic skills in standing up for herself. She can learn to be assertive, aggressive or a nice girl. She can develop skills in all of these. She can choose times to be a nice girl and times to be a bitch, or make any number of choices somewhere in between.

The agoraphobic client wants some immediate relief from the panic attack. Did it occur last week? Does it occur every time certain situations arise? We want to directly alleviate the panic symptoms. We use symbols to neutralize the butterflies and the pounding heart. The symbols must be para-sympathetically active symbols in order to calm the activity of the autonomic nervous system.

Relaxation itself is not necessarily a useful thing, unless we find the right context. Because we want to be very purposeful about what we are doing, we choose para-sympathetically active symbols. We get these active symbols from memories, from the times the client had almost the opposite physiology. The symbols can be all sorts of things: a dove, a soft cloud, water, a moon, a person's face, the father's hand or a glove. The right symbol is active in such a way that it has the exact isomorphic properties that are the precise opposite of the originating sympathetic physiology. Often we find, particularly with agoraphobics, the fear is so overwhelming that symbols are just a palliative, part of our approach. At least then the client gets some experience of comfort, even if it is only for the time that he is in the session.

We listen to the way the client presents, to his orientation in time. It may well be that it has been a good number of years since the client has had a full-blown panic attack. Perhaps it has been a number of years since he has left the house. The client fears a hand will strike him from out of the blue. It is this expectancy, the anticipatory anxiety, that is important.

We format this because it will have a different physiology to the panic attack: "Behind every door a hand is lurking to get me and to chop me." This is not the same as the panic attack. The anticipatory anxiety is prodromal. The full panic attack comes later. We work to alter that with psychoactive symbols. The agoraphobic has a propensity to live in the future. Although he knows something about some of his experiences and the previous panic attacks, he does not know much about living in the present. He 'knows' a great deal about living in the future. He is really good at catastrophizing experience. We want to know if the client constructs metaphors or symbols in the future. How does he enter the future, and how does he project those future memories? Is the client repeating the same memory, about the same thing happening, or does it vary day by day? If it is consistent, we can apply a routine restructuring technique. The client can have his scenario. In addition, we give him many others that have better outcomes than the one he has been catastrophizing. It may be hard to stop that sort of rumination, but quite easy to dilute it so that it loses its effect.

An agoraphobic is sitting about the house fantasizing that the next trip to the supermarket will bring on the panic attack. As he arrives at the memory of going to the supermarket, we develop a number of functional alternatives. Eventually we want him to fantasize a pleasant and agreeable trip to the supermarket, and we might also want to provide him with fantasies that have nothing to do with the supermarket. Absolutely anything that will interfere in the mind with this particular obsessive memory can be useful. We do not want him to practice the panic-laden trip to the supermarket, despite the fact that some eminent therapists say that this would exhaust the phobic response.

A better solution is to have the client achieve that exhaustion by looking at all the possible permutations of the scenario. This exhausts the phobic response by rehearsing every possible bad thing that can happen, rather than just the one bad thing. This gives the client a whole range of possible scenarios and that plays a useful part in loosening the structure. Were a therapist to say: 'Now, think about going to the supermarket very positively,' the client would be likely to have a new positive thought along with the negative one. The negative one, however, is much stronger. We prefer to ask the client, as he has so much energy invested in going there in a panic, to go there in a panic, but in an *inordinate number of ways*. By extending the ridiculousness, it will be easier to restructure the different negative scenarios. Rather than exhausting the pattern, we loosen the pattern by using the imagination, by having the client generate many scenarios.

The memories can have a slippery quality like a nightmare. No matter what we do to circumvent the bad element, something else appears and it is perpetuated. No sooner do we kick disaster out the door than it comes back through the window. We need to have positive symbols so that as the client catastrophizes these, good elements come in. The positive symbols can be built up to have positive powers and these will help alter the negative elements.

With the agoraphobic client, it is important to obtain a panoramic view. Where in time is the density of the symptoms? Is it expressed more in the future or more in the past. Or is it more about an immanent panic attack? The agoraphobic tends to feel understood if he is allowed to talk about his symptoms exactly as he experiences them. There is relief that someone at last understands that he is not crazy. This is an important part of the treatment. Often the agoraphobic feels he is going mad. It is comforting to know that in the chaos of his experience there are some concrete features that we can map out and name. There is power in a name. We can name this a butterfly, this a carousel that spins, and establish the details. This in and of itself can be comforting, regardless of the intervention. Clients tell us this is an important part of feeling understood.

If we wish to influence someone, we first give him a name. After he begins to respond to his name, we can place a hand on him. That is what we do with the management of the feeling physiology. Each element is given a unique name, each has a unique part to play. We eventually come to know the parts and their characteristics. The client learns to alter the feeling physiology and the internal, usually chaotic, experience. The different aspects of the client's panic that we have charted in the catastrophizing are now landmarks and the client has a map to help him get around. The land may still be unsettled and the volcanoes may still erupt, but the client may learn how to shape and contour the terrain, and what vegetation grows in strategic parts of that territory. These landmarks can help stem the panic attack and we can find vents to gradually release the pressure over a long period of time.

This agoraphobic lives in a city that is gray and full of concrete. There are very few people in the city. This is what her life is like. Sometimes she can see that it is green outside. There are doorways that connect to various houses. She cannot go out because she is afraid of the door: there is something at the door that prevents her from going out. She does not know how to unlock this door. When she gets into an agoraphobic situation and goes into a panic, it is as if she soars to an upper level of this city. The city is full of concrete. There is no green: there is heaviness and there is frozenness. Nothing moves; everything is frozen and she feels like concrete. When she comes out of the panic attack, it is like walking ever so slowly down a multi-story garage. She walks down the circular ramp, descending from the upper level to the middle level, and back to where she started from.

Underneath is another city. It is not very often that she is able to visit this city. Being in this city is like being outside: she can see the green of the woods, the trees, and the animals; the sun is shining, all of the people are free and happy, and nobody is locked in. Only rarely does she have that happy experience. What she knows most is the city on the middle level.

What can we introduce into the middle city that will give it some of the lower level's happy green qualities? This is her metaphor— the panoramic view of this client's experience— of what it is like to experience agoraphobia. It is a very *concrete* experience for her. Because of this pervasive pathology, it is difficult to work directly with her images and metaphors. We have to strike a balance between making small changes in her metaphor and the normal counselling, modelling, and desensitization techniques.

Airplane phobia. An airplane phobia is frequently a complex phobia. It is complex because it may not be just the fear of flying: it is often also the fear of being enclosed in a space over which the client has no control. As we gather historical information, we have the client establish the feeling physiology of his symptom. We format that into its symbolic form and direct the client to previous occurrences of this feeling physiology. If it is a simple fear of flying which first occurred when the client was in a plane, it may not go back any further: there was a time when there was an air pocket, and that's all. Or a relation died in a plane crash and: "I have never been on a flight since." These simple cases call for the simple approach of taking the memories, restructuring them and altering the physiology.

For the complex phobic, the physiology goes into the past beyond an actual event on the plane: "I got that same feeling when my brother helped me out of the water, or one time when my mother locked me in a cupboard, and that is exactly the same feeling." We obtain a list of the pre-phobic sensitizing memories. These memories, which have the same physiology as the phobic memories, relate to a different type of experience; they do not have anything to do with airplanes. The client makes one list of these and another with the airplane-phobic incidents. It may be that some of the events that occurred before the original phobic event may have had a different physiology, related to different experiences, and that actually revolve around some independent issues. We treat these separately and restructure the events in order to undermine the historical aspects. These sensitizing events will often be a lot easier to work with than the phobic events. We restructure those memories and only then attend to the bad experiences related directly to airplanes. We then alter the feeling physiology using para-sympathetically active symbols.

Fear of elevators is also often associated with being in a confined space and not having control. If we just talk about elevators and the client goes back and searches for information to do with them, this is by no means necessarily where the sensitizing events are located. We therefore use the feeling physiology as a magnet for gathering the pre-phobic experiences.

As the client shortlists memories of phobic incidents, she works at a verbal, cognitive level. We get a list of the incidents during which the phobic experience was at its worst: three to six intense experiences, perhaps. We have the client establish the sequence of where and when the worst moments occurred. With airplane phobia there is often an anticipatory anxiety that can occur as the client learns she has to fly. This is followed by the actual anxiety *in situ* in the plane. These may present two different sets of symptoms. Both sets need to be explored.

We have the client select a convenient flying incident. Usually the last one is a good choice, although it may not necessarily be the strongest incident. Using clean questions, we get the client to tell us the details. As she tells us these, the feeling physiology is induced. After she has talked about it, we invite the client to identify the worst moment of the experience. When we have the worst moment, we listen for additional details that will be related. We observe carefully to see where the physiology actually affects her. Is it in her chest, her stomach or her head— the most likely places— or does it occur in her knees? We spend some time at the surface before going into her matrix: 'Where does it affect you?' We locate it: 'In your chest? Whereabouts in your chest? Does it have a shape, a color?' We want to put it into a simile: 'It is like what?' What we will probably get is not just one thing but a sequence, and so we have to go back: 'So you get this tightness in your chest that is like a vise. Does anything happen before that?' "No." 'Does anything happen after?' "Well, my knees start going." 'What does that mean?' "They start shaking." 'Shaking like what?'

"Shaking like jelly." 'What sort of jelly?' "Like a green jelly." 'Like what sort of green jelly?' "Like a moldy sort of a slimy jelly." 'So you get this vise in your chest, then you get this green jelly, then what happens?' "I don't know, I get all confused." 'Confused where?' "In my head." 'Where in your head? In the middle of your head? Confused like what?' "Well, it is like spinning." 'Spinning like what?' "Spinning like a top." 'So your head spins like a top? Then what happens?'

We are getting a sequence of physiologies, feelings in different locations. We have identified three things that occurred internally, and we get an external phenomenon such as: "Then I freeze, I run, I sweat or do something like that." We are looking for that moment between a stimulus and a response in this one incident. We are in the matrix. We move laterally and find out: 'Now, you had that feeling when you were on the plane. Was that similar to the feeling you had before you got on the plane, or when you first knew you were traveling on the plane?' We take that feeling back and determine: 'Or was it a different feeling?' "When I am thinking about getting on the plane, I just have the wrench in my stomach. When I get on the plane, that is when my head starts spinning." 'And which is worse?' "When my head starts spinning, it is really bad. I mean I can live with this wrench, but when my head starts spinning, I can't talk, I don't know what." We take the sequence back and determine which physiology is the most intense. We go back through the other memories and use this physiology to pick up more memories: 'Now think of the last time you know you had the feelings. Now what about the time before that, and take some time.' We want the client to do this internally: 'Now think of that *wrench*, the last time you had *wrench* and the other times, and just take some time to go through your history, right back to the very first time that you can remember having *wrench*, and then just give me a number.' All we want at this stage is a number of how many actual memories there are. We get a number around five. 'Now go through again, take *wrench* and use that to pick up any other times when you had *wrench*.' There will be additional phobic times and the client lists her memories of *wrench*. We are not talking about the phobia now, we are talking about *wrench*. These incidents presumably occurred during airplane trips or contemplating airplane trips, but also in other contexts. That is where we take some time to repeat it at least three times. We are looking for that very first time. It might have happened when her father was playing with her, throwing her up in the air, catching her and then letting her go. Although he caught her at the last moment, it gave her a big fright and that is the first time she had a wrench. That is the one we want.

The client gets a list of memories and puts it in order of intensity. Under *wrench* we have all these memories. She may also have another series which is *jelly*, when her legs went like jelly, and yet another when her head spun.

If we presuppose that the client is to tell us all these memories, we are going to get her talking to us and we do not want that. We have to train the client to stay inside. It is no accident when she restricts herself to dialogue. It is probably at least in part predicated upon the questions we ask (unclean questions may demand verbal answers): 'Just think about those memories and then just give me the number of how many there are. And go through each one so you know all the detail.' By saying that, we are teaching the client to stay inside, not to communicate details. All she tells us is a number. There are six of these incidents when she had *wrench*: 'Now, okay, if these six *wrench* events never happened in your life, do you think that you would still have a phobia?' If she says: "Well, no, of course not," we have got the first building block for the intervention: 'We know that these six incidents have occurred and we know that they affect you in these memories now, because when you get on a plane you have *wrench*. Does that make sense?' "Yes." 'Is it possible that these six memories could change in some way? I do not know how that could happen, but if it were possible, and in them changing in some way you did not get that feeling of wrench, would that be useful to you?' "Yes." 'So how would it be useful?' "Well, if I did not get that feeling of wrench I would not get upset when I knew I had to fly." We then get the behavioral components. When we have those, the intervention has been prepared.

The object is for the client not to have *wrench*, and we are using memories as a way of mitigating *wrench*. We have the client take the smallest memory, the weakest one. We may want to spend some time on this to teach her to be internal. Our instructions presuppose that the client is going to go internal and do the work herself. We have her change a point, alter the memory, and go through one memory at a time. We know when she has changed a point by the first instruction, and the client says: "Yes," she can do the whole list: 'Take that memory and freeze-frame it, or see if it runs like a movie. Go through the protocols that I have already outlined and do whatever you can to make alterations.' We spend more time on the first memory and less time on the second. By the third one we may say to the client: 'Now go ahead and change numbers three and four, like you did numbers one and two.' And then we wait. When it comes to the strongest memory, we may only say: 'Well, go ahead and do number six.' When she has done all the memories, we come back to *wrench* in the stomach. We want the client to go through the memories now and test her work: 'Go through and check each memory, go through as it is altered and see if *wrench* comes back, and if *wrench* comes back, then alter the memory so *wrench* is not there.' We tell the client in absolute terms to make *wrench* come back and when it comes back, we tell the client to alter the memory so *wrench* does not come back. It is a double bind, a recursive loop. We instruct the client to go very securely through each memory several times and make all these adjustments, so that no matter what she does to remember any of those memories, she can no longer make *wrench* come back, no matter what she does.

The client has resolved the past memories because, as she recalls those past experiences, *wrench* does not come back. Now we ask in the present: 'Is that okay?' "Yes, that is okay." Then we go to the future: 'Now think of a time in the future in which *wrench* could come back, or might occur as in the past. As you do that, take your knowledge into the future and make the adjustments that you need to make so that *wrench* can no longer be there.'

'We are taking the resources that you have learned, those six memories there, and translating them into the future and changing them so that *wrench* does not occur. Now that you know how to do that, go and do that now.' That is the pattern, so she does it and we ask: 'Well, can you do that successfully?' Now we begin to doubt that she can actually do what she did. We want the client to convince us that she did it, and we say: 'I wonder how you could do it so quickly. Go through it again and really make sure, because you have had it for many years.' She goes through the memories again and checks her work, but we are still a bit doubtful about this whole thing: 'Well, so all right, you have been able to do this in your mind and you did not get this *wrench*, so what about real life? You better make up a real-life task that you can do that will really convince me that this has worked.' "Oh well, if I am going on a flight here." 'If you are going on a flight, you know that before you go you get *wrench*. And now you have some ways of changing *wrench*.'

We may find that by doing the memories, the client only gets half or three-quarters of *wrench* to go. If that is the case, we then work in the present. With this approach we work directly on *wrench*: 'What would it take for *wrench* to go?' We can run through the symbol intervention pattern. We operate directly on that physiology, using other physiologies. We forget about memories and just concentrate on wrench. We want something to occupy the place that the wrench occupied. We want either a flower, or water, or something else there. Perhaps the client can put this flower here, these butterflies there, in exactly the same position as this *wrench*. Rather than trying to make the wrench go away, we want to have that hurt go away. We teach her the skill of putting this flower there, and when the flower is there the wrench cannot occupy that same physiological space. That is likely to be a good intervention.

We translate the phobia into another language, one in which the client is less accomplished. We want to drop the structure down into the physiology and talk about *wrench* instead of the incidents themselves. The incidents, and all the client's verbiage, help to fixate the phobia and make it live. We want to translate the structure of the phobia into another level, where the client is not as well defended. This is what Erickson sometimes did with symbols and metaphors. Clients are not interested in maintaining their symbols or metaphors, but they may be interested in maintaining their pathology. We are working tangentially to make the changes.

When the client produces a lot of verbiage, we steer the procedure out of it because clients may be very adept at maintaining their pathology in the verbiage. The client says: "I feel afraid and I feel bad, nervous." We relate it directly to some event. If the client is out there talking about it, we let her talk about it until we extend this evidence down into the epistemology. We stay with the narration until we find the worst point and we go right with the energy so the client has the feeling of: "That was the worst there." 'And so what happened?' "Oh wow! It was like this, so oppressed, and the feeling came upon me." 'So this oppressed feeling came upon you, and that was the worst part, that experience?' "Yeah, as soon as I stepped into the plane, it was like this oppressed feeling came over me." 'Where was most of the oppressed feeling upon you?' "Well, it came down on my chest." 'So it was mostly on your chest and not on your back?' "No, on my chest." 'On your stomach, or just the upper part of your chest?' "Just the upper part of my chest. I could not breathe." 'You could not breathe?' "Yes, it was like this weight came upon me and I could not breathe." 'And this weight was like what? Did it come from the outside or the inside?' "Oh, it came from the outside. It is like somebody standing with a foot on my chest and it squashed all the air out and I just could not breathe, I was gasping for breath and I wanted this weight to come off me." 'So you have got it, you have got this foot on the chest, and this weight, this weight like what? What was the weight like?' "Like these steel bands on my chest and they just came and gripped me." 'So you've now got the steel bands. Can you work with the steel bands?' And we relate to these steel bands. That is what we want: the real word. We take that word and extend its significance. We find out when the client has the feeling now: 'So when you have these steel bands, that is the feeling, that is the very worst as you board the plane. Are these steel bands worse than the wrench?' "Yeah, they are worse than wrench." We ask: 'So which would be best not to have, the wrench or the steel bands?' "Oh, the steel bands." 'The steel bands, okay. So you could live with the wrench?' "Yeah, I could live with the wrench. I mean, I do not like the wrench, but if I could have the steel bands off, I think I could get on that plane." We keep going until we have this alternate form, this symbolic form that makes sense to the client through the whole of the phobia. We want to get to the syllogism: 'If you did not have these steel bands, would you be able to get on the plane?' "Yes, yes, that is the one!" 'If you did have this jelly in the legs, would you still?' "Well, a jelly, yeah I think so, the jelly, well, it is all right. I do not want to make a fool of myself, but with these steel bands, I think I am going to die."

Claustrophobia. Treatment for claustrophobia and airplane phobia is similar. We get the feelings, the incidents of claustrophobia. We format the historical aspects, alter the internal experience, and alter the presenting physiology. We go on to the future for anticipatory testing of the new learning. We want the client to go into the claustrophobic situation not with great expectations, but with the right amount of trepidation; of going into something for the first time. We do not expect a sense of jubilation. The client can go into the situation with a certain trepidation that there would be with any new experience. Now we want the client to go in for the first time to *discover* what feeling he is going to come out with and what his response is going to be.

Fear of heights. Treatment for fear of heights also resembles that for airplane phobia. We get a list of memories that are actual experiences of being in high places: we get those which are the worst, and we search for some previous sensitizing events. We are not going to allay the fear of heights. We alter the feeling physiology. Then the client can be in the situation and be comfortable about the normal degree of discomfort he experiences. We want the client to be reasonably comfortable in the presence of warning signals. This allows the client to take appropriate action for safety. That is our criterion. Often with a phobia, clients think that in order to be rid of it they ought to be able to go and handle a rat, handle a spider, or touch a snake. Now, that is not normally what people do. We want the client to be in the presence of those stimuli, but without the overwhelming responses. Many phobics suffer from painful fantasies regarding objects that are not generally present in the environment.

Incest and child abuse. These presenting complaints have to do with event-related anxieties. Particular events have occurred in the client's life, and from then on he is no longer the same. There is a broad spectrum of presenting symptoms and complaints through which the client's life is now limited in some way. Whether it be unwanted thoughts, behavior or feelings, the client wants a change because the complaint limits or burdens the way he operates in the world. The method of our intervention is to alter the way the client stores and processes the information of the particular events. We want to change the infrastructure for the processing of information and the way the data is stored. If possible, we want to free the client from the tyranny of his unwanted thoughts and feelings.

Clients present their surface complaint. Underlying that they have information that is stored and acts in a way that limits life. The intervention creates a healing environment so that the stored information can be altered and the way that it is processed changed.

The client presents in his own language. The symptom's own language has a unique meaning. Can we decipher that language and those symptoms so that they make sense to the client? We interrupt patterns or otherwise intervene helpfully with the elements that we have deciphered. It is important to locate the exact moment of the greatest density of the pathology.

Rape. There are a number of moments which we want to establish in order to find out which physiology seems to be most strongly valenced for this client. For instance, there is a point just before the rape occurs when the client usually has an awareness that she is in danger. There is another, earlier, point at which she may have engaged in some particular behavior or activity which has its own element of excitement. This edge of excitement might be a typical tingling feeling inside her abdomen, or the feeling of being in an exciting place. This would be particularly true with assaults from friends and relatives. (A majority of rapes occur from a known partner.) Often in these cases there is a particular physiology present before any indication of the rape: the client, for example, experiencing a tingling feeling of excitement that she likes.

In a case where the woman is attacked by a complete stranger, we do not observe this precursor. Rather, we notice a moment of fear when she knew that something foul was about to happen. She may not have suspected it was to be rape. We get this particular moment anchored to a feeling physiology. This might be a recognition, an 'Aha!' Suddenly things became clear. It might be that her mind started spinning. So there is one moment in time. It may be that one second, two seconds, ten seconds, a minute later there is another key moment at which something occurred that perhaps had to do with the actual rape. This is a different matrix because, here, where the act is being perpetrated, the client might be struggling and: "It felt like a demon was unleashed as I scratched and bit him." The client may have been catatonic with fear. She may have been so afraid that she completely dissociated and it was as if she had floated out of her mind while someone did this to this body. The client was dissociated out of her body. After the rape there may have been a feeling of safety, of when it finished, or a time when the client was in the shower. There may be a moment in the shower in which she had a different feeling from that of the fear, and: "This was the first time that I started to feel safe." The boyfriend found her and got very angry, berating her for being in that situation. Or her father found her and she did not want to tell him. A number of things could happen. It is important to locate these moments and to find the exact feeling physiology for each happening.

It may be minutes or hours after talking to someone that the client overcomes the fear and starts to feel angry about what has happened. Now she is flushed with anger, which is directed towards the rapist and perhaps men in general: "The anger is like a *burning desire in my cheeks* and the rage I feel inside *grips me like a vise.* I want to kill him for what he did to me." Another client who is at the same moment may have a totally different physiology. She is so dissociated, perhaps, that nothing seems real. This client suffers from post-traumatic shock and, "It is as if everything is floating on a cloud and people are floating by." She hears voices, but they do not reach her because she is still partially out of body. That is a different feeling physiology.

With another victim it may be that she has been desecrated. She was going to be a nun, but that is impossible now because she has been violated. These are all very different feeling physiologies over a period of seconds or hours. We gather this information and find out where the greatest density of the client's experience is located.

The symptoms expressed in telling the story, right here and now in the office, may be one set of symptoms: "I shake when I am telling the story of my rape, and I shake and I wobble like a jelly." In dealing with that, we find that this is mainly an overlay on the experience as stored in memories.

A rape victim has nightmares of the experience. In the nightmares she is frozen like concrete with fear. Another client is flushed with fire and full of anger at the event and for the rapist. Yet another is depressed because this thing has happened to her, and because of the implications that it holds for her future: now she has to change her life plan because this event has changed her life.

Where to intervene depends on at what moment the symptom originated and which is the most prevalent symptom. If the greatest density is the replay of the actual rape scene, then healing with memories must be a good intervention. If it has to do with the physiology of anger, memories may be a useful aspect, but not as useful as dealing with the physiology of fire and giving her some ways to alter the anger internally with physiological symbols. If depression is the central issue—she is unworthy— that may present in terms of metaphors of unworthiness: "My life has been blackened; there is a black mark against me; I can never be pure any more." The issues come in different languages. There are different events on which we may choose to intervene, depending upon how the client presents.

There is little use in trying to work with the memory if the client is feeling depressed. The physiology of the depression, of a black cloud, has nothing to do with the concrete feeling she felt when she was being raped. The same applies to working with the anger; a very different physiology from the concrete feeling of fear during the rape.

We follow the client's experience. We do not say: 'You have got to let your anger out.' The client who is feeling depressed may not necessarily feel anger for the rapist. She may see the rape as an act of fate. If we were to focus on anger, or relive and talk about the rape to get catharsis, we may be on the wrong track. The feeling of concreteness around the actual rape has nothing to do with this depression or the black mark against her. The depression and the black mood are more future-oriented than past-oriented.

We listen to the client's language. Is it expressed more in terms of the physiology, the feelings, the memories of the event as it actually occurred, or the language of metaphors? Is this client speaking in metaphorical constructs, in terms of the future, or is she semantically oriented in terms of righteous indignation at the idea of how somebody could do this: "And what sort of person is this that could do such a thing?" When we identify the language, we make the intervention in the language of the complaint. The object is to alter the internal structure of the experience, the way the client processes the information about this event and the consequences of the initial rape. We may need to direct our attention to different moments in time, such as the rape and the avoidance behavior. The subsequent events that occurred as a result of the rape are sometimes perceived as experientially worse by the client.

First we format the physiology, then we learn from the client what we have to achieve, in the client's own language, in order to effect a significant change. Working with the traumatic experiences toward restructuring the memory may loosen the fabric of the experience. The rape can be a very vivid memory and we seek to make a change within it. The change is likely to be non-logical; it can take liberties with the facts of the rape. As a result, the attendant feeling of that memory can alter. To do that the client may modify some visual aspects of the memory. A woman who was gang-raped by five men is dissociated in her memory, and we have her freeze-frame the event so that she can see the five men at a particular moment. We cause an alteration in the way that this event is remembered. She needs comfort, something comforting in that memory, so she conjures a chair that belonged to her grandmother. She sits in that chair and she wraps herself in granny's robe. As she is watching the rape from that position of comfort, she can then see herself on the bed and what happens to her. She decides that she would like to make the bed using fresh, clean sheets. She lines up the five rapists beside the bed and, taking each perpetrator in turn, she looks at their features and begins to change their features into a cartoon-like form. One is very fat, so she turns him into a wax candle because he is fat and flabby. Another has curly hair and so she distorts his features, turning him into a bushy mop. Now she has a whole parade of these characters in her memory. She puts a shower into the top right-hand corner of the memory. She has a light coming out of the shower, where she was able to wash herself and feel clean. The light permeates the scene and illuminates the characters. She now has a composite memory which has little to do with the actual event. What has happened is that the actual memory of the rape has now been evolved into this new visual representation.

This is different from using guided imagery or asking the client to imagine. If we were to ask clients to imagine, they would still have the original memory and they would also imagine a new one. Our way is to evolve the original memory so that it transforms into an altered one. The old memory is no longer there. As we test the intervention, we find that, as the client looks at all these distorted figures, she laughs. That is the change in the physiology. Now it has evolved. What she has now is a *knowing* of the original event. She can describe exactly what happened in an appropriate way. In her memory, however, what she sees and feels is the new recall. The feeling physiology accessed by memories of that rape has been altered into this new pattern.We used the memories surrounding the actual event to alter the affect and replay so that the only thing that plays now is this revised version. For many days after she would tell others what happened. She could tell what happened in a matter-of-fact way. Distorting the features of her attackers was just the evolution needed to help her.

Another client put a shield around herself that protected her from the rapist. She had a train run through her house and leapt on board. The train sped her to her neighbors and they accompanied her on her train journey. She was safe then because these were good strong bonds in her life. Obviously this had nothing to do with objective reality. In this way, however, the client was able to restructure her memories and rid herself of unwanted thoughts and feelings.

We have the client alter the structure of the internal experience and translate that into external behavior. We want the internal alterations to manifest themselves in a new external behavior. This helps alter the memory of the event and the thoughts, patterns, and feelings associated with it. We want the client to act out that internal work in terms of the external reality. What she could not do before, she will now be able to do without excessive and unwanted feelings.

Child abuse. With the abusive parent, in addition to restructuring the memories, we format the physiology: 'Just before you hit your child, what happens? The instant before you know that you are going to hit your child, what happens?' The client responds: "I get a feeling of rage like this explosion in my head and then I strike out." Our intervention is to alter the explosion in the head.

'When in the past did you have that explosion in your head? Use the explosion to go back to pick up the memories.' The client responds: "When my father used to hit me, I would get a different sense of feeling." The client picks up the memories of the abuse and heals the memories of being abused. If the parent has changed, we can use the 'new' parent, as he is now, to go back and help heal the memories of the abused child.

When the abusive parent is dead, he may; "Come back and undo the wrong that he did." There may have been a time when the abusive parent treated the child very well. We have the client take that happy period in early life and have the 'young' parent come and heal the wounds that the 'old' parent inflicted. Working with the past helps loosen the structure of the experience of *explosion* that the client has before hitting the child. Next we work to gather new physiological para-sympathetic symbols that help alter the aggressive sympathetic feelings that are the precursors to the abuse.

Incest. In rape cases we often find eidetic images which the client recalls with great, great clarity. In incest that is mostly not the case. Certain parts of the incestuous relationship are remembered. If an incident occurred at a very young age, often all we get are vague impressions: it just seems like a dark tunnel, or no memories of anything that happened before a certain age, or that a piece in the client's history is no longer there. It is just a blank: "I do not know." We work with this blank. We have a blank, or the dark tunnel, and that is the language of the client's experience. To force the client to recover these 'lost' memories can be harmful. Whatever protective mechanism has functioned for this client, she is now no longer able to recall in detail what happened. She may not have the strength to face the events that occurred at that time. Therefore, we work solely with what the client freely gives us. If she only gives us a hazy memory, then a hazy memory will do.

When the memories are not all that clear, there is an inherent danger in our questioning or in the client's attendance at an incest group: as the client listens in to other victims' stories of their abuse, she may suffer trauma and contamination. When other clients' stories feel the same, they can be damaging because the client may fill in her blanks with other people's material. She can construct false memories with things that she feels happened to her. She constructs the scene, reifies it, and it is as if it really happened. There is little difference in our experience between the effects of what really happened and the client's perceived idea of what happened. A construed event can be just as strongly limiting as any actual event. In trying to uncover something, we are very careful not to retraumatize the client. The event is covered over for a reason and uncovering it is not necessarily good therapy.

We do not uncover memories unless we have a way of protecting the client, and of healing what we have uncovered. What we do not want to trigger is a vicious cycle in which the client wants to find out more and more of what happened, and gets memory glimpses and flickers as we talk. We do not raise the issue of the incest as if it was some ordinary presenting complaint lest we set off a vicious cycle of the client reaching back in memory to relive what happened to find out if it really happened: "I have some sense, there is a smell there. You know I can feel a beard and I feel like I have been touched." Often all we get is a piece of fragmentary evidence, and that is what we work with. If the client has a feeling in the genitals that she was touched, we have her shape that into a specific physiological form. That feeling physiology is what we want to alter. The feeling could also be there when the client is with her spouse. The physiology replays and we want, therefore, to alter that physiology.

With incest clients we often choose to proceed indirectly. We may not want the client to relive the memories, and we do not go back to get the client in touch with her anger. We do not feel that would be a prudent or humane intervention. If the abuse presents itself in terms of a metaphor such as: "It is like a dark deep cave," we want to heal that dark deep cave and we work symbolically to do so. If it is a smell, or, "I get this strange sensation in my stomach, like a square box, and it goes right down inside my genitals," then we work with a square box that goes right down inside the genitals. That is what we are given and that is what we work with, not with the memory of when the client first got *square box,* unless that memory is readily available. It is a great deal safer to work with a square box that goes into the genitals than to work with uncovering what her father did to her. This way we value the client. We are respectful of her process and we are respectful of the defence that is in place and which has enabled the client to survive. We do not have any right as therapists to undo that defence without putting something more useful in its place.

What can we do with that cold, hard, rectangular, tearing metal box? If there is no readily available memory to restructure, we work on the aspects and qualities of the box. The symbolic intervention is to address little bits of the box: to alter its shape, its hardness, and coldness. When does this box appear in relation to external events? "Just when my husband touches me on the shoulder, I know he is up to something. Or when I think about something." We ask the client to list those events. How can we soften the edges of that box? Could we make it just one degree warmer? 'When is that box softer, or is it always this degree of hardness?' We work within that: 'Now you can see me across the room and you can see that memory?' "Yes." 'Now you know the difference between me and the memory?' "Yes." 'What proportion would you say is more present, can you give me a proportion? How much are you there with the memory and how much are you here in this room?' The client might say: "The memory is eighty percent real with me right now and I am only twenty percent in this room." The visual information in the memory is stronger than the visual information coming from being in the room here and now. This memory is persistent. When we get a good change, we help establish that new reality. Although some of the old story line comes through, accompanying it is the aura of having been healed. The physiological analogue is altered and there is excitement in the way that the client describes the new memory. Yet, at the same time, the factual basis of what happened is also there. The old memory is now like a doormat. The traumatic memory is altered. It has the valence of a doorknob. The client can describe it, she knows what it looks like, and yet it does not limit her life. She learns to operate that doorknob. It has an experiential quality. Yet, every time she thinks about it, it leaves her rather indifferent.

In working with some traumatic memories, we do not have to distort what occurred. We deal with the feeling physiology and the memory stays undisturbed. Restructuring memories can be the client's choice as an intervention when the client presents in the language of memories. A physiological, metaphorical or semantic intervention might change none of the memories, nor the architecture, nor the ways that memory is stored. The mind can be facile. We look for its most facile part, the part that will alter with the least effort. Some clients can easily distort the historical events in their memory. Others tend to reject that very natural process. It seems to us that there are many people who continuously evolve their memories without benefit of therapy. Others are realistic in their response if we say: 'Now change a point in there, in that memory, so that it can become different.' "I cannot change anything in there: that is what happened." The client is absolutely right and we will go along with her. We will work with her in another way.

7

Technical Notes and Clinical Observations

Precis

One of the steps in this therapy is to discover ways in which the therapist can help the client alter his internal experience and reality, enabling change to manifest itself in a desired way. We want to develop the way in which the client structures his reality as described in his unique language. We want to accomplish this without emphasizing an information-gathering process that may distort the client's conceptual reality. This process should be catalytic and not distort the principal elements. Rather than using external parameters for a diagnosis, we initially want to give form to the client's internal material.

Mythology. At the ontological level of the matrix, we find the beliefs, the mythologies that clients use to organize their experiences. One of the objects of working at deeper levels may be to change and alter the mythologies that clients use to construct their experience. We may want to reweave the fabric of those experiences to create a more useful and usable mythology. This requires a delicate intervention and one in which the therapist utilizes the material, the warp and weft, that is already there. By taking apart and reweaving the existing material, the therapist enables that mythology to speak in a different way without the trauma brought about by replacing it with something else. This is where great care is taken with language. As the therapist prises apart and creates an environment in which mythology can be rewoven, it is important not to introduce new material until the therapist has been able to reorganize the material that is already there. The therapist can later decide what new material needs to be introduced from the external world. This is an important factor in designing our interventions.

It is easy to make suggestions with all good intentions at the beginning of the therapeutic process, but clients may or may not integrate that information. If they do, the therapist has changed their experience to a certain extent and may make it more difficult to encompass the meaning of the mythology. The therapist may have changed only one sentence, but has already created a different context. What we are seeking in changing the client's mythology is a nodal point, a point at which we can make the least amount of change that may bear many ramifications. This requires patience and skill. The therapist should not intervene too early because one of the objectives of this therapy is to allow the client's self-healing abilities and resources the opportunity to work before the 'clever therapist' does something to heal it.

A forty year old man is driving down a road and has a vision of his father dying. This vision haunts the client, and as we discuss this the client is taken back into a memory. It is an incident in which he got angry with his father at age eleven and went off against his father's advice. This had angered his father. Thirty years later, when he comes back, his father has just died. He always felt that he had seriously wronged his father. Over the past thirty years, he has carried a feeling of guilt for anything associated with his father. The client is taken back in the memory and introduced, as the man he is now, to the time when he was standing next to his father and then walked off. The intervention consists of formatting this memory with the memory of seeing his father dead in the hospital.

Just by leaving the client in that memory, to look at what happened, the mature man is able to evolve. He is now a father, and if his son did the same thing to him, he would forgive him. At that moment, that epiphanic moment of recognition, he realizes that it really did not matter. A father's love can overcome that hurt.

The client's mythology is that, "I hurt, damaged or treated my father unjustly by going off." The client's complaint is: "I am carrying the guilt, I feel guilty." The therapeutic intervention is to enter into the client's matrix at the moment of the disobedient act and allow him to introduce his adult self into that moment. The process of the adult self allows the client to take a new view of the childhood disobedience, to reframe the disobedience as harmless and to forgive. A father's love would be very forgiving because the client already knows the experience of being a father. Now the client has a new mythology, one in which he can remember his father in a very different way.

The underlying myths are at the ontological level rather than at the verbal cognitive level. The ontological beliefs may emerge from a faith, or from family messages, family rituals or social settings that carry particular norms of behavior. In his poem Prometheus Unbound, Shelley writes about four cardinal virtues which seal the serpents in the pit. They are: gentleness, wisdom, virtue, and endurance. When we are dealing with the client's ontological mythology at this level, it is the myths that seal the demons in the pit. If, because of some crisis, the demons escape, the client is distressed or confused. If he presents for therapy as a crisis client, to get at that level we need to search for the virtues that are going to seal the demons and snakes back into the pit. Other cultures have totem poles on which their mythology is centered. When the totem pole is in the ground, the center of the tribal being is in that pole. The base of the totem pole goes through the head of the serpent. When disaster strikes, the totem pole comes out of the ground and the demons are unleashed. When we talk about mythology we are talking about that deep level: the mythology that goes through the very middle of experience, how that experience is molded, and how a client is founded ontologically. This contrasts with a client's epistemology, which is how he knows he knows something.

Narrative is a surface process. It is a verbal process about knowing. The surface aspect of mythology is what Beck terms, 'Rules, beliefs, and expectations'. In his cognitive therapy he appears not to delve far below the thoughts and behaviors that are influenced and generated by these rules, beliefs, and expectations. In the course of our interventions, we sometimes become aware of the epistemological and ontological origins which can be truly mythological, and which we find in deeper layers of the mind. We may sometimes want, or have, to deal with these directly in order to achieve a powerful and effective intervention.

Our work consists of delivering focused, precise interventions. We strive to focus our work at a particular experience, a particular moment, a particular fraction of a second, or at a precise level or levels in the client's mind. We proceed in such a way as to have the client focus his mind on that particular experience. We use precisely selected words, delivered in such a way as to facilitate the client's process and the client's experience of his mental process. We examine this mental process. The ways in which we make interventions are dependent on the language in which the client expresses his reality.

Which is the predominant language in representing the complaint? We will look at the characteristics of each of these languages and the types of interventions that are unique to the different languages. Our intervention can be designed to use two, three or four of the languages to achieve a complete experiential change within a client. We use rules of thumb to discover problem-solving techniques. We only know if it has worked empirically once the intervention has been delivered.

Analgesia. Language is important in achieving analgesia during the intervention. The therapist must keep the conditions clean. Analgesia is facilitated by various modalities:

1. The therapist obtains it through a process of visual dissociation, keeping the client distanced and separated from the memory.

2. The client is kept oriented in the past.

3. The client is kept internally oriented throughout the intervention. The therapist does not 'exist', only his voice is there.

4. The sound of the therapist's voice is used in structuring the intervention spatially, and verb tenses are accurately oriented to the client's location in time.

These are some of the ways of giving the client analgesia before and during an intervention on the traumatic memory. This we call keeping the client *there then*.

These techniques are to be used judiciously in discovering if they work for this client. If our approach does not make an impact, we strive to find another way. It may be that, given the limitation of our knowledge, we cannot facilitate a useful experience. The alteration in this particular memory will not work and that is when we move to another language. We might go on to physiological symbols, with which there need not be a conscious cognitive process directly involved in the therapy.

Delivery and design. How we deliver the intervention is of importance. We need to have inert wording around the active intervention. When the client is well defended and there is vested energy in maintaining the pathology (for example, if the client is depressed and it is apparent in his behavior) it is going to be harder to work on the behavior than on the feelings. Clients do not have much vested energy in maintaining their metaphors or their symbols. However, they do invest energy in maintaining their affective state, or their behavior, or their thought pattern. Working indirectly with the metaphor or symbol of the depression, we often can affect the depression more easily.

We format the memories and provide a simple injunction to alter that memory. Having dissociated the client by focusing on the memory, the latter becomes more amenable to that alteration. We start off with as little invasiveness as possible . Some interventions cannot be handled entirely internally: they need some structural elements and we have to introduce some support. This is where we may introduce an outside factor into the matrix. Our I-ness as a therapist is at an absolute minimum at this stage, because we as therapists are out of the client's matrix and out of the time period that he is working with.

At this stage we are not part of the internal process and this keeps the operation clean, so that the client can discover for himself the way in which he needs to heal. We need to keep this in mind to enhance the effectiveness of our intervention; of forming and delivering it to the client in order for the intervention to have a direct impact upon our specific target.

It is often best to work peripherally at first, rather than going directly into the abyss. We work around it and only gradually work our way in. If we expose a client to his pathology immediately, we may encounter heavy resistance or strong emotion. We want a controlled reaction because it is no accident that the client has a particular locus or nucleus of disturbance that is protected by a shell. If we enter too quickly or too directly, the client has no protection. We soften the shell and give the client the opportunity of gradually being able to peel it off. As the shell comes off, the client learns some new ways of protecting himself against the content. As he learns these new ways, the structure starts to unravel and the pathology begins to change very naturally. That is what we are striving for. We work gently and peripherally and this allows the client to evolve his protective mechanism.

If the client feels like he is on the edge of an abyss, this is his metaphor. If he is too scared to look down, the intervention should not be one where we are going to drop him into that abyss. We teach him about the generic aspects of an abyss, explore the edge of an abyss. We explore how sharp the edge is, what lies along the abyss, what sort of terrain is there. Are there trees or flowers or shrubs away from the abyss? Is it a crumbly edge? And as we explore the edge, we help the client to look for some footholds. What is there on the terrain that the client can use? Is there some rope? Can he make a ladder?

We teach the client to explore the first inch of the edge. He can always come back to the safety of the edge. We give him that protection so that he can have a new means of protecting himself if he should decide to go into that abyss. Is it actually necessary to go down there? Just because a client has a black hole full of a deep dark past, it is wrong to assume that he necessarily needs to go down into that past; regurgitating it all, exploring it, and understanding it in the process. That is only one possibility. Another possibility is to cross over it. The client can do so by walking over it. He can build a bridge and cross over in safety, leaving the black hole behind. The client does not necessarily have to get over it by going into it. What would the other side be like? We may teach the client about a bridge and about what is on the other side, and how to secure that bridge so that he can pass over his abyss.

These are some of the considerations when we are planning an intervention. We do not start out by assuming that we have to uncover memories and talk about the past. It may be entirely possible to construct an effective intervention; one in which it is not necessary to refer to the past. We will get some of that information from the inherent structure of the language, from the metaphor that the client brings. As we interrogate that process, the client does not want to go down there. He may only want to go around it or across it. This is the way that the client knows how to heal himself most naturally within a metaphor. We may need to use that information in deciding to build a bridge or in getting around an abyss.

Guilt. Guilt may resolve itself if we heal the memory about guilt. Guilt is usually about some action, thought or deed which was done or not done. The client can go back in time and work inside the matrix, resolving his sins of omission and commission.

A son disobeys his father. When he comes home, his father is dead. It was the first time the client had angered his father. He carries that guilt for a long time. We create an environment around that guilt so that it can alter. As the client goes through the memories, the memories of the father's love, we may find occasions when the client really knew that his father loved him. We get the symbol of that time when, "Father made this toy boat for me." We have the client take the memory of disobeying his father, and the father's anger, and introduce that toy boat into the memory. This may transform the situation and make a paradoxical change in the memory. Rationally the toy boat has nothing to do with guilt. Yet by causing that juxtaposition, we may obtain that kind of conversion experience, that change that just happens, that paradoxical change. Guilt can sometimes be resolved this way.

Sometimes guilt can be healed in spiritual ways. If the client has Christian faith, then the Cross or Christ coming in, or introducing Him into the memory, can sometimes heal it. If the client is of another faith, the words to comfort or heal that guilt could come from the Koran or the Torah.

There can be various causes of guilt, and as we find them the client defines the physiology of the feeling. Guilt may also be present in the form of a metaphor. A religious client may say that he has done bad, and in doing bad he has committed sins that are unpardonable. We may have to translate the concept into a metaphor and then elicit an image that that sin can be pardoned or that guilt can be washed away.

Anger. A way of dealing with unwanted anger is to transform it internally by working directly with the thoughts, physiology, feelings, symbols, and metaphors that the client uses to evoke his anger.

A thirty year old woman has been in therapy because of the abuse that she has had from her mother. What she wants to do is to confront her mother and act out her anger. She wants to blame her mother for the damage that has been caused in her life by the physical abuse her mother gave her. So she presents with this anger and she already has a plan of what she wants to do, predicated upon previous therapy.

Asked what she wants, she replies she wants to get angry at her mother, but that she cannot do that now. We take her back to the times when her mother abused her, and to what was the worst time. We regress her into that memory. We let that memory develop and then put her as a grown woman, as she is now, back into *there then* in that memory. Now for the first time she, as a thirty year old woman, is in that memory, looking at herself as a six year old girl being beaten by her mother. As she watches her mother beating her, she chooses to take a side-on view. Originally her memory was of this big woman overpowering and beating her. Now she is watching her mother beat her and she can see her brother Billy in the background stealing cookies out of the jar while her mother is distracted. She can see all the messy pots and pans in the kitchen. She can see the worn vinyl on the floor.

She sees how dishevelled her mother looks, she sees the unkempt hair and the absence of make-up. She sees the holes in her mother's slippers. As she looks at her mamma, she realizes for the first time that her mother is simply not equipped to have kids. Indeed, it is a wonder her mother survived. Even as she sees her mother beat her, she realizes at this epiphanic moment, this moment when she is in the memory, that she now no longer wants to get angry at her mother. Her purpose of going into the memory was to see if she really wanted to tell her mother off. As she tried to do that, she found she no longer wanted to. At that moment her anger with her mother over the abuse has dissipated and she orients back to the present. She has a whole new perspective about her mother and the abuse. Consequently she was able to have a different relationship with her mother.

There is the client that says he never feels anger. He cannot feel anger, or when he feels anger he cannot express it or use it in any kind of healthy, practical, acceptable, normal way. We believe him absolutely. We ask: 'When you cannot feel it, what is that like?' Naming can be important. Here we may want to call it something other than anger. We may not want to apply the usual names to experiences and force clients to use our labels. Some therapists might say: 'If you have this feeling, that is anger. Look, anyone in their normal, right mind would be angry if this was done to them. What you have got is anger.' Working in the spirit of clean language, we think that the client has what he has: 'When that happens to you, what is that like?' We would rather work with watermelon in the stomach than deal with the word 'anger', so: 'You have watermelon when you see her, and is that the feeling you do not like?'

We map out the experience in the physiology of feeling. When the client says he does not have anger, we believe him: 'What do you have when you don't have anger?' "Well, I have, I have, I don't know. I just get a funny feeling when I am around her, but it is not anger." 'Okay, what is that funny feeling like? Can you put it into a form?' Now we find out what the client wants to do: 'Do you like to have that watermelon in your stomach? Or is there something that you would like to do with that?' "What I want to do is when people push me around, I want to speak up." 'What stops you from speaking up?' "I do not know." 'So does watermelon stop you from speaking up, or is it something else?' "Watermelon is part of it." 'Okay, what is the other part?' "I just never have." 'So you have never spoken up at any time in your life?' "I just never have." 'So you have never spoken up at any time in your life?' "Not really against grown-ups." 'Okay, but you have spoken up against other than grown-ups?' "Yeah." 'Okay, and when you spoke up then, did you have watermelon then?'

Some clients report that they have no inner sensations in anger-producing situations. Others experience a sensation and do not realize that this sensation is anger. Others still are aware of an internal experience that they sometimes label anger. They then do not know what they can do with it, unaware that it may be useful, constructive, appropriate, or just might feel good to them.

The client reports no inner reaction in 'anger' situations. He does not say: "I do not have anger." We find that he has an external metaphor: "When somebody takes it away from me, to me it is the life forces, it is fate, and fate, when she smiles on me, smiles, and when she rains, she rains. I accept fate in whatever she hands me." It is about the metaphor of fate.

Another client has an 'awareness', an inner reaction. However, he does not realize that this is anger. He does not express his anger or show it. When the client is in that situation, he "...just gets confused" and "...his mind starts spinning." What he has is confusion and the mind spinning like a carousel. The client cannot stop it and it takes a long time for the carousel to slow down. Here we do not deal with 'anger', we deal with a 'carousel' that spins. This is the internal physiological feeling reaction. It does not have to be labeled anger.

When he is angry, the third client does not know what to do: "I do not know, it is all bottled up inside of me. And I really stew and I am miserable for days and I tear myself apart and make myself sick, miserable." 'And what is inside the bottle and how is it bottled up? Is it a green bottle or a black bottle? Is there a cork in the bottle? And does something need to happen to the things inside the bottle? Does it need to stay in the bottle or does it need to come out? Has anything ever happened to the bottle? What happens when you get this experience of being bottled up? And does bottle move?'

We first establish the metaphor. We might say: 'What would have to happen in the real world for that to be unbottled, or for you not to get bottled up?' We relate it to events in the real world and other things the client might say: "I do not want to have that feeling. I get bottled up every time I see her." How can we depotentiate that bottled feeling? We work to alter it: 'Then what has to happen, given you see her again, so you will not get bottled up?'

Migraine. For headaches we have the client map out a physiology of the feeling of pain. That puts the pain into a form: "My head is like a golf ball, and when that golf ball is cut in half above my eye, that is when I know I have pain." When we get the pain in that form, we take the sensations and have the client give names to them and we perform symbolic interventions.

The basic principles are to put the pain in a form, find out where it is located and identify all the modalities while working to reduce them. Some migraine can be dependent on chemicals in wine, nougat, chocolate, etc. Some clients get migraine in certain pressure situations. In a well-formed intervention we make sure that in the presence of these stimuli the client still has permission to have his migraine. We are searching for ways of helping the client to control his pain. One of the tactics in the treatment of migraine and headaches is to shorten their duration. Instead of having migraine all day, we want to speed up the process. It may be that the headache first starts as a pea, increasing to the size of a golf ball, then to that of a grapefruit, and, finally it gradually shrinks away. This process generally takes a day to complete. We try to help the client to make it happen in an hour. If he can do this, he can then make it happen in ten minutes, and then reduce this to possibly just two minutes. Can the onset of migraine make all the symptoms occur very quickly? Our object is to teach the client, in the language of his own pain, to ameliorate the symptoms naturally, using the resources that he has.

Slippery mind. The slippery mind has to do with particular phenomena that make our therapy ineffective. Agoraphobics are particularly prone to this condition. It might also manifest itself in clients with characterlogical defects, and in cases of pervasive pathology. With these clients a symbol or a metaphor, when it is obtained, does not seem to stand for very much. It keeps changing into something else. It can start out with a feeling that is like butterflies and then the butterflies, as we try get a description, go to: "Perhaps they are like leaves. Yes, they are more like leaves on a tree." When the leaves float down, the client gets an uncomfortable feeling: a tree transforms into a river, and we end up with a river when we started out with butterflies. This transformation goes on and on. To a certain degree, this process occurs in other clients. Nonetheless, in those instances we usually reach an end point and then the infrastructure remains fixed.

The problem with these slippery clients is that once we get a symbol or an image, it is not a strong representation of the pathology. The altering of the representation does not have the experiential and physiological impact that we would normally find. The images, symbols, and metaphors will alter. When they alter, there is very little in the way of an experiential change. This phenomenon is also found with clients on tranquilizers or antidepressants. We find that slippery clients can shape the images into some sort of form, but we observe that there is very little affective quality to it. When we bring the symbols together to integrate and restructure the memory, the images combine for a time but then spring back to their original form. If that happens there has been no lasting integration, no transformation. If the client can make an image go from one form to another and then *reverse* it, little is accomplished. The purpose of this therapy is to make an alteration within the infrastructure of the client's experience. We want that change to be manifested physiologically. Most commonly, we want to induce an alteration in the way the client evokes his autonomic nervous responses.

If a client is heavily medicated, the drug is already occupying the receptors that we want to influence by our intervention. As the drug got there first, it is likely to interfere with the impact of our words on the client's reality. Effective change can be particularly difficult when it requires a physiological change and a tranquilizer is blocking the manifestation of feelings. In this case, when the images come together, or alter, only the images change and the client does not manifest the experiential shift.

Sexual dysfunction. First we establish the feeling physiology; establish if it is performance anxiety: 'What happens? What does it feel like?' "It feels like concrete in my stomach, or I have this buzzing sensation that goes on in my head." It may not be located in a genital area. There can be some feeling physiology that is a precursor to sexual stimulation. We simply go through memories: 'When did that first happen?' We get a list of the memories of when it happened, put the client into old memories and restructure each memory so that he can complete the activity successfully, or in some altered way. Then we establish the physiology of satisfaction and build up symbols— para-sympathetic symbols— that will alter the concrete or the buzzing. We can test the intervention, project that into the future and see if the client can do it successfully *in matrix*. We then have him do that behavior *in vivo*.

First we intervene internally and do what we can with the client's internal structures. Only then do we determine what behavior is necessary. The main operation is to desensitize the negative physiology by using the para-sympathetic symbols.

Rather than desensitizing in a behavioral or a cognitive way, we perform the desensitization experientially, internally, with the use of para-sympathetic symbols. Although this is desensitization, it is internal desensitization that does not necessarily use imagery *per se*, but any obtainable para-sympathetic symbols. In our experience, the attachment of the physiology is more important than the imagery.

Generic language. The client has a rock in the stomach and may not know how, or in which direction, to evolve it. We have enquired and the client does not quite know what to do. He knows the rock is there and it seems to him that it would be helpful to make it disappear. We want to help the client evolve the rock. We start by speaking about rocks; we employ a generic pattern about rocks.

'And as you think about that rock and about all the possibilities of *rock*, it is interesting to just wonder about that rock there and about qualities that rocks have. Rocks can be hard and some rocks can have air inside, or are hollow and have some precious mineral or gem inside. And that there is a surface of a rock which may not look very pretty, but it is what could be inside that rock. Is that rock different inside from outside? About how smooth and how rough is that rock? What sort of little hollows could there be? And what things could there be on that rock? And things that could be inside? And what is rock material, and what is other than rock material? And about those things in there, about how it is possible for that to be surrounded by that rock, and to wonder does that rock protect what is in there? Or does that rock hide what is in there, so that what is in there could allow its beauty to be discovered? It is interesting to think about rocks and their size. And there are big rocks, rocks that are the foundation of buildings. And there are small rocks that can be single, and many rocks together. And are there other rocks around those rocks? Or is it just one rock? And all these properties of rock are sometimes quite interesting, so take some time to consider about that rock and what that rock knows. And so you can take some time to discover those things that you could know about rock.'

This generic language is not making any presupposition that there is anything inside *that* rock. We are just talking about generic rocks. We are not addressing that rock directly and if we make one particular point, we may also make the opposite: 'It is interesting to think about what could be inside a rock, something precious, or that it might be just plain rock, perhaps.' We talk generically about properties of rock. We talk about the surface of rocks, about rocks being in position with other rocks, and sizes of rocks.

These statements have the special quality in the tautological sense of being very hard to oppose. There is not much to argue about in the generic properties of rock. We want to find out what the client discovered once he comes out of matrix, and this will give us some direction, some new information with which to formulate the intervention. With this generic approach, we remain clean. We make no presuppositions that rocks should be smashed, or whatever. We initially value the rock. There is a rock there and the client is going to learn to think of many things about that particular rock.

We then use external factors to make an impact on that rock. This could be in terms of cognitions. We describe certain matters directly to the client, or we discuss what *rock* is doing inside him. It may be behavioral. We get the client to perform a task, some work with the family, and see if that will make some changes in *rock*. We may simply give some straight factual information about the external things which pertain to the rock. That is introducing elements into the inner experience in the expectation that they will have an impact on rock. Here we use direct language and the qualities of cleanliness that we had before are now no longer necessary. We can use elements from either inside or outside the matrix. We could take the client back in history and memories, or he could go to a spiritual experience, or some expectation in the future and bring these resources to bear upon rock.

We do not necessarily require information from the client because our questions are primarily directed at sculpting an experience inside him. We are not asking questions to inform the therapist. Our questions are informative for the client and this orientation is important. The questions direct the client to search his experience and put the experience into a form. A "Yes" or a "No" is a very appropriate response to these complex questions. The questions are so shaped that a simple response is required: 'Now can you see if you can make that ball just a little more oval?' That requires a response of "Yes" or "No"— not some long explanation. 'Or is there any other shape that you could make it?' Alternatively we give direct suggestions. We often suggest three possibilities and allow the client to come up with a fourth. This way we narrow the field for the client to search for a direct solution. We give the client alternatives. These can be quite ridiculous, as long as we include the fourth possibility: that perhaps the client can come up with a better one.

These questions, particularly in gathering the information, have the quality of encouraging the world to stop. We want to shorten time. We do not want the client to go into a whole narrative about his experience. We want to freeze that moment in time and extend the significance down into the matrix. The questions are oriented towards two types of information. We want similarities and differences between two particular states, and also between relationships. What sort of relationships exist between this, there, and that? In what sequences are the data stored? This is different from getting information about the item *per se*. We are searching for some meta-information: similarities and differences, and the relationships between items.

Clean language allows the client to do some evolving. We use generic language and generic metaphors to accomplish this. This client has an oval jelly in his stomach when he does not understand something: 'Now go back in the past and think of times when you had that jelly, when you did not understand something.' "No, I did not have any times like that, because this jelly is related to the anticipation that I might misunderstand something. That has not really happened to me, so I have not had that feeling when that has actually happened in the past."

We rephrase it: 'So go back in the past when you had that jelly feeling, when you thought you might not understand something in the future.' We go back into the past, to when he had a future anxiety in the past.

Client's tense. The clean questions need to be formulated in the right tense. When we move resources over time, or take the client back in memories, we must do it in the right tense.

Client:"I feel surrounded by a black cloud." 'When you felt surrounded by a black cloud,' puts the client in the past: he felt surrounded. As we ask that question, we regress him: 'Where was the cloud?' "The cloud was around my head." 'How far around your head did it go? And was it above your head as well as all the way around?' "It was above the head to the tips of my ears." 'Okay, so from above the head to the tips of your ears, and did it come in front of your eyes?' "Above the eyebrows." 'And what shape did it seem to have?' "It was doughnut shaped." 'In the middle of the doughnut shape, was there anything there?' "A black hole." 'And what color was that doughnut shape with the black hole?' "The doughnut shape was dark gray." 'Dark gray and a black hole?' "Pitch-black." 'And were there any other features to that?' "It was cold and fuzzy." 'Was the black hole cold and fuzzy, or was that different?' "The black hole was cold and smooth." 'Any other qualities?'

Dissociation. Dissociation can be achieved in a number of different ways and modalities. When associated, the client has a memory, which is seen through his own eyes. When he is dissociated, he can see himself in the memory. A good many traumatic memories are associated. Dissociating the client will be of benefit in presenting the information from a different perspective. In presenting traumatic memories, the client is often dissociated and this is a state where he has little affect as he recalls the event. Although the client is traumatized, he is dissociated up on the roof, looking down at what is happening to him. It is like an out-of-body experience. In this case we may want to move the dissociation to another point of view, to another perspective in the room. The client can still be out of his body. We want him to view the scene from a different angle. In this visual form of dissociation the important thing is to let the client find a new place from which he can view the scene: 'And as you look at that there, then just see if you could find another point of view, another perspective; a different angle that you could look at that from. You might like to go up or down or around so that you can find just the right place that would seem to be different, and as you do that you can notice how different it is, and notice some new things you did not notice before.'

With this pattern we give the client permission to go a number of different ways. We also deliver the presupposition that when the client looks at something from a different angle, a different point of view, there will be new items that were not available before. One of the purposes in using dissociation is to put the client at some distance from the feelings, so that he does not feel the incident in the same way. With non-visual clients we have to deliver sufficient permission in our injunctions so that the client can dissociate physiologically: 'So that as you *know* about what happened *there then* and about what that was like, you can *know* about how that felt.' The words we use give the client the opportunity to leave those feelings back in time, or back in a particular place.

The injunction is delivered by talking to the eye and ear. When we change the qualities of voice, by lowering it and resonating it, this adds the non-verbal qualities that can help modulate the client's experience. The acoustic qualities also help to obtain analgesia: softer, lower, slower, and so on.

The words we use are words that can also carry an implicit sense, as in using conjunctions: 'And as you begin to think.' Here we are gently joining the client's reality rather than saying: 'Now I want you to.' As we join his reality, we can gently curl the client into a different perspective: 'And as you begin to think about so many ways that those circumstances might have been different, that scene might have been different, that that experience could possibly have been different for you.' The words *think* and *know* are useful because they help to verbally dissociate the client from the feeling: 'As you *know* about what you felt, *there then.*'

We use orientation in time: 'So as you know about what you felt then,' will put the client back in time and keep him oriented in time. When we add the word *there*, not only do we put him back in time but also into place: 'As you know about how you felt *there then.*' We can dissociate between the office and the place where the trauma happened. For a traumatic memory we may want to direct a client to just before the incident, or just after, when he reaches a position of safety. We direct him either side of the trauma and gather the resources we find there without dropping the client into the memory.

A further element of dissociation is that our statements have no reference to external reality. We do not use 'I', or 'I want you to'. We do not draw attention to the environment, nor do we evoke the non-verbal cues in such a way as would bring that to the client's mind. What he is doing out here physically is not what he is doing inside. Referring to the outside reality can distract the client into the present and outside the matrix.

The elements of dissociation serve to keep the client internal, inside his head. We diminish the external reality so that our voice, and only our voice, is reverberating inside his head. It is as if our voice was with him inside, back there in time, at that place. We are paralleling the client's experience and watching it with him, as opposed to his coming out and describing his experience to us in the here and now. We establish the reality that is in there and the non-reality that is out here: 'And as you know about that, *there then*, and begin to think of all those things that happened and how they impacted on your life,' keeps the client inside his head and oriented in there. That is quite different from saying: 'I want you to go into your memory and find out about all those things.'

A further tactic of dissociation is that we do not refer to the present. When the client has finished, we bring him back. We do not seek to bring information from the past into the present to gain insight, or for any other reason. We seek to make the present here and now, not be. We regress the client into the past, leave him in the past and perform the intervention only in the past. If we need things from the present, we leave the client in the past and allow him to briefly come to the present to fetch those resources and take them back to his past: 'And as you know about what happened then, you can think about the people that you know now, and how the people that you know now could go back to then and change then in some way. And the knowledge that you knew then, how different that is from the knowledge that you know now, and how the knowledge that you know now can go back to then and change then.' That phrasing is bringing people and knowledge back from the present into the past. We are linking people and knowledge together and facilitating the client's access to his knowledge. The word knowledge has to be delivered very slowly so that the client will search for a specific item or a person or resource.

We are shaping an environment that allows the client to go safely, without trauma, back into the past. We are giving the client some skills to do that. His only connection with the present is our voice. Our voice accompanies the client and delivers information that he can take into that experience in the past. It is a split reality. We act as if the past is the only thing that exists. When the client returns from there it will take some time for him to reorient to the present.

When we have completed an intervention with dissociation, we want the client to come back. When the client has finished his work he will come out when he is ready. We give the client enough neuro-physiological time to change, alter, and process the information secured. All this is facilitated by allowing him to stay inside. We do not bring the client out when it suits us. Nor do we count him up and out: that is artificial and imposing. We leave him to have control of his experience; all we do is shape it.

Mermaid. A male colleague, aged forty two, married, father of two school-aged children, presents for therapy. Seven weeks ago he remade the acquaintance of a young woman. There has been no intimacy between them and only a few meetings, but her effect has been great: "This young woman is constantly on my mind. It interferes with my work, marriage, and home life."

During a psychotherapy workshop a participant is presenting a case. He becomes very open in the hypnotic environment and learning situation. His defences gently diminish. This psychologist, happily married and successful in his field, has not succumbed to the charms of clients who are attracted to him and who want to become more intimately involved. He has integrity and is well defended against these clients. In this training program, and in the ethereal atmosphere of this afternoon, he notices an acquaintance. Suddenly, something happens in his chest and heart. He is affected and there is a thud. It is as if something has come from this acquaintance and caught him like a lance or a spear in the heart. There is an immediate sensation of fear and wounding. And as he knows about that, he begins to daydream about this woman.

She has blond hair and a self-absorbed, rather vacant expression on her face. He later invites her out for dinner. Much to his surprise, she accepts. At that stage his heart is beating furiously, his mouth is dry and he becomes quite speechless. He can think of nothing except that he has asked this woman out. During dinner he remains quiet. It is a very awkward evening. She is oblivious, unaware of anything that is going on inside him. To Julian that is part of the fascination. His immediate attraction to her is unrequited: she is just there. He takes Kari Ann to the railway station to see her off. Kari Ann hugs him good-bye and, at that moment, she stands on tiptoe against him. He feels her warm softness, her hair brushing against his face. He feels that hug and is profoundly affected again. He turns and walks away wondering what has struck him. It is a searing, painful experience. It is bittersweet, tinged with a pain. That evening Julian is unable to sleep and obsessive thoughts begin to gather. Julian's night is filled with those last few hours with her.

Julian has crying spells; it is as though he is drowning. He feels as if he has been flooded: "It's overwhelming. My wife and children seem to drag me down, drown me, and I want to go walk about. I want to swim, but I don't know how to swim. My work suffers as I cannot concentrate. And there are times when I go home, or on the way home, I just cry. I sit in my car and cry, and that seems to add even more to this lake. It is so heavy. I just don't know what to do about it."

Julian's thoughts go into the future, about seeing her again. He has this intense feeling of pain in his heart and down his left side. He envisions the future: what would it be like to see her again? What was in that warm hug? Was there more to it, or is it just his imagination? His mind continues into future thoughts about what it would be like to be with her. For two or three days he fights the urge. He has his own life, yet the feeling is intense. The pain that he wants relief from is like being poisoned, and yet he wants that poison again. The only way to get that poison is to see her again. The ambivalence of should he or shouldn't he haunts him. Haunted by that experience, he succumbs and calls Kari Ann— much to her surprise— and they arrange to meet again.

He meets Kari Ann and spends time with her. Her impression of it is that it is as if he is not really interested in her. The sweetness of that experience means much more to him than to her. He is bound up in the experience of being near her. In those moments in her environment, the smell of her perfume, the proximity of her femininity, he finds complete and utter relief. It is a heady experience. They read poetry together. They share Keats.

Julian has again been profoundly affected. He sought some relief in that experience so that he could get over it. That was his purpose. He thought he would get relief from the pain by seeing her again and so he did. Then he left to go back home to his family and hoped that he would get over it. After two weeks, the experience comes back even stronger and haunts him. He loses all interest in his family and in his work and friends: it is like a roaring in his ears; a sound he cannot deaden or turn off. He has an ache that throbs on and on, that will not leave him alone. He throws himself into long hours of work to try to get over it. After four weeks it still will not let him go. He is caught in this experience. He thought that he had dealt with it, having faced the pain of his experience and wrestled with it. Yet it still hangs on. He thinks only of her. The pain in his chest intensifies and his thoughts become even more preoccupied with this unattainable woman. It is a paradox: here is a woman who has no interest in him, who never makes a move, who gives no sign at all of being interested, and yet he is totally caught up. How is she different from all the other women who had used their charms to influence him or attract him?

It is in this state that he comes to the therapy. Kari Ann is petite, almost anorexic: she has slim limbs and melts into the background. She is quite still. Her long hair falls about her face, almost hiding it. She is twenty eight, a psychologist working in an institutional setting and devoted to her work. She has many friends and is not seriously interested in any particular man. She has an elegant way of moving: graceful, very fluid. She is smooth and measured, has a quiet confidence about her, and speaks with a lilting voice. She is asexual, dressing in garments which do not reveal her figure. Her flowing dresses extend down past the knees. There is no overt sexuality about her. Kari Ann is almost a little girl by nature, just a quiet presence. She does not attract through vivacity, yet Julian feels even more drawn towards her. She feels easiest in the company of women and is given to thought, having an interest in art and artists, and intellectual pursuits. She is not a homemaker or a mothering woman.

'And is there something you would like?' "What I want is, I'm not sure. I want to get rid of these feelings I have inside me for her because they are destructive to my work. I see her in everything I do. I hear her voice, but I have my own life and family. What I want is to get her out of my experience, I want her out of my thoughts and I want this pain of her in my heart to leave." 'And when you have pain in your heart that you want to leave you, where in your heart is that pain?' "Before I answer that question, I want to say that although that's what I want, I'm not sure, and although I want all that to go, and would like to forget about it, there is also a part of me that wants to keep her, and wants to get to know her, and desires her. I have an ambivalence about it and I'm not sure. All I know is what's good for me. If I could just get rid of this feeling in my heart and thoughts, then I think that would be the best thing."

'So when this pain is in your heart, is it the outside of your heart or the inside of your heart?' "It's a bit of both." 'So, what's that bit of both like?' "It's like a cut." 'And what kind of cut?' "It's like a gash." 'And what kind of gash could that gash be?' "It's sort of big in the middle and it goes off to the sides, almost like an oval." 'And when it's almost like an oval, are there any other qualities to that oval?' "It's oval and it's like there's something in there." 'And what could that something be that is in there?' "I think it's round." 'And round like what?' "It's round like a stick." 'And what kind of stick could that be?' "Well, it seems like it's made of vine." 'And what kind of vine?' "Like a shiny vine." 'And how long could that shiny vine be?' "It's long like a spear." 'And so it's long like a spear, and is that spear there now?' "No, it's like a hole that has been made by a spear, and I still have the wound left by its shape in my heart." 'And so it's like a wound being made by a spear, and that hole is in your heart. What else is there about that hole?' "Well, it seems to bleed on the outside and it's like blood that has dried." 'And about the inside?' "And the inside is different, the inside is not blood. It's like fluid." 'And what kind of fluid?' "It's like water, but it's not quite like water." 'And that's on the inside?' "Yes." 'And when that is on the inside, then what's that like?' "The fluid is inside the heart, and the fluid seems to be disturbed, and it is shaking about, and the shaking and the slopping of the fluid is very painful." 'And what is that slopping fluid like?' "It's like somebody stirring it all up." 'And who could that somebody be?' "It's Kari Ann." 'And how is Kari Ann stirring all that up?' "It's like she is swimming in there." 'And what is she swimming in there like?' "It's like she is disturbing the water when she is in there and it laps up on my heart and is very painful." 'When she is disturbing the water like that, how is she disturbing the water?' "She is swimming like a mermaid." 'And when you have *mermaid* what happens?' "It's very painful because her swimming disturbs the lake and in disturbing the lake it hurts. And I can't get her out because I like her being in there, and it hurts at the same time." 'And so what could happen next?'

The therapist works with the mermaid in Julian's lake and examines the ways in which any ambivalence associated with him wanting her in there, and yet wanting her out, can manifest itself: "Well, it's like an inlet, like a lake. More like an inlet where it's very peaceful and beautiful and this water laps up on a beach." 'And what else is there about that?' "Well, it feels very nice and I want to be there on that beach, but although it's nice on the inside, I can also feel the pain of the wind in the heart and the blood on the outside." 'And what else is there about the inside?' "It's all lovely and ethereal. It's like there's this beautiful garden away from this beach and there are mountains and palm trees. There's a lot of promise and hope; it's an idyllic scene. Around the corner there's Kari Ann and I can see her sitting there, and there's something strange about that. She looks just like mermaid." 'And what else happens?' "I'm not sure because as soon as I try and get close to her, she dives into the water and escapes." 'And so spend some time finding out what you would want to have happen there.' "What I want is to be there with her. I want to be there. But the pain of being there at all: because on the other side of the beach where mermaid is… is the hole in my heart. The blood is dripping down into the water and its spoiling it, and I can hear the sounds of my wife and children."

"I can see them on the other side of the beach and the water there is red. And I can see them all, and there are these long threads which are attached to me. Even though I can see them, I can't hear them any more; I just want to break away." 'And go to the mermaid?' "But I can't do that because these threads hold me back. And my wife, she has the biggest thread. And so I am caught between my desire to go across to the other side to mermaid, or to Kari Ann and the ties that bind me. The more that I keep looking towards Kari Ann, and to the beautiful scenery on the other side, and I see the barren wall where my family is, as I keep looking, the more blood drips into the water. I just don't know what to do." 'And so take some time to discover about what would have to happen so that you could know about something different. And what could be different about Kari Ann on one side and a wife and family on the other? And so just take some time to discover what could happen next.' "The conundrum of what to do. Mermaid begins to move. And as she swims across to the other side, her hair becomes entangled with the blood from my heart and from my family. Her golden hair becomes matted with the bleeding of my heart. And as it becomes matted, the blood from that side collects in her hair and the water becomes clear. As the water becomes clear, the strands that connect me to my family begin to shrink and start drawing me to the other shore. Kari Ann travels back to the other side. Now her appearance has changed and her hair is red and matted, and she looks old and wizened and I become drawn towards my family."

'And then what would need to happen next?' "Well, I have the hole in my heart. Something needs doing to it." 'And mermaid: could she go to the hole in your heart, and what could she do to a hole in the heart like that?' "Mermaid goes across to that side and she takes her matted hair and she shaves her head, and applies a twisted end, her matted hair, with the blood to bind the side together. When she does that she now comes back to the middle of the beach, and she begins to transform. As she begins to transform her hair, and the hole in the heart, she gets it to contract and the wound begins to heal. And mermaid begins to transform into the sand. And there appears a rock. On that rock in the middle of this sea, mermaid turns inanimate. And the wound begins to heal. Now I can begin to hear the calls of my wife and my family."

And as Julian stares at the sea, the beach gradually changes. The trees change and become the yard of Julian's house. His wife and family begin to move down and start occupying the middle ground. As soon as they walk along the beach they find this rock and they become fascinated with it. Julian walks over and sits on the rock and begins to play with his children. His wife comes over and joins him.

The lake begins to get shallower and mermaid no longer enjoys being there. Julian's family begin to empty out the lake. The mermaid becomes more and more unhappy and begins to fade away because the water in which she was able to play no longer has the depth she needs. The water begins to drain away and we strive to further reduce its level: "I want to have her swimming there and I also want my family, and I can't give her up." 'And so you want both of those, and so take some time to know about both and see what happens.'

As Julian takes that time, the water continues to ebb. His family, his wife and children, on the other side start drawing off the water, and as they do so they take away the water that mermaid plays in. The needs of his family regain his attention. As the water drains off, mermaid loses interest, and she turns to rock.

As we establish a relation between the water draining out and mermaid losing interest and growing old, and Julian's ability to concentrate, the wounded heart starts to heal. As the water starts to disappear, Julian's thoughts become less preoccupied, because the lake becomes an arid environment. As the waters recede, Julian wants mermaid and wants his family. The resolution comes through the third alternative, which is giving up neither the family nor mermaid. The family causes an arid environment in which mermaid can no longer live. The desire for mermaid begins to fade as the emotions of the water flow towards the family. Julian turns his attention to giving the water to his family, creating a new, nurturing environment for the family, but without forgetting the experience of mermaid. Draining away the water constitutes a distraction a third dimension.

Julian talks about the changes that have occurred with the water in his heart: "I can't believe what has happened. But very, very strange: it's almost like a dream. Each day the water level is just a little less, and sometimes it would get more and eventually Kari Ann would come back and haunt me. But, mostly I could get the water level down. I can do that by taking my kids out to a ball game, or I could do that by taking my wife to a restaurant. Each time I did things with my family, the less water there was in that lake and the less time I devoted to it. What was useful for me was that I did not have to give up mermaid, she was still part of my experience, and now it's like she has just transformed into this beautiful beach, and now she is a rock and I don't have to forget about the experience I had with her. As long as there's no water in the lake, she can't play. I have found that now there is a fertile valley where the lake used to be, and my family are living there. They are just beginning to find new blades of grass. Now my family have joined me and they are where that water used to be, where Kari Ann used to frolic. I am not sure, but sometimes I think it's going to flood in again, but when it does I know what to do. I really keep concentrating on doing things with my family, and with my boy. Then I can keep the water out."

'So when you do things with your family the water level goes down?' "What I have found is that I've been too involved in my work recently and so it left that hollow, and it was that hollow that Kari Ann could occupy. The more I can put my family in it, that is going to create a nice new field for the flowers and trees. Kari Ann will still be there because that's part of the rock, that is a very central part; but at least it's not hurting me any longer. I don't feel that pain any longer. Some of the thoughts come back, but they don't last very long and I can just put them onto that rock. When the water starts coming in, I now know how to drain the water out."

'You now have a way of dealing with the unwanted feelings, and you find that you are spending more time, and doing more things, with your family. And what is different about your work?'

"What is different is that most of the time I don't have the obsessive thoughts, and as soon as I do get them, I put them down onto that rock. And when they go into that rock, they just stay there so I can concentrate on my work. My mind is not preoccupied with Kari Ann, and the pain in my side seems to be replaced. Where it was like a spear had gone through me, it's still a little painful there. I can still feel the touch of my family and wife, it just seems to be gradually healing, it's about half healed at this stage. It is now a river flowing through there, not a lake, so there's less water and it's more manageable for me."

'So it's about half healed, and is there anything else that you would like in relation to your family?'

"As long as I can keep spending time with them, and don't get too carried away with workshops and work, then I think that is how the rest of it is going to be dealt with. Sometimes I am scared it is all going to come flooding back and flood over and drown everything, so I am scared to even think about it. But I am going to test it out and I am going to call Kari Ann when I feel strong enough. I think this is going to be important to me, that I know that I can still talk to her, yet it won't just come up and flood everything else in my life like it did before."

'So you have now told us how your thoughts are and how your actions are in relation to your family. Then how are these things in relation to your work?'

"I think the difference in my work is that I now understand some ways of helping people who get caught in the same kind of double bind, in that they want something, they want both things, but these are mutually exclusive. By concentrating on how much water is needed to reduce the lake to a river, then to a stream, it becomes a lot more manageable. I will also know that I have a way of telling whether I am going to get affected by anyone in the future, and it will no longer be an out of control experience. I am not going to be afraid any longer, that I might fall, or be affected by, say, a Kari Ann. I can tell whether my lake is going to reach a flood stage or not. Now that I know how, I'll continue to be very, very careful."

Clinical Notes

Agoraphobia. This condition requires a family, behavioral, and intrapsychic approach. The client catastrophizes in the future. We act to impact on prodromal metaphors. These are the metaphors that occur before the strongest component of the panic sets in. These components can be a sinking feeling like: "Going down a well in the stomach." This intervention is of help to the client in gaining control of the physiological components of the panic.

Dissociative disorders. Formatting the external metaphors will define the structure and mechanism of the dissociative phenomenon. There can be metaphors layered upon metaphors in complex structures. These metaphors can constellate separate contexts of different ages or different personalities. We would strive to depotentiate the traumatic events, and to give clients control over their dissociations. Metaphors and symbols provide a language for interacting with various functions and personalities. Abreactions are contained.

Grief and loss reaction. The client often keeps the departed (person, memory, place, illusion or circumstance), as though still alive, within the inner world. The intervention consists of dissociating the good, loving, positive feelings from the memory and making those positive feelings available to the client in internal physiological symbols. This can be a satisfactory way of resolving grief and loss.

Incest. Because childhood memories of incest are often vague, it is quite usual that incest traces will be stored in internal physiological symbols: "I have this empty, hollow feeling inside of me." Formatting the symbol will often gradually unfold elements of the experience. Most commonly a frightened 'little girl' is hidden in the inner world. Sometimes she is 'frozen' in a specific memory. The wounded child is also found behind a physiological symbol such as a rock on the heart or a lump on the throat. Often the intervention entails allowing this child to feel real and valued. This can be accomplished by giving the child the opportunity to alter the circumstances *there then*. The child can then guide the therapy, which may act on memories, metaphors or symbols.

Obsessive compulsive disorders. The approach consists of formatting auditory, visual, and tactile perceptions from memories relating to the first occurrence of obsessional thoughts, and from prodromal sensitizing memories. The method can be used to extinguish unwanted sensations and perceptions. The content of voices and images is often best avoided and the therapist confines himself to formatting those manifestations. The successful treatment of compulsive behavior usually requires that these internal strategies of evolving metaphors and symbols be continued with paradoxical, behavioral, and pattern interventions.

Phobia. The memory of the last phobic response is used to establish a sequence including the specific physiological symptoms. These symptoms can be represented by physiological forms: rocks, fists, butterflies. Simple phobias respond well to this approach. The symbols are used to evoke memories of past panics. Restructuring the memories can result in changing the physiology of the panic.

Post-traumatic stress disorder. Although specific memories are easily identified, they are extremely resistant to direct clinical intervention. The epistemological metaphor will often be an external construct associated with an internal physiological symbol. Both metaphors and symbols can be used to recover pre-trauma sensitizing events. When working with PTSD, intervening on memories is generally useful only for loosening the fixed patterns of the unwanted behavior, thoughts, and feelings. The resolution of this pathology most often results from evolving the internal physiological symbols.

Rape. The psychological consequences can often be treated successfully by restructuring the appropriate memory of the moment of maximum emotion. There are often various persistent unwanted emotional sequelae such as anger, fear, guilt or shame, which will be associated with distinct and separate metaphors. Each of these independent metaphors has its own origins in times and sensitizing circumstances unrelated to the rape. Formatting these metaphors can serve to recover the relevant emotional incidents from the client's pre-rape history. These incidents can be used to work with the unwanted feelings. This can be much easier for the client than dealing with the fresh anger from the rape.

Depression. The metaphors typical of depression are not readily evolved. When such a metaphor is successfully impacted it is important that a new and more positive structure is evolved and left in place. In our experience, these evolving interventions may have to be repeated a number of times so that enduring behavioral improvements are obtained.

Contra Indications

Psychotic and borderline disorders. We are unambivalent in advising clinicians against the use of these methods. Metaphors and symbols easily lead the client and therapist into a different and dangerous order of reality. It becomes very difficult to control these patterns as clients move rapidly between logical levels and adjacent symbols and metaphors. Clients and clinicians are in danger of being overwhelmed.

Medication. Clients may exhibit interesting imagery. However, this is unlikely to be associated with valid physiological or behavioral response. The therapeutic benefit, if any, is minimal.

Therapy Verbatim

Golf Ball Heals Knife: Two Traumas Resolved

**The client complains of a pain in the heart caused by
two separate experiences. One symbol (golf ball in head) is
used to heal another (knife in heart). Both memories are
stored in metaphors (a slice, criss crosses).**

'Do you know what you want?'
"Yes."
'What's that?'
"I want to change the effect of the two traumas."
'And which trauma do you want to change first?'
"The one that I am conscious of, and then the one that I am not
consciously aware of but I know about."

**The therapist asks the client to establish the epistemology
of the memory. Content is not asked for.**

'And so, how do you know the one you are conscious of?'
"Because I remember it."
'And when you remember it, how do you remember it?'
"I picture it."
'And when you picture it, where do you picture it?'
"In my head."
*'And when it is in your head, and you picture it, whereabouts in
your head do you picture it?'*

"In the front of my head."

'And when it is in the front of your head, where in the front of your head is it?'

"Behind my eyeballs."

'And does it have a particular shape to it when it is behind your eyeballs?'

"Round."

'And it's round like what?'

"Like a used ball."

'And it is round like a used ball.... And what kind of used ball is that round like?'

"Like a hacked up golf ball."

'Like a hacked up golf ball. And whereabouts is the golf ball hacked up?'

"All over."

'All over. And what other qualities are there to that golf ball?'

"It's dirty."

'And it's dirty. And do the hacked up parts of the golf ball have any particular pattern to them?'

"It slices, it curves."

'It slices and curves. And are those slices and curves sliced and curved in any particular way?'

"Some are separate, and some are criss crossed."

'And do you know which ones are separate and which ones are criss crossed?'

"Yes."

'And might it be possible that you could separate the separate ones and separate them from the criss crossed ones?'

"Yes."

'And so just let the criss crossed ones and the separate ones be together in a way that just seems to make that sense to separate and to criss cross and to let them do that and be together in a way that can be separate and criss crossed. And just what could you discover when that happens...?'

The therapist asks the client to let separate and criss cross evolve. Golf ball spontaneously moves to heart.

"It moves."

'And it moves. And just how does it move?'

"It moves down."

'And it moves down to where?'

"To my heart."

'And it moves down to your heart. And so just let it move down to your heart. And that's what happens when you separate separate and criss cross, because the golf ball like that doesn't want to be separate. And then it doesn't have to be criss crossed like that. And so just let that golf ball move to just above the part it wants to go to, and just what a golf ball like that would want to do when it goes to a heart in that place. Just what would that golf ball want to do there?'

A new metaphor (knife) develops from the word hurt.

"Stop the hurt."

'And so when it hurts there that the golf ball wants to stop, what's that hurt like?'

"Like a stabbing pain."

'Like a stabbing pain. And when it's like that stabbing pain, what kind of stabbing pain is that stabbing pain?'

"It's like a knife in the heart."

'And that stabbing pain is like a knife in the heart. And what kind of knife in the heart is that?'

"A thin, tiny knife."

'And it's a thin, tiny knife. And what sort of handle does a thin, tiny knife like that have?'

"Smooth, gray."

'And it has a smooth, gray handle. And are there any other qualities to that knife?'

"It's shiny."

'And it's shiny. Is there anything else around that knife...?'

"Darkness."

Therapist's words join the two metaphors (golf ball, knife) in the heart.

'And there's darkness around that knife. And so, take some time, to know about that knife, and about all the qualities of that knife in the heart. And as you know about that knife, know about golf ball, and about separate and criss cross and about just what would need to happen. And just what would need to happen so that golf ball could know about what to do with the gray knife like that, and darkness, so heart would not have to have a knife like that? And just what could a golf ball do? So just take some time to discover that.'

"Golf ball could invite the knife in."

'And the golf ball could invite a knife in. And as a golf ball invites a knife in what could happen next?'

"The knife would be in the golf ball, not in the heart."

'And would a knife be willing to go into a golf ball like that, that had criss crosses and slashes?'

"Yes."

'And so a golf ball and a knife could come together in that way. And then what would need to happen next...?'

"Remove the golf ball."

'And could a golf ball know just how to be removed with a knife in it? And just where would a golf ball want to go when it was removed with a knife from a heart like that?'

"Out."

'And a golf ball could go out. And so just let a golf ball go out. And where would a golf ball that would go out, go out to?'

"The water."

'And it could go out to the water. And would a golf ball with a knife know just what water to go out to?'

"Yes."

'And can it just go to that water with a knife? And just what could happen when a golf ball and a knife would go to that water?'

"It would sink."

'And it would sink. And as it would sink with that water, what could happen to a golf ball and a knife?'

"It would disappear."

'And it would disappear. And as you know about a golf ball and knife that disappears, what do you think that a golf ball might want to do that could be different than disappearing?'

"Get smaller."

'It could get smaller. And would a golf ball and a knife in it... could it get smaller in such a way that that golf ball could begin to know about water and knife? And what ways could a golf ball and a knife begin to become different?'

"It could change."

'And it could change. And how could they change?'

"Into a marble, into a pea."

'It could change into marble, into a pea, a hard pea. So just see if a golf ball would be interested in being in water as a marble or hard pea. And what could happen to a knife...?'

"I don't know."

'So take some time to discover what could happen to a knife, and what could happen to a hard pea when it was in water. And what could water do to a hard pea like that, and about a knife that's gray that has that shape? And how could a knife like that begin to change so that it could be useful to a hard pea that was in water?'

"It could pluck it out."

'It could pluck it out. And could a knife do that to a hard pea?'

"Yes."

'Then just let that do that to a hard pea to pluck it out. And then what would need to happen?'

Therapist intends to evolve metaphor (pea). This fails. Metaphor must be evolved, not destroyed.

"Throw away the pea."

'And the pea would be thrown away. And just where would you throw away a pea like that that had been plucked out, and was in water?'

"In the garbage."

'And what could happen to a pea like that that had been thrown out into the garbage?'

"Picked up and taken away."

'Be picked up and taken away. And would a pea like that want to be picked up and taken away in garbage? Or would a pea like that be interested in being put somewhere else? And just what could happen if the pea that had been in water was put somewhere else? What would happen to a pea like that?' (pause)

"I don't know."

'So take some time to discover about what might be more appealing to a pea like that than being put in the rubbish. And what could a knife do that could be useful with how to decide? And so just let a pea and a knife decide what will happen. Take your time to do that.' (long pause)

'And so what happened to heart, pea and knife?'

"The pea was washed by the water, it began to grow, it changed to a tiny apple on a tree. And it grew and grew and grew until it was ripe for picking. And knife can be laid beside it to be used as a carving knife and that apple can taste sweet."

'And that's just the right thing to happen to a pea. It can grow and it can have an apple. And the knife beside an apple and that's just the thing, then an apple can be useful. And with a knife beside it, it can be sweet and that's just like **apple-beside-her** isn't it?'

"Yes."

'And to have a knife beside her as well. And so what else would a knife and an apple need to have happen?'

"To be used."

'And how could they be used?'

"To satisfy a taste. To be used in the kitchen or elsewhere."

'And to be used in a kitchen or elsewhere. And so would you like to take a little time to learn and discover all the uses that you can use an apple and a knife for?'

"Yes."

'And then just have them teach you all the things that they have needed you to know, and that you can know now about apple and about knife, and all those uses. And how different that is from a golf ball and from a knife in the heart.' (long pause)

'Umm, how did you get on?'

"What?"

'What did you discover?'

"Umm. The pain stopped."

'Okay.'

"It didn't hurt anymore."

'So what do you have?'

"Lots of new things."

'And what are those lots of new things?'

"I don't know all of them yet, but they are going to be new lines and new experiences."

'Okay. And so did you get what you wanted in terms of the first memory, and about being able to change that?'

"Yes."

'And how do you know that it has changed?'

"Because it was a pea and it changed to apple. It don't hurt any more."

'And the apple is more appealing than a pea?'

"Yes."

'Okay. And it doesn't hurt any more?'

"No."

'And you are sure about that?'

"Very sure."

'Okay. And so about the other memory.'

"It was the knife."

'So you didn't change those memories without telling me?'

"Yes."

'What sort of person are you?'

"A changed person."

'How do you think that makes me feel, I mean I think I'm doing one memory and you are working with two.'

"I'm sorry about that."

'Well, guess I'll learn to live with it. So take some time to check through and make sure that both memories you would have wanted them to have been changed in a way which just seems to be the way that you would like them to be. So just take some time to do that.' (long pause)

'So how are you getting on?'

"Okay. Fine."

'What do you mean fine?'

"I feel great."

'Did you check through those memories? Okay. And is that how you want them to be?'

"Yes."

'And you are sure about that?'

"Yes."

'Okay. Are there any questions that you would like to ask this gentleman about the experience? Is there anything else you would like to say?'

Client relates content as an effortless afterthought to the intervention.

"I can share with the group what the two traumas were. The first one is a conscious memory of having to go into surgery when I was seventeen on my right knee. Ten days after surgery it was very painful. I asked for the doctor and he came to me that morning. As soon as he took the bandage off he told the nurse to go and get the operating room ready and to bring in the emergency equipment. And there wasn't time to get me to the operating room. They were all trying to get the blood out, there on the spot, but they didn't have time to do anything to anesthetize it and they began to stick needles in to drain the blood. It was very, very painful, and not knowing what the pain was until that day. They stuck needles in my leg to drain the blood for fifty minutes and all the needles like this.... And the other trauma was when I was told, with regard to my birth, I was born two and a half months premature because my mother contracted German measles and I was born with German measles and weighed less than two pounds. I was told I was only given 24 hours to live. So the trauma of that premature birth... and the other traumas have been physically related to that. The golf ball, the knife was the pain from all the traumas. And I felt the pain in my heart over the years."

'So by getting the golf ball then, what happened when the criss crosses separated?'

"Well, when they separated the two traumas became linked and the slices represented one trauma and the criss crosses related to the other."

Knots: Headache From Family Rules

The client complains of headache and fear. The metaphor (hurts) is derived from the symptoms. The therapist's questions deepen the information contained in knot. The client obtains insight. For the first time he discovers positive family messages.

'Do you know what it is you want?'
"Yes, I want to find out how to be free of very occasionally giving myself a headache, right back in here at the base of my skull, and when that happens feeling a tightness in my shoulders, in my stomach, in my forehead. It has some kind of ominous fear and I don't know what the fear is."
'So when it is there, whereabouts is it?'
"It's right in here."
'And when it is right in there does it have a particular shape or form to it?' (pause)
"Umm. The only shape I can think of is that it feels just like sore knots right there in both sides."
'And how many knots?'
"Two, one on each side. Most often though... I answered too quickly. Sometimes it is just one, right on this side, on the right side, other times it is on both sides."
'So sometimes it is one, and sometimes it is two. And are those two knots different from each other? What are the differences in the qualities of those knots?'
"The one on the right is more painful and is bigger and has more power."
'And the one on the right is more painful. What are the different qualities of that?'
"Somehow it makes the back of my neck hurt, the back of my head hurt...."
'And when it makes the back of your neck hurt, what kind of knot is that knot?'
"I would say there's a knot with all kinds of fibers in it... a ball of string kind of knot."
'Like a ball of string kind of knot.'

"Yeah."

'And what kind of ball of string...?'

"It appears to be made of flesh, but the flesh seems, it is almost like nerves that are all struggling together, all tied up and tied in, just struggling, pulling together. Pulling hard. There's this tightness."

'It's a tightness and it's like flesh pulling together. And is it just one knot or is it just many knots?'

"It's one knot made up of all these different strands, which are strands of flesh or nerve that are about 3/16th of an inch in diameter."

'And how many strands could there be there?'

"Fifty... thirty to fifty all mounted together. It's like they are all struggling."

'And so they are all struggling and they are knotted together. And any other qualities to that?'

"They are kind of tan flesh color."

'Okay. And so knowing about that knot, and about all the qualities to that knot and the other knot, and what is different about it?'

"He is not as important."

'He is not as important. And so knowing that he is not as important, is he made of similar things to the other knot?'

"He has very little fiber, he just agrees with the big knot."

'So he has very little fiber and just agrees.'

"She's right."

'So she's right. And so what does that knot have that has very little fiber?'

"All it has is the ability to add to my pain or to say yes, she should be hurting."

'So he just adds to....'

"...his support...."

'So he adds support. All right. And is there anything else about him?'

"The nothingness."

'So there's a nothingness. And where is that nothingness?'

"It is just in that little tiny marble size something ball."

'And so the little tiny marble size. What kind of little tiny marble

size could that be?'
"It is more like a cyst, just a membrane... oh, probably 3/16th inch thick. That is just filled with mostly opaque but fluid gel-like substance. It's the nothingness.... No, the struggle is not there, the struggle is in the bigger one that is a little bigger than a golf ball in size."

'So the nothingness is in the cyst and the struggle is in the bigger knot that's little more than a golf ball in size. Any other qualities to that bigger knot?'

"That bigger knot is always squeezing, pulling, struggling, moving, never at rest until somehow it leaves. When it is there it is like it is trying to close in on itself and it just tries so hard it hurts."

'And so that bigger knot is trying to close on itself. So take some time... to know about that bigger knot, and all the qualities of that bigger knot, and about its size and about its closing in on itself, and about the flesh and the little tiny knot, and about its size. And as you know about that knot, about the nothing, and the cyst, and the membrane, and all the qualities of that nothingness, and as you know about that, that you take some time to discover about just what it is that knots like that want to do, and about what would they need for you to know so that they can be different and can be other than knot.' (long pause)

'So what did you discover?'
"I discovered that all of those strands in that knot in the back of my head were fearful commands of what I should do, and what I should be and what I should think, what I should believe, how I should be. And when I opened those up and turned those strands over, what was written on the other side was the opposite. I could be what I wanted to be. I could be me. I didn't have to be perfect. I didn't have to know what was exactly right, before I would say what I thought. I could think my own thoughts. And then I discovered that there were some strands that ran from that knot down to my forehead, which said I want you to see things just exactly the way that I see them instead of the way that you see them. And I want you to feel very, very tight and very anxious until you see them the way I

see them. And I could never see them that way. Again, opening up that lot in my forehead, on the other side of those strands, was the other wish that was that I should see things clearly the way I see them, and think clearly, and see things clearly. And then I also discovered that from that knot at the back of my head there were strands that ran down right here in a knot right in the pit of my stomach and the knot said: 'If you love me you will be me,' and that was very scary, because I didn't want to be me. I didn't want to be that me, I wanted to be me, me."

'And so that can be scary. About knowing which knot not to be.'

"It seemed as if I was going to be the me that she wanted, I would have to be afraid like she was. And I couldn't even be me. And somehow as I turned that knot inside out there was the message there that she really did love me being me. And then I looked at the other knot, the small one and that one didn't seem to connect in my forehead, but it did have some kind of connection to that knot in my stomach. And the scare was that I shouldn't grow up, because if I did I would make mistakes and somehow he wouldn't love me if I grew up and made mistakes, he would be afraid and I would be afraid. And again turning the knot inside out was all of the blessing of saying he wanted me to grow up and be me."

'And so it can be quite interesting to find out which side not to be.... And when you find out which side of the knot should not be on the outside, and should be on the inside, and what was not on the outside and should be on the inside, and how when you do not know that what a difference that makes about how you do not know how to be and to be or not to be.'

"That is the question!"

'And that is the question! And so what do you think would need to have happen next; now that you know about inside knot and about messages there, and about messages outside knot, and about knots to be you, and about she knots and he knots, and what knot...?'

"I can take either side of the knot, I can let the knot be what I want the knot to be."

'And just what side of a knot would you take to begin with so that you could let a knot be what you want a knot to be?'

"I would take all three knots, open them up, and lay them out, and turn them over. And now that both sides were given, then I can choose to look at, be aware of, feel and live with either side."

'Then take some time about those three knots, and about turning them over, and taking them out. And it might be interesting, as you do that about those knots, and how they connect to eyes and to chest, and about when you take them out about what ways those knots may be able to get together in some way so that the strands and the pieces of the different knots may be interested in how they relate to each other both on the inside and on the outside. And the inside out becomes the outside in. And just what ways once they know that could they be interested in knotting together so that they can knot-ice what each has? And that could make a knot-iceable difference.' (long pause)

'Hello! And so what have you got?'

"What I have is that the pain of the knots really were the family rules. And the scaring, tightening, badding, and negative from Mom and Dad and knotting them up and turning them over was the other side which was really nice, and that was the permission and the blessing from each of those people; and that's also in me, to figure things out. That's the one in the back of my head, the big one. To see things clearly that's the one in my forehead. And the one in my stomach was the one... and what I got was a new knowing that each one of those people really did and do bless me to be me.... And I like that."

'So that was not a bad discovery was it?'

"It was a good discovery. I don't like knots and I don't need knots."

'And so what do you have now that is not knots?'

"This open permission from all kinds of people. The true permissions to be, to think, to see, to feel, to enjoy, to have figured things out, to cope, to be moment by moment me."

'And so do you still have some knots left?'

"I don't think so. The knots are the sheets of permission."

'So what you have is sheets of permission. And what kinds of sheets are those sheets?'

"Those sheets are the knots taken all apart, rolled out and turned over. With all kinds of permission written all over them."

'Okay. And what are those sheets made of?'

"Fiber, up there; reality in my life. But, the positive, the love that they have for me; but they just love me, and like me, and want me to be me."

'So you have those fibers?'

"Uh huh."

'And that's very interesting, to be able to have those fibers on those sheets with those messages. And so what would happen if those sheets would begin to turn the other way and become knots again?'

"I don't think that they will."

'How do you know that?'

"Because somehow I know that I received both the rules, the frowns, the tightness, the fear, and also the love, the blessing, the permission, the freedom, I received both. One side was I love you if, the other side is I love you. And I knew at a different level. I know that I always had and now know it, that they love me. No conditions."

'And how could sheets trust you, that they could be sheets and that they would not have to go back to being knots again?'

"The sheets just know I'm okay."

'And do they have any conditions about you being okay?'

"No, I think they have trust. Not conditions, trust that I am okay."

'So they trust that you are okay, and that you are not likely to short sheet them?'

"That's not likely."

'But it is likely that you are not likely, or you are not likely that you are not?'

"I think that's strong."

'You think that's true, but you couldn't not be really sure?'

"I am sure."

'Okay. So is there anything else you want to have happen...? Do you have a sense of completeness that you got what you wanted?'

"Uh huh. Thank you."

Saw Finger: A Case of Anticipatory Anxiety

The client complains of flash-backs to her accident with a power-saw and the feelings of horror/shock associated with future images. The feelings (horror/shock) lead to a memory at age eight or nine (trapped inside house). In the intervention the child frees herself from the house. This resolves the feelings. The negative images are extinguished.

'And what is it you would like to have happen?'
"This summer I almost cut my finger off with the table saw, and I still have flash-backs. But more than that I get images. My husband still uses that saw and I get images of him doing something more horrible than what I did, which bothers me a lot."
'And so when that bothers you a lot, where does that bother you a lot?'
"Visually. I see it there."
'And when you see it there, where do you see it when it's there?'
"I see it in the sense of horror, shock."
'And when you see it in a sense of horror, shock, whereabouts is it when you see it in the sense of horror or shock?'
"In the gut."

This somatic memory operates the anticipatory images.

'And when you have horror or shock in the gut, whereabouts in the gut?'

Better question might have been: 'And when you have a sense of horror or shock, where do you have it?'

"Dead center."
'And when it's in the gut and it's dead center, what's it like when it's in the gut and it's dead center?'
"It's terrifying."

'And it's terrifying. And when it's terrifying and it's in the gut and it's dead center, does it have a shape or a size or a form to it when it's terrifying? And what kind of terrifying could that terrifying be?'

"Gripping. It's gripping."

'And when it's gripping, it's gripping like what?'

"Like it's controlling, very controlling."

'And so it's gripping like it's very controlling. And when it's gripping like it's very controlling, is there anything else about that gripping and it's very controlling?'

"It's controlling and yet I have no control."

'And when it's controlling, what kind of controlling is that controlling?'

"It's that sense of helplessness."

'And what kind of sense of helplessness is that sense of helplessness?'

"It's wanting to be able to reach out and change the situation and the images, and yet not being able to."

'And when you want to reach out and you're not able to reach out, whereabouts are you when you want to reach out and you're not being able to reach out?'

"Inside."

The client gives a series of feeling attributions (terrifying, gripping, controlling, helpless). This is possibly a clue to a child within. The information is chaotic, coming from both the adult and the *child within*.

'And whereabouts inside?'

The client responds with a memory.

"Inside the house."

'So take a little time to know about that house, and where you are inside that house and about all the qualities of that house. And so take some time to know about that house, and just how old could you be when you're in a house like that and you want to reach out?'

Reach out is the first clue that there's a child within. The *child* is within the client's memory.

'And so how old could she be?'
"Eight, nine."
*'And when **she's** eight or nine, and **she's** reaching out, what is it that **she** would like to have happen?'*
"It's confusing because what I want to happen is for something not to happen so that I don't have to know that it happened."
'Where is it confusing when it's confusing?'
"The denial."
'And when there's denial, where is the denial when there's denial?'
"My back."
'And so denial is in your back. And where in your back is denial?'
"Shoulders."
'And it's in your shoulders. And when denial is in your shoulders, whereabouts in your shoulders?'
"All the way across."
'And so when it's all the way across, what's it like when it's all the way across?'
"A yoke."

The metaphor (yoke) belongs to the child. Now questions are asked to develop yoke.

'And so it's like a yoke. And what kind of a yoke?'
"Oxen yoke."
'An oxen yoke. And what could that oxen yoke be made of?'
"Wood."
'And what kind of wood?'
"Rough, big heavy wood?"
'And so it's made of wood. And is there anything else about that wood?'
"It's blond. Gray-blond."
'And about that yoke. Is there anything else about that yoke?'
"Just that it's heavy."
'And it's heavy. And what could there be around yoke?'

"Nothing."

'And so is there anything else that could be attached to yoke when a yoke is on shoulders? Or how is a yoke of gray-blond wood on shoulders?'

"Fixed."

'And when it's fixed across shoulders, how is it fixed when it's fixed across shoulders?'

"Permanently."

'And when it's fixed permanently, what's it like when it's fixed permanently?'

"Terrifying."

'And whereabouts is it fixed permanently, when it's fixed permanently?'

"Across the shoulders."

'And when it's fixed permanently across the shoulders, then how is it attached or fixed permanently?'

"Nails."

'And how many nails?'

"Two."

'And what kind of nails are those two nails?'

"Big brown spiked railroad nails."

'And is there anything else?'

"Just permanency."

'And when there's permanency?'

"There's no escape."

Escape is the metaphor.

'And so when there's no escape, how do you know there's no escape?'

"Because there's blockage; can't move, can't go through doors, can't move out."

'And when there's blockage, and you can't go through doors and you can't move out, whereabouts is the blockage when there's blockage?'

"The whole body is blocked."

'And when the whole body is blocked, what's that like when the

whole body is blocked?'
"That's the helplessness."

This is the origin of *helplessness* that belonged to the *child* trapped within this memory. *Helplessness* recurs when the finger is cut and with the sound of the saw.

'And so the whole body is blocked and that's the helplessness. And is there anything else?'
"That's what keeps me from going out."
'And is it the yoke that keeps you from going out? Or the block?'
"The yoke."
'And so how does the yoke keep you from going out?'
"Because it's so heavy and wide, and so permanently attached. It can't get through the door."

The therapist's words surround the memory by reiterating the situation. Change becomes possible.

'And it can't get through the door. And so take a little time to know about a yoke that's permanent, heavy and attached. And as you know about a yoke like that, of rough gray-blond wood, a yoke that's permanently attached, with brown spikes, and about how you can't reach out... and as you know about a yoke like that, and how a yoke blocks, and it might be interesting to take some time to discover what that yoke wants you to know, and what it is a yoke like that could teach you, and about what would need to happen so a yoke like that could be different. And how could you learn about going out through a door with a yoke, and whether or not you could learn to turn so you could go out of a door sideways with a yoke, or whether something would need to be done before you went out of the house with the yoke. And just what could happen. And about a finger. And about what a finger saw. And about a saw finger. And about what a finger could teach a yoke about saw. And whether a sore finger could go to a yoke, and about the sound, and about what could be sore....'

"I think the finger could remind the yoke that they are both for service."

'And could a finger teach a yoke that?'

"As long as the yoke was careful."

'And how could a finger know that a yoke was careful?'

"When it protected itself."

'And so what else might a finger like to have happen?'

"The finger could possibly help remove the nails, to remove the yoke, to remove the terror."

'And would that finger know just which nail it would want to remove first? And a finger can know some interesting things because a finger knows about... a fingernail. And can a finger know about a fingernail that might know about just which nail a finger....'

"Probably remove the left one first."

'And it could move the left nail first. And what would it do when it removed the left nail first?'

"It would take it out, pull it out from where the nail had been in the heart."

'And it could do that. And then what would that finger want to do with that nail?'

"Throw it away."

'And as that finger could throw that nail away, is there anything else that that finger could think of to do with a nail like that? And how could a finger with a fingernail know what to do with a nail like that?'

"It would just know that it's not necessary."

'And what would that finger like to do next?'

"Remove the other nail."

'And could it remove the other nail?'

"Yes."

'And what would it like to do next?'

"Remove the yoke from across the shoulders."

'And would a finger be able to take a yoke from across the shoulders? Or would it need a hand?'

"It would need a hand."

'And what hand would it need?'

"It would need its own hand. Matter of fact, it would need both hands."

'And it would need its own hand and both hands. And so as it has both hands, what could happen next?'

"It would perhaps motion to another hand, a third, fourth hand to come help."

'And could that finger know just the right motion?'

"Yes."

'And that finger could motion for a third or fourth hand to help. And then what could happen?'

"And then they could remove that heavy, gray, broad, rough yoke from across the shoulders."

'And could they do that?'

"Yes."

'And as they do that and whether or not they'd want to use the nails, and what would they like to do next with a yoke like that?'

"Just take it off and put it down."

'And when they put it down, is there anything they'd like to do about that yoke so it could be different in some way? And what could be done about a blond, gray wood?'

"Well, the hands could pick it up, take it outside and saw it up."

'And could those hands do that?'

"Yes."

'And when those hands did that, how could that be used? And what could happen about wood like that that was sawn up?'

"It could be usable, but not heavy and not burdensome."

'And so what could be made out of wood like that?'

"A doorstop."

'And could nails be interested in going to a doorstop, or would they need to be elsewhere?'

"No, they don't need to be there."

'And so if yoke was now a doorstop, then yoke could keep a door open, so a door would not stop someone who wanted to reach out. And a yoke stopped someone from reaching out. And a yoke was permanent, and now a doorstop can keep a door open, and a door open then doesn't have to stop someone from reaching out.... And what would she like to do?'

"Go through the door."

'And as she goes through the door, could she notice about an interesting doorstop?'

"Most definitely."
'And so it's different having a most definitely doorstop than a permanent yoke.'
"True."
'And what would she like to do next?'
"Stay out for a while."

This solution makes sense to a child. It transforms the negative metaphor (yoke) into a positive metaphor (doorstop).

'And does she know what she wants to do when she stays out for a while?'
"Move and be free and not restricted."
'And are there any other clothes she'd like to have, or does she like what she's got on?'
"She's fine."
'And so now she can move and be free. And is there anything else she would like to have happen?'
"I don't think so."
'And so take a little time to know about how she can move and be free, and she doesn't have to have yoke and permanent and terrifying. And as **she** *knows about that,* **you** *might like to go into the future about times when a husband uses a saw, or into the past when a saw and a finger, and about what* **she** *could do about that memory. And about a stopper, and what that memory might be able to do with a stopper, and about going into the future, and about a husband using a saw, and whether having a stopper and a doorstopper could make that fear be different in some way.'*

The new learning of the child (move, be free) resolves the adult's memory. This liberates the client from the negative images and the fear of the saw.

"Yeah. She could go in and out at will and check and know that everything is okay, which would be better than staying in the

house and being terrified that it might happen. So the freedom
is there to go and come."
'And did you get what you wanted?'
"Yes."
'And is she all right?'
"She's fine."
'And did that work out all right in the future?'
"Yes. Thank you."

Three Blobs: Assuming Responsibility

**The client frees herself from the men in her life. She
discovers her metaphor for the three men (blobs). Through
memories and feelings she discovers her new metaphors
(rod, star) which represent her desire to control her own
life. The intervention consists of introducing the new
metaphor (rod) into the old (blob). With her new metaphor
(star) the client assumes responsibility for her own life.**

'And do you know what it is that you want?'
"I've been thinking about several things, but I think basically
I want to really truly feel happy."
'Okay. And how do you know that you don't really truly feel
happy?'
"Because I worry a lot and...."
'And when you worry a lot, where do you worry a lot?'
"Kind of in my chest.... Just feels kind of stifling, right here."
'And when your chest feels stifling right there, whereabouts in
your chest does it feel stifling right there?'
"Close to the heart."
'And whereabouts close to the heart?'
"Close to the right side of my heart, I guess."
'Close to the right side of your heart. And when it's close to the

right side of your heart, what's it like when it's close to the right side of your heart?'

"It's kind of like a choking-like..., a stifling, suffocating feeling."

'And when it's like a choking and suffocating feeling, what kind of choking and suffocating feeling?'

"Like I can't breathe, can't think straight."

'And what else is there about that?'

"I find it difficult to trust. I can't think straight, and I worry."

'And when you can't think straight and you worry and you find it difficult to trust, whereabouts do you find it difficult to trust?'

"Within my own self, within me."

'And whereabouts is that?'

"It's all over."

'And is it all over more on the inside, or more on the outside?'

"I think it's more on the inside."

'And whereabouts more on the inside is it all over?'

"I guess just inside the upper part of my body, it's got a tightening feeling...."

'And it's a tightening feeling. And what kind of tightening feeling?'

"Like something that can't get out, like when I want to scream."

'And when it's like something that can't get out and like a scream, what kind of something that can't get out could that be?'

"Just a feeling that I shouldn't be feeling this way. I can't explain it."

'And when you have that feeling where is that feeling when you have that feeling?'

"It's in my head, that I shouldn't be feeling that way, is in my head."

'And whereabouts in your head is that?'

"Somewhere in the back of my mind."

'And when it's in the back of your mind, where in the back of your mind?'

"It's way back in the back of my mind."

'And it's way back. And when it's way back in the back of your mind, what's it like when it's way back in the back of your mind?'

"Like something evil."

'And when it's like something evil and it's way back in the back
of your mind, does it have a shape or a form to it when it's like
something evil?'
"It really doesn't. It just appears to be a sort of a blob."

**This matrix concerns existential issues (happiness and
evil). Therefore the metaphor is vague (blob). An attempt
will be made to follow each idea down to a significant
metaphor.**

'And it's a sort of blob. And what kind of blob could that blob be?'
"Just something that's constantly moving."
'And it's constantly moving. And when it's constantly moving,
how is it constantly moving?'
"Just back and forth and around. Just always there."
'And it's back and forth and around. And is it constantly moving
more back and forth or around when it's always there?'
"Back and forth."
'And back and forth like what?'
"It comes and goes."
'And when it comes and goes, how does it comes and goes?'
"Just as a reminder, and then it goes back."
'A reminder, and then it goes back. And when it comes and goes,
what does it come and go like when it's a reminder?'
"I don't know."
'But you know that it comes and goes and it's like a blob. And
when it comes and goes, and it comes as a reminder?'
"I can't trust it to stay gone."
'And so it just comes and goes, back and forth.'
"And it makes me unhappy."
'And what would it like to do?'
"I don't know. To see me unhappy."
'It would like to see you unhappy. And so what does it need to
do so it can see you unhappy?'
"Bring thoughts of it into my mind."
'And how could it bring thoughts of it into your mind?'
"Just makes me see things or imagine things."
'And when it makes you see things or imagine things where does

it make you see things or imagine things?'
"In my mind."
'And whereabouts in your mind?'
"In the back, in the recesses of my mind."
'In the recesses of your mind. And how many recesses does it make you see things in the back of your mind?'
"Three."
'And so it could be three.'
"I want to be free of this worry and mistrust. It's like a constant burden I'm carrying."
'And when it's like a constant burden, whereabouts are you carrying it when it's like a constant burden?'
"Just weighing on my shoulders, my back."
'And does it have a shape or size to it when you carry it on your shoulders or your back?'
"Like rocks, two rocks just resting on my shoulders."
'And what kind of rocks?'
"Sometimes like heavy big boulders, and sometimes just a nagging little pebble."
'So sometimes it's like big boulders, and sometimes a little pebble. And is there anything else about those boulders or pebbles?'
"Sometimes they fall off and I'm okay, but I always worry that they'll come back."
'And they do come back. And so what would those boulders like to do?'
"Just keep me down."
'And what else would they like to do?'
"Keep me unhappy."
'And can they keep you down and keep you unhappy?'
"Not all the time."
'And so what would those boulders like to do?'
"Those boulders would really like to go away."
'And what would need to happen so they could really go away?'
"They would just need to fall off."
'And when they fall off, can they come back again?'
"They do."

The therapist uses his words to have the client develop additional information about boulder, pebble, and blob, as well as to evoke antecedent memories.

'And so they can go away and fall off and they do come back. So take some time to get to know those two boulders and what they're made of, and what could be inside of boulders like that. And about pebbles, and about all the times that you have boulders. And you take some time to get to know those boulders, and take those boulders back in your history, right back to the very first time that you first got those boulders, and about what happened when you got each one of those boulders. And you take some time to discover what happened there then when you got those boulders, and about blob, and when blob goes back and forth and when blob has those pictures in the recesses, and when blob reminds you and how blob does that, and about if there are three recesses or if there are more. You take some time to know about that and about any other that you might have. And as you know about boulders, and about blob, then take some time to discover what would need to happen for boulders to be different and how boulders could change, and about blob and what is it that blob needs you to know so that blob can be different, and what is it that blob can teach you and if blob can know that you know, then blob might not have to be blob.'
"But if it goes away... it's just a part of my mind."
'That's right. So you just take some time to discover what blob wants to do so that blob doesn't have to go away. But what could blob do so that it could be different and that it wouldn't have to go away. And whether or not blob could go down to rocks, or rocks could go to blob, and just what could happen if blobs and rocks were to get together in some way. So take some time to discover that.' (long pause)

'And so what's happened?'
"I feel that I'm stuck and probably have been for a long time. I was able to come to the conclusion that the three blobs, the coming in and out, reminder of good and bad, represents three significant men in my life: my father, my ex-husband, and my

present husband. And for some reason with each one of them I felt some pain, and I always felt I didn't deserve the pain that I felt, and that I sometimes now still feel. And then you talked about the small pebble and the big boulder, and what I'm beginning to realize is that the boulder represents a lot of anger and resentment that I feel because of what happened, and I think I didn't really deserve it. And then the small pebble I view as myself: insignificant, even though I do things I feel are worthwhile and rewarding. I get stuck in this feeling that people that I really care about don't see that. And I want to know where to go from here so that I won't spend the rest of my life appearing to be happy or having it all together when I have these feelings."

The client's insight (relating three blobs to three men) leads to a new set of feelings (undeserved pain, anger, resentment, insignificant, stuck). These give rise to a new metaphor (rod).

'And so when you have those feelings, whereabouts do you have them?'

"It just seems to consume my body.... It's when I give in to those feelings in my body, they're in my chest, my neck, my shoulders, my back."

'And so where are they most when they're in your body and you give in to them?'

"It's just like an all-consuming feeling I get... overwhelming feeling that I get."

'And when it's overwhelming what's it like when it's overwhelming?'

"Feels like I'm about to explode."

'And when it feels like you're about to explode, where are you about to explode when you're about to explode?'

"My head."

'And when you're about to explode in you're head, what's that like?'

"It's like losing control."

'And when you're about to explode and like losing control, what

kind of explode and losing control could that be?'
"Irrational... asking why."
'And when it's irrational and asking why, whereabouts in your head is it irrational and asking why?'
"My brain, my mind."
'And where in your brain or your mind?'
"Right in the center, it just takes control... it's just right there."
'And when it's in the center, is there a shape or a form to it?'
"Just sharp."
'And sharp like what?'
"Sharp like a sword."
'And what kind of sword could that sharp be like?'
"Like a piercing thought."
'And what could that piercing thought be made of?'
"Events.... Something.... Metal."
'Events or metal. And what kind of metal?'
"Durable."
'A durable metal. So take some time to know about a durable metal and about events and about if it's like a sword, and what kind of sword that could be, or if it's about durable metal and events. And about what else is there about durable metal like that.'
"Can't penetrate it. It's there."
'And when it's there and you can't penetrate it, what's it like when it's like that?'
"It's like, this is what you have to live with."
And when it's like that does it have a shape to it?'
"It's just straight."
'And straight like what?'
"Straight like a rod."
'And what kind of rod?'
"It has no **end**. It just goes on."

The therapist asks for the polarity (beginning) of end. This evokes the client's new metaphor (star).

'And so a rod that has no end and just goes on and is durable. And does that rod have a beginning?'

"Yes."

'And what's it like when it has a beginning?'

"It's... good."

'And the beginning is good. And good like what?'

"Like happy thoughts and happiness."

'And when a rod has a beginning that has happy thoughts and happiness, what are they like when they're at the beginning of a rod?'

"They're like new and exciting, like shiny."

'And shiny like what?'

"Like a star."

'And is there just one star, or more than one star?'

"Like one bright star."

'And so at the beginning of a rod is one bright star. And so what would that bright star at the beginning of a rod like to do?'

"Shine brighter. And show."

'And what would happen to a rod if the beginning of a rod was to shine brighter and show?'

"It would reflect the brightness."

'And what could happen when a rod begins to reflect the brightness?'

"Happiness would be there. I can't believe this."

The client's new metaphors (rod, star) are brought together with the old metaphor/symbol (blob).

'Take some time to get to know that star and that rod and about when a rod is made of something as durable as what that is, and when it has such a bright, shiny beginning, that could that rod be durable enough with such a beginning like that, and to shine brighter. And take some time to get to know that rod and that star, and about a rod and star, and about where could that rod begin to shine like that star, and could it be interested in going way, way back to blob, and about what would happen if star and blob were to get together?'

"Oh! Good things— forgiveness, happy times."

'And if a rod was able to go to the three recesses at the back of your mind, and be able to go far, far back to blob and to three

recesses, and about if a rod and pebbles were to get together, and two boulders. And just what could happen with something as durable as that rod, and what could it do about two boulders and pebble? So take some time to discover all you can know about a bright beginning and a star and a rod that's durable and goes on. And take some time to discover that, and about what else can happen.' (long pause)

'And so what's happened?'
"Well, I came to the conclusion that I'm that bright star. The insignificance I felt was because my self-worth has always been tied up in what others think of me rather than what I think about myself. The long rod that's durable I see as the marriage I'm in right now, that it will stand the test of time because I'm right there. I came to the conclusion that in the dark recesses of my mind there are some guilt feelings, perhaps that I wasn't good enough because of my mom's failed marriage and my first failed marriage, that there was something wrong with me. But now I see myself as important, as a star, that might be able to affect what's going on in my life. The question I'm wrestling with now is: what do I need to do at this point? I feel better having realized that I am important."
'And so what's happened to boulders?'
"The boulders disappeared. The heaviness that I felt was my own insecurities, and the star kind of enclosed itself over the boulders and pushed them away, like a hand. About the blobs— I don't know what the blobs can do as far as a star— sometimes I feel that's out of my control."
'So take some time to know about the blob, and about a blob that can be out of your control, and about where a blob is and all the qualities of that blob, and about a star and a rod, and a star that can do things with boulders and pebbles, and about how could a star and a blob get together or what could a rod and a blob do. And about just what could happen.'
"A star and a blob could get together. They could mesh and become one."
'And could a blob be interested in meshing with a star and becoming one?'

"It could be."

'And could a star be interested in doing that?'

"It's possible."

'And what about rod? And if a star was at a beginning and could begin to mesh with a blob, then what would a rod do?'

"Hold them together."

'A rod could hold them together. And would a blob need to come to a star and a rod? Or could a star and a rod go to blob?'

"The blob would need to come together with the star and the rod. Just one blob I'm talking about."

'And could that blob do that?'

"Yeah."

'And then what would happen?'

"Then it would become a part of that star."

'And could it become a part of that star?'

"Yes. Still, the rod could also serve as a divider so the blob and the star could still maintain their identity."

'So even though they're together, you could know the difference between a star and a blob. And you'd know just where a blob was, right next to a bright star, and divided by a rod.'

"This is amazing...! This has been so fulfilling. When I came I was feeling so torn... (like I was) going in fifty different directions."

'And how do you know you're still not going to go in fifty different directions?'

"...There's a new feeling of control..., I can breathe easier.... It's just there. I've thought about some things I had refused to really face up to this point. They've helped me realize how important I am."

'And when you feel that, does that make a difference?'

"It makes a difference."

'And do you know what that feeling is that makes that difference?'

"It's a feeling of relief and acceptance..., kind of peaceful."

'And so have you got what you wanted?'

"I got what I wanted."

'And how do you know that?'

"...I feel serene right now, and hopefully this will carry over."

'But is it durable?'

"According to that rod that's made out of durable metal, it is."

Exit Interview

"It's really going quite well. Last night after I left... the two blobs I had not really dealt with kept coming back, so I felt that I needed to explore that just a little bit further and I do have some idea about what I would like to have happen. The fact that they were fading in and out of my life— one represented my father whom I had witnessed walking away when I was about eleven years old and the other is my ex-husband who from time to time will say that our marriage could have worked if I would have given him another chance. So I would like him to kind of release me from that kind of pressure, but I understand that he will be in my life because my son (from that marriage) is definitely there. Then with my father— he has kind of removed himself. But if I came to the conclusion that I really did not have any power to prevent his leaving, I would like to continue to have him in my life and just accept that."

'So, did you get what you wanted in terms of what you started out with?'

"Yes, I did. I have come to the realization that by not assuming responsibility for my own actions I had reduced myself to an insignificant person and given other people power over me. But now I realize that the power lies within me and that I can make a difference, and the star represents what I can be. With accepting that responsibility for myself, I accept that I cannot control anyone else, just myself."

Sex = Guilt: A Case of Sexual Inhibition

This intervention uses metaphors trapped in the child's body and introduces them into the client's constructed memory.

'And do you know what it is that you want?'
"I know what it's about. I can't get clear on what I want to do about it."
'And when you know what it's about, how do you know you know what it's about?'
"I want to record over an old equation that I've had in my head from a very early age that says 'sex = guilt'."
'And when that old equation is in your head, whereabouts in your head is it?'
"Right here, on the right side of the back of my neck. I can feel it."
'And when you can feel it, what's it like when you can feel it?'
"It's a tight knot that won't relax."
'And what kind of tight knot is that tight knot that won't relax?'
"A very stubborn one."
'And what's a stubborn knot like that made of?'
"I guess it's made of gristle, very tough gristle, that's all wound around and around."
'And as you know about a knot that's very stubborn and that's made of very tough gristle, is there anything else about that knot?'
"Yes, there are times when it isn't there. But I have to go far away— out to the West Coast— for it not to be there. And when I'm out there, it's not there. And when I'm back here, the knot is back."
'And is there anything else about that knot?'
"It has tendrils or things attached to it that go down my right arm and down my back between my shoulder blade and my spine."
'And when it goes down between your shoulder blade and your spine, what else is there about that?'
"It's very constricting, and it hurts, and it drains me of energy."

'And when it goes down there and it's constricting and it hurts, what's it like when it goes down there?'

"It's like an adversary that's at war with me and, too often, it wins the battle."

'And when it's like an adversary that's at war, and that too often wins the battle, what else is there about that adversary?'

"It's very sneaky. It hides in dark places, and I think it's gone, and then it sneaks up on me when I least expect it."

'And does it want to be very sneaky now, and hide in dark places? Or would it like to do something else?'

"I don't know."

'And so, do you know where it is now?'

"It's still there."

'And is there anything else about it when it's still there?'

"It thinks that it is part of me, that it belongs in my body."

'And as it thinks that it belongs in your body, what would it like to do?'

"I'm afraid it would like to stay there."

'And when you're afraid it would like to stay there, where are you afraid when you're afraid it would like to stay there?'

"All over."

'And when you're afraid all over, are you afraid all over more on the outside or all over on the inside?'

"Inside."

'And when you're afraid all over on the inside, whereabouts on the inside?'

"In my chest."

'And when you're afraid all over on the inside in your chest, what's that like?'

"I breathe faster, and I have trouble catching my breath, and I get shaky, and my voice gets squeaky, and I feel paralyzed, like I'm frozen and I can't move."

'And when you're frozen and you can't move, what kind of frozen is that frozen?'

"It's just like being frozen, wherever I am, being glued to the space I'm in."

'And what kind of glue is that glue?'

"Super-glue."

'And whereabouts is that super-glue?"

"It's from almost the top of my head all the way down."

'And what else is there about that glue?'

"It holds me in place."

'And when it holds you in place, how does it hold you in place?'

"By just immobilizing me, just like... frozen."

'And when it's just like frozen, is that what it's like when you have super-glue?'

"Yes."

'And when it's just like frozen just like that, is there anything else?'

"Everything gets all cold, and the feelings start to die."

'And when everything gets all cold, and the feelings start to die, whereabouts does it get all cold, and the feelings start to die?'

"In the trunk of my body... in my breasts, my stomach, my abdomen, my genitals...just die."

"Just die" is the first clue to a *child within*.

'And when they just die, what do they just die like?'

"Like they've been sedated. They know that they're not dead, but they feel like they're dead, and they can't move."

'And when they know they're not dead, and they feel dead, and they can't move, is there anything else about them when they feel dead and they can't move?'

"They can't speak, and they can remember times when they didn't feel this way, but they can't do anything or tell anyone."

'And about how old would they be when they know that?'

"About seventeen."

'And when they're about seventeen, what would they like to do?'

"Play on the beach."

'And what would need to happen so they could play on the beach?'

"They would need to go to the beach and have moonlight and water."

'And could they go to the beach and have moonlight and water?'

"Yes."

'And as they go to the beach and have moonlight and water, what would they like to have happen next?'

"To lie down under a weeping willow tree."

'And could they lie down under a weeping willow tree?'

"Yes."

'And then what would they like to do?'

"Listen to the waves beat upon the shore, and listen to the wind blowing through the trees, and watch the lights of the boats far away."

'And would they like to do anything else?'

"They would like to be free to do whatever they want to do with someone they love."

'And what stops them from being free to do whatever they want to do with someone they love?'

"They don't stop."

'And what would they want to do?'

"They would want to swim naked in the surf and feel how good the water feels."

'And so would they like to do that?'

"Yes."

'And so take some time to let them do that, and to find out what they'd like to do next after they've swum in the surf, and where they might like to go. And about what it is that they can teach you, and about a knot and gristle.'

Therapist has attempted to move the child's metaphors (knot, gristle) into the memory (beach). This fails.

"It's very scary."

'And it's very scary.'

"And they might drown."

'And they might drown.'

"And they're very scared."

'And when they're very scared, how do they know they're very scared?'

"They feel frozen. And they don't want to stay there. It's too scary."

'And so what would they like to do when they feel frozen?'

"They'd like to move from that place and never go back."
'And how can they move from that place?'
"I don't know."
'And they're frozen.'
"And they're frozen."
'And they can't move from that place. And it might be interesting that as they know that they're frozen and that they can't move from that place, about what could happen if a knot and gristle could be interested, and could go to them....'

Therapist introduces the child's metaphors (knot, gristle) into the memory (beach). The client transforms the metaphors (into rope) and uses this in her scenario.

"Yes! It could be like a rope to throw them to hold on to and pull them in."
'And that's what that knot and gristle have been waiting to do for such a long time. And it's got just the right length, and just the right amount of stubbornness, and just all the qualities that they need.'
"They're holding on."
'And as they're holding on, what happens next?'
"They're gliding through the water like someone holding on to a ski rope, and they're taking a ride through the water."
'And they like going in the water when they've got something to hold on to.... And as they're gliding through the water, what would they like to do next?'
"They'd like to keep gliding through the water for a while."
'And just let them take all the time they need to glide through the water with something to hold on to. And take some time to discover what could happen to gristle, and how different that can be, and how it doesn't have to be in shoulder any longer. And about what it is that gristle needs them to know so gristle doesn't have to be gristle, and about what it is they can learn about super-glue so that super-glue doesn't have to be there like that. And what can super-glue and gristle do together? And about them, and about water, and about gliding through water. And so take some time to discover about all these things, and about

what can happen.... And is there anything else they need?'
"They would just like to play there awhile. Well... they would like to know that they could come out safely somewhere, but I'm not clear on that."
'And so take some time to find out how they can know and be clear that they can come out safely, and about how that knot might be able to teach them about that, and so they can glide and play for as long as they like.' (long pause)

'And so were they able to get out of the water all right?'
"Yes. And they've been many places around the globe, in the air. They've been in many happy situations. And the gristle, and the ropes; the ropes... have become more like ribbons, and the gristle is no longer pulling them. They go pretty much where they want to go, and the ribbons are attached, for a kind of anchor or a means to be pulled— in a kind of safety device— maybe. And it feels kind of right to just let them do that. And they've been going back and forth between here and San Francisco, and feeling more and more at home in both places."
'And do they need to do anything else?'
"I think they need to just experience that back-ness and forth-ness, so that the two lives don't seem so opposite. They're not too concerned about the gristle, they're having such a good time. But I'm concerned about where those ribbons that started out as gristle are anchored— if they're anchored in my shoulder, or if they're anchored anywhere, or if they need to be."

'Concerned' is a new feeling. It is formatted into a metaphor (rod and reel). Rod and reel will be transformed later.

'And when you're concerned, where are you concerned when you are concerned?'
"In my right shoulder."
'And whereabouts in your right shoulder?'
"Right here, where the gristle was for so long. It feels like there's a little bit of it left, and I wonder if that might be like the anchor."

'And when there's a little bit of it left, what's it like when there's a little bit of it left?'

"It's like a rod and reel, And I wonder— if the gristle decided the feelings were having too much fun, if it would reel them in, and then that would make the knot again, and I don't want that to happen...."

"But I want to tell you about the super-glue. The super-glue isn't needed with the gristle or the ribbons. Super-glue is just a nice thing to have at home in a drawer, or maybe at the office, but not anything that you need to carry with you."

The following six questions serve to store the client's new metaphors (rod, reel) in a safe holding context.

'And so that's about super-glue... and what about a rod and reel?'

"Seems like the rod and reel need to be somewhere, just so they're safe... it's confusing, whether there needs to be a rod and reel."

'And so what would a rod and reel like to do so rod and reel could be different than being in a shoulder?'

"They would like to be available."

'And where could they be so that they could be available? And where could be just the different place where they could be available?'

"Maybe somewhere in my house. Maybe somewhere on a wall...."

'And could there be just a wall where rod and reel could be available?'

"Just a wall...?"

'Just the place....'

"Yes. On the wall of my laundry room— just kind of there, available."

'And would rod and reel like to check that ribbons are okay? Or is it all right being on a wall?'

"It's all right being on a wall."

'And so ribbons are all right...? And rod and reel is all right...?

And feelings are all right playing?'
"They're wonderful playing."
'And do they need anything else?'
"They just need a lot of time."
'And so they can take all the time they need....'
"Yes. I think they'll take a long time."
'And they can take a long time.'
"Some of them are getting a little tired. They might like to just stop and rest where they are, without having to be pulled in by rod and reel."
'And it's nice to have that choice... and that's a reel choice.'
"Yes!"
'And did you get what you wanted?'
"Yes."
'And how do you know that?'
"Because of how light I feel, and how the room and everything disappeared, and because the pain in my shoulder disappeared, and because I feel very calm and settled and very okay about it. Very okay."
'And does that give you what you wanted?'
"Yes."
'And you're sure about that?'
"Yes. I'm sure about that."
'And it's taken care of the guilt?'
"Until you asked me just now, I forgot about the guilt."
'So do you want to check and make sure?'
"Let me check."
'Just check and make sure.'
"It's like the guilt may still be floating around out there someplace. But it's very far away. And I don't know where it is, and it doesn't know where I am, so... if it's out there and it doesn't touch my life, maybe I don't have to worry about where it is. That's how it feels. Maybe it didn't cease to exist, but it went far, far away."
'And is that going to be good enough?'
"I would like it to die, to be gone completely. If it's out there floating around, it might attach to someone else."
'And so take a little time to find out where it is, and where it's

*floating far, far away, and about what you could use to catch
something when it's floating far, far away. And how you could
be sure about where it is, and if you could catch something
floating....'*

"I see where it is. It's over a body of water, like an ocean. And
it's very gray there, and the guilt is very gray, like a low-hanging
cloud. It even has its name on it in capital letters, g-u-i-l-t, on
like a little gray cloud."

'And what would that little gray cloud like to do?'

"Hmm. I don't know. It's looking at a fisherman down below in
his boat. And the fisherman is looking back at it. The fisherman
has a net. Maybe the fisherman could catch it in his net."

'And could a fisherman catch a cloud like that in his net?'

"I think so. But I don't know what he'd do with it when he
caught it."

'Then that's for a fisherman to find out.'

"Right."

'He just has to see if he can catch it.'

"Uh huh. But I think he can."

*'And take some time and see if that fisherman can, and about
whether he likes to use a rod and reel, or whether he likes a net.'*

"Oh! Well..., he could be very creative, and use the rod and reel
to cast the net. And the cloud of guilt has a kind of funny
expression on its face, almost like it wants to be caught."

*'And could it be caught by a fisherman who could cast a net with
a rod and reel?'*

"Well, I'm not clear if he needs to do it with the rod and reel but
I think he can do it with the net."

'And just see if he can do it with the net.'

"The fisherman is very strong. Maybe he has one of those cane
poles on the side of his boat, something to hold the net up
high..., and... yes, I think it's happening— the weight of the net
is pulling the cloud of guilt down, only the net slips a little, and
it's not covering the whole cloud."

'And so what would need to happen?'

"Maybe now the fisherman could take his pole and kind of scoot
the net over... and now it seems more like the net's got it, like
the net has some power of its own."

'And so it would be interesting to know about a net that can catch a cloud that's got guilt on it. And a net can know a lot of things about... gills. And how interesting to have a... gill net.'
"Yes."
'And when you have a gill, and a gill net, that's how you can breathe.'
"That's right. That's right!"
'And so all you need to do is to take a "U" out of that "GUILT".'
"Yes."
'And you can drop that guilt.'
"Yes. And it can just fall into the water. Or not."
'And gills can breathe in water.'
"So they'll be okay."
'And so they'll be okay. And "you" doesn't have to be there.'
"And that feels very good, that feels very wonderful. I feel sort of warm and nice. And I can breathe."

The client's inhibition is resolved. The new memory (fisherman, cloud, net) contains the old negative metaphors (knot, gristle) in new positive forms.

'And just take some time and check to be sure you've got what you wanted, and to know about guilt differently, and about knot. And so now you can have a... knot guilty.'
"Yes. Knot guilty. Not guilty."
'And so you have a net gill-ty instead.'
(laughing) "Yes. Not gross, but net."
'And the net is the bottom line, after all.'
"And it feels very good to laugh about it."
'And you got what you wanted?'
"Yes. Yes, I got what I wanted."

Farewell To Arm: Child Sexual Abuse

Client complains of headaches. This is her admission ticket. The metaphor ('C' shaped spear) for headache is developed. It travels from the head into the stomach. In the stomach another metaphor (belt and ratchet) is discovered. This metaphor contains information about, and memories of, the sexual abuse. Another metaphor (withered hand) appears. This metaphor leads to further information about the abuse.

The memory of the abuse is changed as the 'little girl' is revealed. The client realizes that the abuse has caused her to feel small and vulnerable in her relationships with men. She now feels empowered relative to men.

'When you have this headache, where is this headache?'
"It's here now, in the upper part of my neck just below my skull and up into the back of my skull and in my ears."
'It's in the upper part of the neck and into the back of the skull and in the ears.'
"It's kind of a 'U' shape round my skull; it takes up about a part of my skull and comes out over my ears and still in the skull and it feels like it goes into my brain a little bit. It feels real thick in my temples, like it's a rounded knob in my temples. And it is only at the top part of my neck, right underneath my skull."
'So what's the knob like that's in the temples?'
"It's shaped like an egg, and it's dense as if it were made out of wood, and it's laid down so the old wood is horizontal like this, and the long end like this on both sides, and on the left side. (pause) There's more pressure from it on the left side, but they are both the same shape on the left and right side."
'What is that pressure like?'
"It's like a pressure cooker. And it's cooking beyond what should have been released."
'So what else is there about that pressure cooker?'
"The pressure cooker just disappeared and the whole headache now has gone into the right hand back side of my skull and down into my neck and it feels like a thick rod."

'And so there's this headache that's in the back of your head that's like a rod. And what else is there about this rod?'

"It's not quite like a rod, it's like a... it is shaped like the head of some kind of ancient spirit, that I have seen, where it comes up into its blade, and it's rounded. And then it has another knife edge that comes over like this to the side and that's how it is shaped. Although it's not that object. That's just how it's shaped. It's thick and round and it is kinda like a log in its size and it's a cream color, at least the main part of it is cream color."

'So it's like a spear with a thing over it and this thing is cream colored. And what else is there about this?'

"It's not a spirit, it is shapes like the spirit, and it's the size of a small log, with a little wing that comes off to one side that's shaped kinda like a 'C', and it's cream colored and it's made out of ivory or stone."

'And it is shaped like that. And so what else is there?'

"It's changed again and it is more like a memory of that being there. And what I am aware of is.... (pause) It's gone into my solar plexus and my stomach. My God, here I am!" (pause)

'So what is in your gut that makes it there?'

"There's a concentrated ball of.... (pause) It's like there's a concentrated center that has radiations that come out of it. And then the center is, it's like it's got a pulsation to it."

'This concentrated center has a sort of pulse coming out of it, what else is there about this?'

"It's round and it's really dense. I think the color might be a cream again or yellowish, kinda like a thick sun of some kind."

'And so this concentrated ball with stuff all round it is kinda like a thick sun. And what else is there about that?'

"It's afraid."

'And when it's afraid, how does it know it's afraid?'

"Because it's there."

'And when it's there and it's afraid what else is there about that?'

"It shows up and at the same time you become aware of being afraid. And it's a special kind of afraidness, it's.... And when I am aware that it's there, then the rest of my body tenses and

I have a feeling really tight across my neck and shoulders. And when it shows up it's there to tell me that the afraidness is there now. What I want to do is get rid of some of the intensity of the pain that's sitting in my solar plexus and it's a radiation of this afraidness."

'And what else is there about that afraidness?'

"It tightens this whole area. I feel like I'm in a vise being squeezed."

'And what kind of a vise is that vise?'

"It's like this belt that goes around my ribs and down into my gut area and it has a ratchet on it in front so it can be tightened like this and it's a real strong cotton."

'So is there anything else about that belt and that ratchet?'

"The ratchet is out of real shiny silvery metal like stainless steel. It's a real expensive item, strong metal and design, and it holds together like a fire-hose, that thick. And somebody else is ratcheting it. I can't ratchet it. And it tightens down. Only I don't have any control over when it gets ratcheted and when it doesn't. Something else is still happening."

'And who or what could that be?'

"I just see a hand."

'So is this a left hand or a right hand?'

"It's a right hand."

'And is the hand connected with arm?'

"It goes up almost to the elbow."

'What happens with the hand at the elbow?'

"I can't see any more."

'And do you know whose hand that could be?'

"Um huh."

'Then what could happen next?' (pause)

"It's tightening the ratchet."

'And so is there anything else that you would like to have happen?'

"I want it to stop."

'And what could happen to make it stop? (pause) And take some time to think about what could happen to make it stop. (pause) 'And just what would a hand like that need to know to be different? (pause) And so what does that hand want to do?'

"It's going to have it's way no matter what."

'What things does that hand want to do?'

"It wants to hurt me."

'And so that hand wants to hurt you. And in what ways does that hand want to hurt you?'

"I'm afraid to say."

'And so you can be afraid to say about the ways that that hand wants to hurt you. And so take a little time to know about all the ways that that hand wants to hurt you, and about that hand, and about the ways it has hurt you in the past, and about all those times. And as you know about that, about what would that hand need to know, and need you to know, so that that hand wouldn't need to hurt you in that way. And so what ways and what things could happen so that that hand could be different?'

"Cut it off at the elbow."

'And you want to cut it off at the elbow?'

"I could take a sword and cut it off at the elbow."

'And if you took a sword and cut it off at the elbow, then what would happen?'

"Then it would go away."

'And then what would happen?'

"Then I wouldn't feel the pain."

'So if you cut that hand off at the elbow with the sword then you wouldn't feel the pain. Would that hand still be there even though it was cut off from the elbow?'

"It would be on the floor."

'It would be on the floor. And if that hand was on the floor, being cut off at the elbow what would happen then?' (long pause)

'So as you know about that hand, and about it being cut off, it might be interesting, that what could energy and radiation in center do if it were to go to a hand like that? (pause) And just what could happen to a hand that wanted to hurt in that way, and that knew about a ratchet, if that energy and that center were in some way able to do something, what could happen to a hand like that?' (pause)

"The hand doesn't get to have the energy."

'The hand doesn't get to have the energy.'

"If it got the energy it would come back and do some more. It wants to have the energy."

'And what stops it from having the energy?'

"I won't give it to it."

'You won't give it to it. And how won't you do that?'

"Give it the energy? It's mine."

'Fine! And so when you take the energy and you won't give it to the hand, then what happens to hand?'

"It dies."

'It dies. And how does the hand die?'

"It just shrivels up and dies."

'And so can hand just shrivel up? And there's hand without energy shrivelled up. Is there anything that you can do with the hand that's about to die and shrivel up without energy? And what could a hand like that do to a ratchet or to a belt like that?'

"They can't do anything."

'They can't do anything?'

"The ratchet just falls off, starts to fall off."

'So just let a ratchet fall off. And the hand that's withering now, and a belt that's cotton; and just discover what could happen to all those things when they come off. And what could be done with them when they come off?'

Taking her energy back that hand withers. Now we don't particularly want to have a withered hand lying around, and a ratchet and a belt. We want to help those to grow and develop into other forms as well. We don't want a lot of debris lying around. It is all still part of her experience, all part of her mythology. They belong to her whether or not she liked those experiences. It doesn't matter, they are her experiences, and they need to be valued as such. And so we have no right to go around exorcising these things and cutting them out. We want them re-incorporated in a different form because they still belong to her.

'And so what can happen with a withered hand and a ratchet and a belt?' (pause)

"When the belt and the ratchet fall away, then I become an adult."

'You become an adult.'

"And then I can turn around and look at the person the hand belongs to. And then I can take the sword and come across his face with it."

'So you can take the sword and you come across his face with the sword. And then what happens?' (pause)

"Two things happen. One is that he knows how much pain he has put me through. And I also feel guilty for causing that pain, for slicing and cutting him."

'So take some time to discover about slicing him and cutting him, and exactly where you would slice him, and exactly where you would cut him. And about the guilt you would have. And about how he would learn how much pain he has put you through. And as you know about that, it might be interesting to know, if there are other ways that you could use a sword like that. And about what could you do, now that you are an adult, and an adult who has turned around. And what would an adult do who knew about a belt and about a ratchet and about a withered hand, and about a sword? And could an adult who turned around know just what to do with those things?' (long pause)

'And so what has happened?'

"I can take the belt with the ratchet on it in my left hand, and the sword in my right hand, and when I turn around and stand up and face him I can take the belt and swing it across my body and down under the left side of his face so he feels the metal slamming against his head. And I can take this."

'That's right. And he can feel the metal slamming against his head. And he can know about your pain. And that's different than a cutting pain isn't it?'

"And I can do both."

'And you can do both, and just exactly where would you want to cut him?'

"With the sword in my right hand, take it across my body and that's just above his right ear and down across his face, across his cheek and down to the shoulder on his left side."

'And as you cut him there, and then what would happen?'

"And then I'd drop the belt, and take the sword in both hands, and raise it above my head, and I'd come right down the center of his body."

'And as you come down the center of his body, and then what would happen?'

"Then I stop it, that's enough."

'And what would happen to him?'

"Then he would know how much pain he's given."

'And as he would know about that, and how much pain you've had, what would happen next?' (pause)

"I start to feel guilty."

'And you start to feel guilty.'

"But I don't want to feel guilty, I just want him to know what it feels like."

'And so how could you let him know what it feels like and not feel guilty?'

"By stopping this thing right and letting him feel the initial pain."

'Right. And if you stop the scene right there, and let him feel the initial pain, and what could you do with somebody who had felt that initial pain? And is there anything you could do with cotton from a cotton belt, or from an energy, or from a ratchet, or from a withered hand? And just what could you do?' (pause)

"I don't need any of those things."

'And you don't need any of those other things?'

"No."

'And what do you need?' (pause)

"I need to heal myself."

'You need to heal yourself.'

"I need to heal him myself."

'You need to heal it yourself. And so how would you begin to do that?'

"It just happened."

'It just happened. And how did you do that?'

"I just saw him whole without his right arm."

'And you saw him whole without his right arm?'

"Yeah."

'And his face?'

"It's whole now."

'And his shoulder?'

"It's okay."

'All right. And so he was able to heal himself. And he is without his right arm. Okay.'

"And so he has to open his eyes now and look at me."

'And can he open his eyes?'

"They are open now."

'Now?'

"Yeah. What I see, and what I need to see, is what he knows, that I know, he knows, and he does."

'And he does?'

"Almost."

'So just take some time, so that he can know that, as much as you want him to know, and even more than almost.' (long pause)

'Okay, so what's happened now?'

"Umm.... He's reflecting back on that shared memory that we have about the times that he hurt me, and didn't know the extent to which he was hurting me. So he knows that now."

'And he knows that now?'

"Yeah."

'And he knows that more than almost now?'

"It looks like it."

'Really? And is there anything else that you would like to have happen?'

"I want to; I don't want to slip back into being that little girl in that pain."

'And so what would need to happen so that you could know that you wouldn't have to slip back into that little girl and that pain?'

"He needs to be seated as he looks at me. And I look into his eyes. And I need to be standing. I just did it. I need to be taller than he is. I need to be willing to remember this too."

'Can you be willing to remember this too?'

"Yeah."

'Okay, and having had that happen, then can you be sure that you can remember that differently, and that you won't have to slip into that as a little girl?'

"Everything has changed already."
'It's changed already? And just continue to let it change, so that you can really know that it has changed. And that that won't need to happen any longer.' (long pause)

'And so are there any things that you can say about that?'
"That's hard to be back here because things are different now. And my insides are jello which usually happens with insight like this."
'And so do you like them to be jello like that?'
"I'll firm up shortly."
'So take some time to enjoy that jello and to enjoy the firmness. And you don't have to be here. And you can be there for a while. And let that jello firm up with that insight. (pause) So would you like to say something about your experience and about what happened?'
"As we were talking about the headache, it started me out on the headache. There wasn't too long after we started describing it, locating it when I could feel stuff in my stomach and it just got worn down. I wanted to kill him. But when we got down into it then I began to realize how much afraidness there was. A few weeks ago I had a dream about sexual abuse I experienced when I was pretty small. And that was repeated several times. And this is the first time I had an inkling of what had happened. One of the things that happened to me in my childhood which was traumatic, and in that dream I remember it clearly now that I've had the dream. I was being held by this man, across with a right arm coming across around my solar plexus and ribs. And so it's not surprising that the belt was a ratchet around that area. I was surprised at how angry I was and how much I wanted to put him in pain too. And it was hard, it was different, I struggled with letting that be out, but once that was there, it was like all of a sudden I was an adult, which I had never been in that place in me. And I hadn't realized that until that moment when I could take the sword and the belt and stand up and be equal with him and face him, instead of having him behind me. And the jello-y place, that I experienced when I was coming out of it, has firmed up remarkably fast. But at

other times the experience is kind of being shaken up internally, and it's taken days or weeks for that to settle down. And it's like it happened days or weeks ago. Umm. When I was finishing it off, I was envisioning it both historically and in the future times when I might slip back into that position of feeling vulnerable and helpless and being held against my will and to be vulnerable and small. And I've not experienced what it was meant to not be vulnerable and small in those situations until today. And I hadn't realized how profound that was to be out of that space. And to know a different experience. So...."

'Okay. So you have some firming up. And how is that in there now? Is that firmed up how you want it to be? Or does it have more to go? Or...?'

"A little bit more to go, probably the finishing touches tonight and tomorrow. It feels ninety percent there. I'm surprised at how fast it has gone. It's something that has shifted my relationship with men, just in that experience. A chunk of me has really shifted. It has really shifted. That I have been struggling with for a couple of years now."

'Can you remember times when that physiology was present in your relationships with men?'

"I didn't realize it's connected to this though. I just realized that... it didn't have to be physically enacted. It could be just in a word, or a conversation, or an action in that experience, where I would slip right back. And I'd feel small and vulnerable, and held against my will and hurting."

'And do you have any ideas about how that headache was related to that?'

(laugh) "You know the only thing that comes to mind visually is those little tiny enchiladas that we ate which may be phallic, I don't know. A couple of times I wanted someone to say: 'What would you like to do?' And what I would have done is I want to scream, and cut this guy to pieces with a sword, and the screaming component was there. That's all." (long pause)

'Right, so was it disruptive when I re-introduced the idea of that energy? So what was the key thing, was there a key word or phrase that let you know that you put energy in that arm?'

"I was ticked off with you for telling me to go back over that stupid arm on the floor that was dying. And then you asked me for the energy and I thought that's the stupidest thing I've ever been asked to do... and then I stopped for a minute and I thought, now why am I reacting that way? And what I got was that I really do not put the energy into it, and I started getting very afraid, so I just sort of played with putting energy in. When I did, the thing started to come alive and started flying at me, you know, just like it's going to start taking the energy away. And it was dead on the ground again, and I put the energy toward it. So that was really useful, because it was trying to rob me of my energy, my life energy, whatever energy was down there that was in pain." (long pause)

"I was getting really uptight. It was like the anxiety in me, about me giving the energy which was just building and building, as you were suggesting that."
'So when you did that and it just flew at you, and flew at your neck or your face or...?'
"It would have killed me. It was angry at me for cutting it off from doing what it wanted to do to me; and that energy would have energized it. My energy would have energized it to kill me; and it was going to fly at my neck."

This operates independently. It was going to be very tricky then. This is not just imagery. But this has an energy all of its own, and a life all of its own. That's why you don't destroy it.

'So where is it now anyway?'
"The arm? It's just lying on the floor, it is slowly dying."
'It is still slowly dying? Is there anything else you want to do with that?'
"No."
'Just let it slowly die... okay. So when something is slowly dying like that is there some other way that an arm that is slowly dying cannot become something else other than an arm slowly dying?'
"Um huh."

'What?'

"It just became a flower."

'*Became a flower?*' *(pause)*

"Yeah.... That's interesting because I didn't want to go back and look at the arm, because I thought it was all finished, but what was lingering was a sense of guilt of having hurt it and wanting it to just know that it hurt me without really totally killing it, or leaving it in that ugly position."

'*So now it can transform into a flower. Right. Now where could that flower go, that flower that has been an arm, and just where would be the place for a flower like that?*'

"It's a light pink lotus and it's sitting in a quiet pond in a forest with the reflections of spruce trees all around it."

'*So that is where that flower can go... and it is sitting in a pond... and the owner of what used to be... the owner of a flower like that... is also sitting... and that's a different situation isn't it...?*'

"Um huh.... He looks old."

'*He looks old?*'

"He looks tired. And he looks sad with the realization of what he had done."

'*So somebody who looks old and sad like that. And about a lotus sitting in a pond. And where could someone old and sad go and be just in a place somewhere?*' *(pause)*

"When I look at him now, his arm is there. But the arm that hurt me is not there."

'*So the arm that hurt you is not there?*'

"But he is still, and he is physically whole with a different forearm."

'*Okay so he has a different forearm than the arm that hurt you. And that arm is now a lotus.*' *(pause)*

Everything is tidying up now, isn't it? That becomes part of her mythology. It no longer is a truncated monomyth which all stops at that age with a belt around her and that same thing over and over again. It is growing and evolved so that the belt and sword are over her fireplace and he is sitting on a swinging chair on a porch. And he has a different forearm. And the forearm that did that is now a

lotus in a pond and reflected with birch trees. Now all those parts are coming together again.

'And that energy and that center, and just where could that be...?'

"Right in the center of my gut, where it belongs when it is not threatened."

'And that is where it belongs when it is not threatened. And the parts of that jello that had yet to set. Has any more of that set?'

"Uh hum.... Changing the arm into a lotus was most important and then putting the sword and the belt over my fireplace...."

'So how much more of that is there that needs to set?'

"Very little. Just a little bit of the memory of the pain and the fear across."

'That memory of the pain and the fear across there, what's that like now?'

"It's like a real thin edge that is slowly... it's like a sunset, the sun is going down and the light is going away from it."

'So it is like a sunset. Just take a little time to let that like a sunset set, set.'

"And it's set."

'Okay. And how has the jello set?'

(laugh) "It's fine. It's green mint and jelly. It's all set."

'It's all set.'

Using a metaphor like that, we notice the use of the word 'set'. It gets beyond verbal report. This is her epistemology of how this experience completes itself. There is ten percent, and there is just a little bit, and we have got the edge of the sunset, and then the jello is all set. There's no more working through. The fact is that it has set. And now a variety of insights will occur and understandings will reach back through her experience. Those insights will be interesting, but they won't be parts that she needs to help her heal. She is not gaining any more insight to help her change. That's happened now. And the insights will simply provide confirmation about the experience, whereas if we had not just done this last ten percent, then those insights

would have been necessary for her to heal. We must not just swap for another complex: rather than being held and the pain and being afraid complex—for here I can hurt him by cutting him and I feel guilty after I've done it. We have to take care of the guilt and the wanting to do the hurt, and him to know how she hurt. It is a neat solution to a whole complex. He is whole, but it is not the whole that he was then. The forearm is a lotus flower.

If we started and said: 'What do you want to do with the headache?' the answer to that question is that the client doesn't know. And she doesn't know because she doesn't have enough information about it. When asking the question cognitively, the answer is: "I don't want it." And she is exactly right. We have to be careful at what time we ask a question like that. At first she has no information other than the pain. We have to get it formatted; which is to find out its shape and size and color and all the characteristics so it becomes vivified by her experience. Then, when it is vivified, then we can ask that question. Notice we ask that question of a hand, not: 'What do you want to do with that hand,' because she can't do anything with it, that's why it is still there. It's a fragmentary part of her experience: 'What does that hand want to do?' "That hand wants to hurt me." And that would also be the difficulty if we had left that hand lying on the floor. In another experience later on, that center gave up the energy and that hand is sitting there ready for that energy. That could happen if she got involved with a man. It doesn't have to be in the same abusive situation: if she got held in a certain way, if someone put an arm round her waist. All of a sudden she might not know what went wrong. She begins to panic. All those events could have provided opportunities for that energy to go back into that arm. Then that arm was going to go right for her throat. That arm has been with her all those years, and it is a strong arm which has been actively involved right throughout her life. An arm like that is best transformed. We just can't leave it lying around. It becomes a lotus flower, that takes care of it. The same with the sword and with the belt. They are on the mantlepiece. They are trophies now.

The whole mythology is all there. Every relic from that experience is there. The energy is back in the center. The energy has shown us where to go and what to do. Let us consider all the communications we have had from our clients, and how these things might have evolved if only we had the ears to listen....

Bibliography

Ashby, W. R., *An Introduction to Cybernetics* (New York: J. Wiley, 1956).

Bandler, R., & Grinder, J., *The Structure of Magic: A book about language and therapy, Vols. 1 & 2* (Palo Alto: Science and Behavior Books, 1975).

Barthes, R., *Elements of Semiology* (London: Cape, 1967).

Bateson, G., *Steps to an Ecology of Mind* (New York: Ballantine Books, 1978).

_____ *Mind and Nature: A necessary unity* (New York: Bantam, 1977).

Bateson, G., & Bateson, Mc.C., *Angels Fear* (New York: Macmillan, 1987).

Campbell, J., *Grammatical Man: Information, entropy, language and life* (New York: Simon & Schuster, 1982).

Campbell, J. (oseph)., *The Masks of God, Vols. 1-4* (New York: Penguin, 1976).

Chomsky, N., *Syntactic Structures* (The Hague: Mouton, 1957).

Derrida, J., trans. G. Chakravorty Spivak, *Of Grammatology* (Baltimore: Johns Hopkins University Press, 1976).

Eagleton, T., *Literary Theory* (Oxford: Basil Blackwell, 1983).

Eliade, M., trans. by W. R. Trask, *The Sacred and the profane: The nature of religion* (New York: Harcourt Brace Jovanovich, 1959).

Factor, D. (ed.), *Unfolding Meaning: A weekend of dialogue with David Bohm* (Loveland: Foundation House Publications, 1985).

Frye, N., *Anatomy of Criticism* (Princeton: Princeton University Press, 1957).

Gallop, J., *The Daughter's Seduction: Feminism and psychoanalysis* (Ithaca: Cornell University Press, 1982).
_____ *Reading Lacon* (Ithaca: Cornell University Press, 1985).

Gordon, D., *Therapeutic Metaphors* (Cupertino: Meta Publications, 1979).

Iser, W., *The Implied Reader* (Baltimore: Johns Hopkins University Press, 1974).

Kristeva, J., trans. T. Gora, A. Jardine & L.S. Roudiez, *Desire in Language: A semiotic approach to literature and art* ed. by L.S. Roudiez (New York: Columbia University Press, 1980).

Lacan, J., *Ecrits* (New York: W.W. Norton & Co., 1976).

Lakhoff, G. & Johnson, M., *Metaphors We Live By* (Chicago: University of Chicago Press, 1980).

Levi-Strauss, C., trans. C. Jacobson & B. G. Schoepf, *Structural Anthropology, Vols. 1 & 2* (New York: Basic Books, 1963 & 1976).

Ochberg, F.M. (ed.), *Post-Traumatic Therapy and Victims of Violence* (New York: Brunner Mazel, 1988).

Sapir, Ed., *Language: An introduction to the study of speech* (New York: Harcourt, Brace & World, 1949).

Shannon, C.E. & Weaver, W., *The Mathematical Theory of Communication* (Urbana: University of Illinois Press, 1964).

Watzlawick, P. (ed.), *The Invented Reality: How do we know what we believe we know?* (New York: W. W. Norton & Co., 1984).

Whorf, B., *Language, Thought and Reality,* ed. J. B. Carroll (Cambridge: Technology Press of M.I.T., 1956).

Wilber, K. (ed.), *The Holographic Paradigm and other paradoxes: Exploring the leading edge of science* (Boulder: Shambhala, 1982).

Wilden, A., *The Rules are no Game: The strategy of communication* (London: Routledge, 1987).

Wilson, J.P., *Trauma, Transformation, and Healing* (New York: Brunner Mazel, 1989).

Index